THE RUINING OF LEMUS DANIEL

LARRY DANIEL

W. Brand Publishing
NASHVILLE, TENNESSEE

Names and places have been changed to protect individuals in the story.

j.brand@wbrandpub.com
W. Brand Publishing
www.wbrandpub.com

Cover design by designchik.net

The Ruining of Lemus Daniel/Larry Daniel—1st ed.

Available in Paperback, Kindle, and eBook formats.
Paperback ISBN: 978-1-950385-21-8
eBook ISBN 978-1-950385-22-5

Library of Congress Control Number: 2019918179

CONTENTS

FOREWORD

In late 1994, I sat across the table from a team of high-powered lawyers after my father's controversial memoir involving a former friend was subpoenaed by a Federal District Court in Washington, D.C. The criminal investigation of the Secretary of Agriculture and his dealings with this friend had caused an ex in-law of mine to bring the manuscript to a local investigator's attention. Suddenly, my sisters and I were forced to make some quick decisions about our dad's exposé.

Eager to protect my father's powerful enemy, these lawyers presented an out for us so we could move to quash the subpoena rather than have the details exposed in a hearing. Handing the manuscript over to investigating officials would have made us the subject of unwanted scrutiny, and I feared the consequences of not cooperating with the attorneys. I wanted to make it clear that I wasn't looking for a fight with my father's former associate.

In the late 1980s, with the help of a friend, my father had penned a raw and unapologetic tell-all. The finished manuscript detailed the nefarious actions of certain individuals whom he held responsible for his misfortune and collapse in the late 1960s. He had very little else to resort to in retaliation that wouldn't result in a prison sentence, so he opted for information warfare. There was plenty of carnage and collateral damage to report and he didn't omit his own misdeeds.

He passed a copy to his children and many more to his friends, but his ultimate plan for the book remained a mystery to me. He died shortly after finishing it, and never knew what would become of it. In spite of our efforts to conceal his book from the court, it was eventually leaked to the press and brought his antagonist a lot of unwanted attention. I could envision my late father laughing out loud from the great beyond.

After the events of 1994, I began thinking about how to tell my father's story in a different way. Publishing a book was a fantasy at that point, but one that would stay with me.

In spring of 2016, I found myself cornered between a herniated disc in my lower back and a serious desire to avoid the knife. After considerable procrastination, I consented to surgery, but the slack time leading up to it provided a springboard to start composing the story that I had longed to write. I'd collected notes about events as I remembered them, but now wanted to make something more complete. After I got started, I found that I couldn't stop.

As a young man, I shared my father's anger and had to go through a series of self-discoveries before I could tell the story without his vitriol. I recalled the dark places and troubling details of my youth and faced my own demons. I had to forgive myself as well as others. This book is my testimony.

Very little was altered in his contribution to this work, and the few changes I made were to add background information that my father didn't include. Portions of his book have been woven into mine to better illustrate my life and relationship with him.

This memoir is about a father who loses everything except for his newly-soiled reputation while struggling to regain his comfortable lifestyle; and his son, who navigates through the wreckage. The turbulent times of the bohemian 1970s serve as the backdrop to this true story of survival, redemption, and coming-of-age under difficult circumstances.

Many of the names and places have been changed. Any resemblance to persons living or dead, are purely coincidental.

The Ruining of Lemus Daniel consists of a dual narrative that runs the length of the memoir. One is from the author, Larry Daniel, and the other is from the father, Lemus Daniel, in italics, copied from his tell-all.

THANKS

To **Kat,** who was there in the beginning, sifting through my amateurish attempts and taught me something every time she handed my work back to me.

To **John,** who was the first to read the roughest of drafts and told me the truth.

To **Mekiya Walters,** who agreed to do a structural edit after reading the words that I'd written. As the edit progressed, he discussed ideas with me and helped me search for voice. I learned some basic fundamentals and he gave me books to read that were also helpful. I learned a lot from him.

To **Fran,** who opened my eyes a little and helped with the final touches.

To **Mary,** for all the help.

To **my supportive wife,** while I went willingly into the rabbit hole of piecing this story together, an eternity seemed to pass with no ladder out before I was at ease with some of the material.

It was worth it.

"I understood myself

only after

I destroyed myself.

And only in the process

of fixing myself,

did I know who

I really was."

– Sade Andria Zabala

PART I

THE RUINING

CHAPTER 1

Something scary looking is wrapped around something I love. I exit the front door, walk down the front porch steps, and head right, toward my tricycle. I look forward to hopping on and pedaling around the driveway, as I suppose I've done a few times since the state-of-the-art, steel tricycle arrived. I always ride far from the street, heeding my mother's warnings from just inside the doorway.

But this time I stop and stare. A large black snake is muscling its way up and strangling my ride. It hisses at me and I retreat quickly to my mother's side. I am three years old and this earliest memory is a frightful one. I don't remember going back to my tricycle that day. All I remember is the hissing black snake.

The year was 1958. My mother, Doris, was a stay-at-home mom who doted on us kids with an easy smile. With one son (me) and three daughters—two of them younger than me— she kept herself busy, but was always there when I needed her. She was raised in the rural community of Elm Springs, Arkansas, a country girl without apology or indoor plumbing for most of her young life, who could look like Liz Taylor whenever she wanted to. My younger sisters are Hazel, with a head of fiery red hair, and Iris, who just turned one, with sandy blond hair like her grandfather. Ruth is four years my senior and is dark headed like me.

My father, Lemus Daniel, was a gregarious man with a buzz haircut and big ideas. Handsome enough to make women look twice, his broad shoulders and big smile towered over us as we clamored for him to pick us up with calloused but caring hands. Some days after work, he'd hoist us up on his feet as he lay supine, and gave us the feeling of flying with our arms spread like Superman. He had a temper but he only rarely let us see it. Born in El Dorado, Kansas, and one of eleven children of Depression-era parents, he endured the 1930s by ignoring an empty stomach and wearing homemade cardboard shoes. These days, he's known by his friends as the hardest working man around.

He prospered as a builder during the housing boom of the late 1950s, and as our family size increased, our living spaces did as well. We moved from the small studio I was brought home to as a newborn, to a slightly larger house in town, before settling in at the spacious red brick residence on West Emerald Avenue. My favorite space in that house became a floor vent that flowed warm air behind a chair in the living room. I found the privacy of the space peaceful when I wanted to avoid the noise of my sisters. Our large backyard was fenced, and a small alleyway that ran behind the neighbor's wooden fence often served as a fort or a castle for me and my younger sisters. My older sister, Ruth, who had her own room and her own, older friends, was usually exempt from these adventures.

When my father brought home a television set, it was met with enthusiasm. Not everyone had one then. I soon became a devotee of *The Little Rascals* and found a kindred spirit in Alfalfa—a central character in the show—who sang rather poorly and seemed wholly unaware of his poor voice. After a year of studying Alfalfa, I knew the routine so well that my father would summon me out to perform it at social gatherings. I'd wet my fine, jet black hair to create an exaggerated cowlick just like Alfalfa, and sing with a squeak in full character. I was the spitting image of him, the party goers all bellowed, and I loved the attention. Another character in the show was Buckwheat, a child of color whose significant role in the production gave me a sense early on that the world might have a lot more kinds of people than I was led to believe, growing up in all-white Springdale.

My father, in his tell-all memoir, described it this way:

"Springdale was a bigoted and racist town in the late 1950s. Large billboards warning blacks not to let the sun go down on them eliminated any notion that there might not be an active Ku Klux Klan membership among the citizenship. The governor was a segregationist."

In 1957, the Montgomery bus boycott sparked the civil rights movement, and while growing up, my father often voiced his stance on race discrimination, stating that the color of a man's skin shouldn't determine how he was treated.

In the summer, we visited our mother's parents in Elm Springs on the weekends. My maternal grandparents were educated but simple country people, with a few superstitions and void of much discussion over race.

The trip took about half an hour, and Granny Griffin, eagerly awaiting our arrival, would be standing by the swing as we pulled in. Their house was wrapped in white lap siding with a porch swing that hung near the center of a small carport across from two chicken houses that they tended. A root cellar lay buried out back by a narrow creek running through thick surrounding woods. The local newspaper—which ran no more than a couple of pages—always declared our impending stay ahead of time as if it was breaking news for the small community.

Granny was short with granite calves that bulged. She sometimes covered her white hair with a colorful bonnet to keep the sun at bay while she directed the communal baths my sisters and I took in the galvanized wash tub in her front yard. We fed table scraps to an old red dog that always came around and sang gospel songs with Granny at the piano, that filled the small house my dad had built for them the year before we started visiting. Sometimes, she would take us swimming in the creek only a short hike away. Clad in oversized panties and safety pinned bra, she'd calmly pull the leeches off of us after we exited the muddy water. At night, I slept with my grandpa Albert with the window open listening to the katydids harmonizing with the fan.

Albert was aloof but could show affection. He was proficient at rolling his own Prince Albert cigarettes and spouting country wisdom. When I asked him if he was a prince like the Albert on the can, he replied, "You bet your socks," and gave me a wink. After my sisters and I got our bearings, it was never long before we started pestering him about going to the general store, and him always promising that we'd go, "dreckly."

Albert had an old black pickup truck with gaping holes in the wooden bed. The truck had a foot starter, three on the column, and I don't think he ever drove over ten miles an hour, whether we were in the back or not. The trip to the general store was fewer than three miles away and took forever, but my sisters and I were content to watch the scenery crawl by from the back, occasionally peeking through the holes to the road. Orange soda pop and candy cigarettes followed, and we drew on the latter just like our grandfather did his cigarettes before we ate them. Albert chained smoked his creations and solved the world's problems with the other old

timers who loitered at the general store while we buzzed aimlessly through the aisles, free to do as we pleased.

I considered Albert a pushover who enjoyed showing us
off to his pals for the price of a pop, but most of the time we
belonged to Granny. She didn't give in to us so readily, and
swung a mean weeping willow switch if we ever got out of
line. We'd routinely walk the short distance to the rickety old
barn, where Granny milked a few cows before marching us
toward the two small chicken houses. After just a few trips
through the chicken houses, the fascination of hundreds of
chirping chicks lost its charm because of the stifling smell
and lack of breathable air. But she usually insisted, so I met
the challenge by holding my breath and walking fast from
one end to the other—about a hundred feet or so—and pretending to check the water and feed system. Whenever she
made the rounds by herself in the additional house in the late
afternoon, she would reach down and snag a full grown bird
for the night's dinner. My little sisters and I would gather on
the other side of the dusty dirt road, barefoot and in our un-
derwear, eager to see Granny coming with a chicken in hand.
Once she reached the yard, she'd hasten her crooked gait and
begin spinning the bird by the neck, winding up like a slinger,
while we giddily anticipated the horror. Round and round its
yellow legs would flail, the intensity increasing, until finally
the whip was cracked. The headless bird would go flapping off
down the hillside for what seemed like an eternity. Mesmerized, we curiously wondered how it could flap its wings like
that without a head for that long. "It's a-dancing," she would
chortle as we looked on.

She boiled some water, brought out some buttermilk,
stirred eggs, flour, Crisco, and finally an iron skillet
sizzled with chicken breasts while she mashed potatoes.

After bringing up a jar of green beans from the cellar, Granny served a dinner that was pretty much the same every evening.

My grandma wasn't the only one in those days killing chickens in Arkansas. Statewide, the business started taking off, with sprawling farms dwarfing my grandparent's coops. Today, the poultry industry in Arkansas is huge, second in the nation in overall production, and my father took the time in his tell-all to describe its unsavory origins:

"I was eight years old when we moved to Arkansas, two miles east of Springdale, and eighth of ten brothers and sisters, ranging in age from three to sixteen. Coming from Oklahoma City, Springdale was a strange place for me. It was my first introduction to the country, cats and dogs, and livestock. When President Roosevelt took office in 1933, he offered—and we accepted—five dollars for our cow for the purpose of putting money into circulation. I remember my older brother Phil and I leading the cow to the stock pen on Hunt Avenue at the railroad tracks in Springdale, to join a few hundred other cows to be shipped away and destroyed, supposedly for the good of the country; although it took ten years and a World War to make it work. That set me to wonder about politics at a very early age. We butchered and ate the pet goat later that year, but the cow would have been much better.

By then, people were starting to find Springdale a good place to live and raise their families. One of those families was the Dawson family. That same year, after a tip from another truck driver, 25-year-old Jim Dawson came to Springdale from Kansas City looking for his wayward wife Margaret, who had run off months earlier with a truck driver from Kansas City by the name of Charlie McCoy. After arriving in Springdale and inquiring at the local gathering places, he found them at the Red Castle Café. Jim walked in and with McCoy's back turned to him and Margaret's eyes as big as silver dollars, he proceeded to pour a cup of hot coffee from a nearby table onto Charlie's bald head and demand that he leave town. McCoy complied, and Jim reconciled with the now pregnant Margaret. A few months later, a son they named Thomas was born.

The town lacked paved streets and boasted a population of 2,000. My parents with their eleven children arrived in Springdale about the same time and moved into a large country home on twenty five acres, two miles east of town. Dawson, after finding his wife Margaret and reconciling their marriage, took residency on Emerald Avenue, Springdale's main street.

Families moved to Springdale for different reasons. My father, Harvey Daniel, after gaining a moderate amount of wealth in real estate and with a large number of children in Oklahoma City, woke up one morning in 1929 totally wiped out financially, as were most Americans during the crash of 1929. Harvey's health was next to go when he was stricken with a kidney ailment some six months after moving his family to a farm in Arkansas. He was financially destitute for most of the 1930s, in fact; a charity case. It was only from the benevolence and generosity of the Walter brothers, the land-owners, was the family able to stay.

Meanwhile, Jim Dawson was fighting for survival in the trucking business in Springdale. Springdale was the truckers' headquarters for a 500-mile radius. The area was becoming famous for its many truck farms, producing the majority of fruits and vegetables that found their way to Dallas, Kansas City, Tulsa, Oklahoma City, and Memphis. Since there was no truck refrigeration in those days, overnight hauling was a must. Truckers lined up to meet the farmers as they brought their product into town without agents: just buyers, sellers, and haulers.

For hauling, the advent of the refrigerated system in the 1940s meant produce from as far as California could be trucked in greater quantities and more economically, and it left the small time truckers out of business and looking for other ways to survive. As a result, the chicken growing industry was introduced to the area, so orchards and fields full of grapes, apples, peaches, tomatoes, and strawberries were being replaced with chicken houses. Jim Dawson quickly decided to change with the times and convert his trucking business into a chicken hauling business. About the same time, Jim and Margaret divorced when Tom was just a toddler. Tom and I would become acquainted after the War.

By the 1950s, the Dawsons had it good, but they were not the only ones in the chicken business. There were a dozen or so broiler producers as big—or bigger—in the area. They were all doing quite well until the chicken crash of the mid 1950s when the price of chicken fell from twenty-five cents a pound to eight cents a pound. Jim knew that just a year at those prices would wipe out the local chicken business, so he called all the chicken producers together and explained how over-production had caused their plight. He persuaded each grower to cut production immediately by half. They all agreed and did just that. But Dawson didn't cut his own production. Instead, he tripled it. The prices soon soared, with Jim Dawson way out in front. He never looked back. The few remaining stragglers were either left at Dawson's mercy or became allies of the Dawson organization."

I've heard it said, when people tell you who they are, listen, and when they show you who they are, believe them—advice my father should perhaps have heeded before befriending Tom Dawson.

He describes this relationship from the beginning:

"When I was a young man, I became acquainted with Tom Dawson. My first encounter should have been enough warning. The year was 1946 and I just returned from a three-year stint in the military. The town of Springdale, now with a population of four thousand, was a busy place, with almost all of its military men returning home. This meant many unemployed young men were looking for something to do.

Our favorite hangout was Herod's Café, a place where you could find all ages and classes of people. The main attraction was a pinball machine located on the west wall toward the front of the building. All the young people would gather around the machine to watch each other trying to convert nickels into Herod tokens that could be used for food or soft drinks. The odds of winning were poor, but I always enjoyed a challenge.

It was my turn to try and beat the nickel snatcher and many spectators gathered around as I played. Suddenly, a young man of maybe 15 years old elbowed his way to my side. In less than 10 seconds, he'd elevated the top of the glass of the pinball machine, inserting a straightened wire clothes hanger, and was making it sing like it was out of control. The tokens added up at a record pace when the proprietor, Hal Herod, rushed over, throwing kids out of his path as he made his way toward me. The young man who manipulated the wire was out the door before I could explain his role in what had just happened. Needless to say, the affair left an impression of me on Hal Herod.

When the smoke cleared, I asked my younger brother, Samuel, "Who was that kid?"

He told me it was Jim Dawson's son, Tom, and that he was here now and staying with his dad after living with his mother and a truck driver and traveling the country for the last few years. I was five years older than Tom, and could see that the kid had been somewhere besides Springdale, Arkansas.

Shortly thereafter, I accepted a job as a truck driver, which kept me on the road and out of town for most of the next few months. As summer school break arrived for Tom, I learned that he had been caught between classes bootlegging whiskey shots that he stole from his dad, and it got him suspended from school. Jim was called to school, and the superintendent told him that Tom would be permitted to take class exams and be credited with completing his junior year, but would not be re-admitted for the fall term. Jim made plans for Tom to enter a military school in Missouri for the upcoming fall.

Later that summer, I left for California and spent the next three years learning the homebuilding trade. After military school, Tom entered the University of Arkansas in Fayetteville, a short distance from Springdale. I returned to Springdale in June, 1950, and hadn't been home long before I ran into Tom. He dropped by to see my brother, Sam, as we nailed shingles on the roof of a house we were working on. Tom crawled onto the roof carrying a quart of beer and he and I were re-introduced. The three of us began to talk and ended up spending quite a bit of time together that summer. My three years of work in California allowed me to buy a new 1950 Pontiac that impressed Tom. He'd never owned a car and always wanted to drive it. If he bought the gas, I usually allowed him to do so. One hot, muggy summer evening in 1950, I drove to the liquor store and tavern on Emerald across the street from the Springdale Theater. I would go there often, usually in the evening if I couldn't find anything else to do because a friend of mine from high school, Don Bender, worked there. Tom walked in and saw me sitting at the counter. We were young and always looking for action of the female variety.

"I know where there's an easy lay in Benton County if you want to go up and check it out," I said, admitting that it would

take $10 for it to become easy. I met the young lady the previous day when I picked her up hitchhiking from New Orleans to Kansas City. She needed money, and invited me back to the cheap motel she called home. I consummated the transaction that day, and I knew that Tom would be interested, too.

He insisted on driving and knocked back a pint of Ancient Age before scrambling behind the wheel of my Pontiac. After another stop for a six pack of beer and an additional pint of whiskey, Tom, while racing around the corner just before the Benton County line, suddenly came to a screeching halt. He tilted the last of the whiskey and chased it with a beer, then dragged me from the car into a restaurant. The place was about to close, but we sat down at the table. The waitress asked for our order. Tom said, "Bring me a steak."

"What kind?"

"Any kind."

"How do you want it cooked?" she asked.

"Bring it like it is," Tom yelled. "Don't even warm it!"

The waitress brought the steak cold from the refrigerator, and he ate it with a piece of bread. He finished it off before I could even get a bag of potato chips down. He would have his own blood dripping down his chin before long, too.

We left with less than six bucks between us. Tom was still carrying the keys to my car, and he seemed to think his gas money was keeping him in the driver's seat. I was too drunk to argue.

We arrived at the motel, and Tom wasted no time in dragging the working girl to the bedroom. I listened from the other room. After a considerable time, the laughter suddenly turned to a more business like conversation. It appeared that Tom was unable to produce the aforementioned $10. She lost her temper and began striking Tom with a determined intent to injure him.

She was swinging everything she could get her hands on. We ran for our lives, with the woman right behind us and screaming for the police.

Tom was already racing the engine as I crawled in. He took off down the road and we were doing what seemed like eighty when we smashed into the rear of a dimly lit Model-A Ford. I didn't even have a chance to warn him. The driver of the Model A and his wife were thrown through the cloth top of their car, but luckily, not killed.

My car careened into the path of two oncoming cars, and nearly a dozen people were injured. I was thrown clear of the wreckage, knocking me out of my shoes. I staggered back to my car where Tom was still under the wheel. He was obviously badly injured, but trying to dial the radio to full blast and laughing. Tom received more than 60 stitches to close the wounds on his face. After surrendering his license, he was released to his father, leaving me without a car. State Policeman Clyde Winston investigated the accident.

The incident sobered me and prompted me to select new friends. In late 1950, I romanced and married Doris Griffin, who was five years my junior. I started a career of building homes, and Doris and I had four children over the next eight years."

Time would tell if my father had really changed his ways.

CHAPTER 2

My dad lost his car in 1950, but his building career proved profitable, and 10 years later, a twin engine airplane complimented the two new cars that sat in his driveway. He often took my sisters and me up to see what appeared to be miniature cows and thread-like rivers below. It was a little scary at first, but we relaxed after he assured us it was safe because he was a good pilot. The entire family could fit into the aircraft and we made trips to Miami, New Orleans, and St. Louis—among other places—for vacations.

After one of these airplane trips, he put up a basketball goal for me at the house. My first love had always been football, and I kept track of my favorite teams on television, but I was starting to gain interest in basketball because I could shoot hoops without needing anyone else. In no time at all, I was able to hit shots from every imaginable angle, even from the top of a two foot brick planter 20 feet away. I'd developed a shot style that was more heaving than anything else because it took all I had to reach the goal. I brought the ball low to my right hip, and in one motion, flung it upward toward the orange rim. The Boston Celtics and UCLA Bruins became my favorite teams.

During the summer months, my mother would often drop me off at the municipal swimming pool where all of my friends hung out. It was located at Murphy Park and a youth center sat alongside it. Sunny days were spent jumping and diving from the low board before progressing to the high board, a good 12 feet above the water. I could do a front flip, back flip, and a variety of other moves by the end of the summer of 1963, but I also suffered second degree burns from lying out on the concrete all day without a T-shirt on. Sunburn protection was lax at that time and more than a few of us walked around red and blistered.

I was still a big fan of football, and I closely followed the Razorbacks, the local college team. Dad took me to a game, and I came to idolize the wide receivers, the position I wanted to play. I was bean-pole skinny and prone to being hurt by the bigger kids, so I preferred to be spread out at the end. Dad encouraged me—if I could touch it—I could catch it. I made this my motto. He would throw the ball just out of reach so I had to dive for it, telling me I'd need to toughen up if I wanted to play football.

As my sisters and I grew, the country atmosphere of Granny Griffins lost some of its appeal, so when Mom and Dad needed a break, we were taken instead to our paternal grandparents who lived in town. My grandmother's name was Vina, but my grandfather called her Mother. She was a compassionate woman with an enormous heart. Every day, a large kitchen put her through her paces as she fed us or anybody else that wandered in. Food never saw a trash can. I'm sure that enduring the Great Depression and trying to feed eleven children and a husband had a lot to do with it. She would pinch my cheek hard and tell me that I was the cutest thing she'd ever seen before cleverly opening my mouth to shove in the last little bit of food so she wouldn't have to put it back in the fridge. Vicks VapoRub was revered as a magic potion in her house, warding off all conceivable forms of discomfort and disease, and just to be safe, she smeared the odorous jelly over my chest every single night that I slept there. My nostrils came alive with the burn of the vaporizing inhalant as she worked her fingers loaded with salve, into my nose, as if I'd overdosed on wasabi. I actively struggled while she begged me to hold still.

My grandfather Daniel was a soft-spoken man with a head of thick, wavy white hair. He was the pastor for the local Nazarene church. As he spoke, the congregation moaned and wailed but I never saw anything too extreme. At his house, he often sat in his favorite chair while my sisters and I took turns brushing his magnificent hair. Being part curious, part ornery, we decided one day to load the brush with Vicks while granddad Daniel took an afternoon snooze. After a few strokes of the medicinal gel through his wondrous locks he woke up startled and quickly stopped the proceedings. Even then, he never raised his voice.

I became acquainted with a few cousins while at Harvey and Vina's. Dad's brother, Sam, had two kids who spent a lot of time there like us, Brett was Ruth's age, and Irene the same as Hazel. Dad had another brother named Phil who lived nearby but didn't come around very much, and another brother who died in the war. Besides that, there were seven aunts who provided a host of cousins for me, all of whom lived in California.

My paternal grandparents provided a carefree and secure environment for my sisters and me, but still, I can see why my father rebelled against them. Granddad Harvey railed against sin, trading his sermons for food and leading his family in regularly scheduled religious doctrine throughout the day. While writing this book, a relative showed me letters written by my dad during the war. They'd been sent to his parents describing what he could of his base in San Diego. I also read the replies, which were simply page after page of scripture references. I suspect that my dad respected his father but resisted this indoctrination. While I was growing up, he never set foot in a church with me, instead recalling stories of the 1930s gangsters that dominated the headlines of his youth. My own formative experiences with religion amounted to a smattering of Sunday school attendances at a nearby Methodist church at my mother's insistence, and a few services at my grandfather's church whenever I stayed with them, but nothing more.

Lemus Daniel did without much of anything as a young man, but after he'd earned a hint of the good life, he wanted more. He prided himself on his early successes in business and his sensitivity to omens, including bad ones like those detailed below:

"With the help of my father and Harold Smith, I started my first house to be sold on the open market. This led to some pretty big adventures in Springdale. My few years of experience in the business in California proved very helpful in bringing the new ranch-style home to the area. My business gained momentum, and I came to be considered a pacesetter in new home construction throughout the remainder of the 1950s.

Meanwhile, Tom graduated with honors from the University of Arkansas, while Jim kept his chicken haulers busy and expanded his assets. Tom married a girl named Joan and had three children—one boy and two girls—over the next few years. We kept track of one another through mutual friends, and offered an occasional 'hello' at social functions. After a considerable time, Tom and I slowly resumed our friendship. Tom, in the interim, expanded his role in Jim Dawson's company and was accepted by many influential people, including local politicians.

In the spring of 1957, Tom showed up at my office with a roll of house plans under his arm. The plans had been drawn by a local architect, Bill Williams, who'd studied design while living in Greenwich Village in New York City. The plans were for a very elaborate house for me to build on Ruby Drive in Springdale. During the building, and after completion of Tom's home, he and I began socializing more. Our wives and children became friends as well.

During the years of 1958 and 1959, Dawson's business continued to grow, and I moved into a new home on Emerald Avenue. Everything was going well until I got a strange call from the local police department.

Back in the fall of 1956, I'd purchased a very old house on Claire Street in the business area of Springdale. I had no particular plans for the property, but as business wheels began to turn a few years later, I considered the investment. After a few weeks, I was approached by David Allen, a mortician from Tulsa, who wanted me to convert the old house into a mortuary and lease it to him. I agreed and entered into a 10-year contract. I was away for a couple of weeks when I got a call from Clyde Winston, who was no longer State Trooper Winston, but now the Chief of Police. He assured me that there wasn't a problem; he just wanted to discuss something with me. I agreed to come down to the station and was led to Winston's basement office. I recognized Gary Clancy sitting next to Winston. Clancy was the owner of Clancy Funeral Home—the only mortuary in town—and an ambulance service that Winston operated for him, from which he made more than a few dollars. I took a chair.

Chief Winston lost no time getting to the point. He handed me a picture of David Allen, a mug shot. "Do you know this man?" he asked. I replied that I did and that I was renovating a mortuary for him on Claire Street. Clancy remained silent as the chief continued. "We don't want him in our town. He has a police rap."

I looked at Clancy. "Who doesn't want him in our town?" I paused before finally asking, "What kind of criminal is he supposed to be?"

"He's been arrested for drunk driving," the chief replied.

"What else?"

"He's an undesirable, we don't want him here."

"That's your department," I said. "And I have no authority to say who can or cannot live in this town."

Gary Clancy remained silent throughout the whole conversation but I understood why he was there.

Chief Winston pulled no punches. "Lemus, Gary Clancy here is ready to make you an offer on that funeral home you're building. He'll pay you more than you'll get from Allen."

"Gentlemen," I replied. "I am not ready to enter into a conspiracy with you against a man trying to make an honest living."

I got up and headed for the door. Before I could exit, Chief Winston stuck his finger in my face. "Lemus Daniel, you'll remember this day!"

David Allen did occupy his new business on schedule; but it would have been better if he hadn't. Allen called me after his third trip to the Winston jail. He needed $500 to post a bond, lest he get hauled back to jail on another trumped up charge. His ambulance had been cited again while responding to another false emergency. He pleaded with me for the money so he could pay and leave town. I gave him the money and took the building back."

I can applaud my dad's defense of Allen, but part of my father's resistance to Winston was bolstered by his association with Tom Dawson, who could protect him from his threats.

CHAPTER 3

Before I started fifth grade, I attended summer camp in southern Arkansas, a top-notch operation that lasted for two months. A first-rate rifle and archery range sat on one end of a sprawling property of pine trees, and on the other end, a sled-like apparatus sat on a track at the top of a hill. Riders would lie on their bellies and race down the hillside to the cooling waters of a clear lake below. Our bunks were designed like forts with old wooden floors and porches that were marked by a Pirate team logo. Youngsters from as far as Dallas and Indianapolis filled the many bunks and became friends overnight. Jimmy Dawson, Tom Dawson's son, had come with me, but because he was older and in a different bunk, I didn't see him much.

By the end of camp, I'd gained a medal for shooting a .22 rifle and a blue ribbon for our bunk winning the most basketball games. I'd also built an insect cemetery under my bunk house, weird burial grounds full of small rocks that marked the demise of various pests I'd come across during my stay.

While I was away at camp, and the girls at Grandma Daniel's, I learned that Mom and Dad had been living the high life with the Dawson's, squeezing in trips to the Gulf and New York, placing high-roller bets at the racetrack in Hot Springs, and rolling dice in Las Vegas. My dad was getting comfortable with his lifestyle and my mother was showing little resistance.

Billy Kennedy was one of my new buddies, and we sat on our front porch when our parents pulled in a few minutes apart to retrieve us. I was introduced to Billy's sister: She had long, brown hair and a cute smile that produced a pair of dimples that made me swoon. My first crush, I mumbled the name Marcia for a few miles before settling in for the drive home with my parents.

The school I attended wasn't far from Emerald Avenue. I liked my teachers and most of my classmates and didn't get into trouble, but I was small and occasionally bullied by bigger kids. To avoid getting beat up, I kept to myself.

I did eventually join my classmates, Kendall and Gary, in their rock 'n roll band. The Beatles had taken the world by storm, but we made *Wooly Bully* by Sam the Sham our go-to song because it was easy. Unable to play any complicated instruments, we used a tambourine, maracas, and bongos, banging furiously as we sang. Our teacher, Mrs. King, encouraged us and led us to believe that we were good enough to someday display our music on the world stage. By late 1965, the band brought me out of my shell and I was walking the halls at Westwood Elementary with a bit more swagger.

I still had to stay on the lookout for hard feelings from some of the kids at school, especially the rural boys hauled in by bus from the outskirts of town. Some of these scrappers would resort to fisticuffs for a variety of offenses, real or imagined. Tom Dawson meanwhile, had already earned his share of black eyes while traveling the country with truck driving strangers and an uncaring mother before being pawned off on his father as a teen. Now, with Jim's guidance, Tom was willing to do whatever it took to be the one delivering the blows. I stayed out of his way, too, and never complained to my father, but I think he knew, often saying not to let anyone push me around. Still, I remained non-confrontational, awkward, and not quite fitting in. At the time, I saw no value in earning a black eye.

By the time I was 10-years old, I was a member of the Cub Scouts, obsessed with comic books and fantasies of fighting crime. I'd have found it hard to imagine the circles I'd be running in a few short years later. Not so for my father, who was already neck-deep. By my sixteenth birthday, I would find myself in a somewhat different situation: immune to hassling, and surrounded and supported by a crew of dangerous criminals.

His memoirs continue:

"I recall that Tom directed me to drive down Willow Street, and pointed to a little white house. He leaned across me and as usual laid on the horn. He didn't let up until an elderly black gentleman came out of the house.

"Benito," Tom yelled, "Will you drive us to Ft. Smith?"

Fort Smith was 80 miles away. Benito said he would for $15.

"Benito's a good driver," Tom said. "You and I are going to drink this booze." I was too weak-willed to say 'no,' and within a few minutes, we were on our way to Tiny Henson's Vegas-style gambling joint just west of Ft. Smith, across the Oklahoma border. Somehow, I felt honored to be included in this excursion.

After we arrived, I sat at the bar and settled in while Tom yelled and screamed at the dice table. A little later, I leaned on the table myself and played until my funds were depleted. It didn't take long, and left me stuck there until Tom was ready to leave. I went out to the car where Benito was sleeping. Black men were not allowed to enter the gambling hall. I relaxed into the back seat, and tried to sleep until Tom came out. Around 5:00 a.m., he emerged, looking like hell. I asked him how he was able to stay up all night without sleep and he pulled out a bottle full of tiny white pills and offered me two.

"Eating two of these is like whipping a tired horse!"

I declined, and he demanded the back seat for himself and closed his eyes as Benito drove us back to Springdale.

After we had been on the road close to two hours, Tom sat up and asked where we were. Since Benito's top speed seemed to be somewhere around 30 miles an hour, we hadn't gone far. It appeared that Benito wasn't such a good driver after all.

"My God, it's 6:45!" Tom shouted. "I'm supposed to be Master of Ceremonies at a fundraising breakfast for the governor at 7:00!"

After I assumed the wheel, Tom told me that he didn't mind missing his role as Master of Ceremonies, but did want to hand the Dawson contribution check to the governor personally. He hoped the governor would help him get his license back after he lost it a second time for reckless driving.

We got there just as the meeting was breaking up and Tom was able to personally hand the check from Dawson Produce to the governor. He then made the request for re-instatement of his driver's license.

Tom told me later that the governor hadn't really refused him, but said that perhaps he might need a favor or two in the future, and Tom agreed. I asked him if he'd ever had any political aspirations.

"Hell no," he told me. "I can buy a politician easier than becoming one."

In early 1966, Dad pulled my baby sisters and me around on an upside down car hood attached to a chain on his car bumper. A dozen feet behind, we swung across the ice and snow and around the corners of abandoned streets, hanging onto the flat device he'd crafted for us, and belly laughing with glee.

The year before, one of the major rivers near town had been dammed, and formed a 50-mile shoreline with more than 400 square miles of water playground known as Beaver Lake. Dad wasted no time in purchasing an 18-foot ski boat in anticipation of the coming summer. We fished, learned to ski, and spent a lot of time on the water. He also enjoyed entertaining his friends with the boat and often held cook outs at the lake.

As I'd hoped, when the school doors finally did swing open, I found myself sitting next to Laura, whom I'd met at the pool and who'd made me forget about Marcia from Dallas. That first day, she drew pictures of me on the chalkboard with a round head, big ears, and buck teeth. It didn't look anything like me until she sprinkled in some freckles. She was the daughter of a well-known family in town, and like me, had an older sister.

One day after school, my father invited only me to join him for a trip to the Western Hills Resort in Northeast Oklahoma with a couple of his friends, Robert and John. It was a short flight, but after we reached altitude, he surprised me, telling me to get in the co-pilot seat and hold the steering wheel. I was anxious, but he encouraged me, and I eventually grabbed the handle, sat tense and wary, scanning the horizon.

After he'd let me dip and veer for a bit, he ended it only after I put everyone's stomach on edge. I wasn't sure how much control he'd really given me, but in my mind, it was a lot. I'd fretted killing us all in a fleeting moment.

At the resort pool, I noticed a couple of women that I didn't recognize. One, Brenda, had long, dark hair and makeup caked on her sun-kissed face. She said "hello," with a voice deep and smoky. There was an ice chest full of beer at the pool and Robert tossed me one. I looked at my father, who nodded his permission. Before I started drinking, I looked again for his consent and he was still grinning, so I turned up the can. The beer was cold and refreshing, and I endured the bitter taste, determined to finish it. They all laughed after I'd downed it, belched, and started slowly sipping on a second. *It was our little secret,* my father told me.

That night, I slept it off in my own room.

Upon returning to Springdale, he let me out in the driveway and told me that he wouldn't be staying at the house as much. He'd gotten an apartment across town because he worked late so often, but would be around a lot. It felt wrong to me, but I couldn't speak to it. I tried to be as grown up as possible about the news.

Behind the scenes, Dad was riding high, making money, and keeping women on the side. This vice was his true weakness. He showed up at the house often enough to keep me from asking too many questions, but was starting to get careless. Not long after the Western Hills trip, he came by to take Ruth to an after-school band practice. He'd decided that we'd all go and drop her off, then enjoy some ice cream at a parlor in town. Mom said she'd come, too.

We pulled out of the driveway with my mother in the front seat and the four of us piled into the spacious, but still limited, back seat. We knew we'd all fit better after we dropped Ruth off, so we tolerated the tight space without much complaining. Less than a hundred yards from our driveway, while heading east towards the school, we felt a thunderous jolt in the back. We turned to see a car that had rammed the heavy, durable rear bumper. It was slowing down and preparing to do it again. And once again, while we braced ourselves in the back seat, we were rammed from behind and pushed forward.

This was being done on purpose. I recognized Brenda from Western Hills, alone, in the car behind. Mom and Dad remained silent while my younger sisters looked to each other trying to figure it out. Ruth and I shared a glance that knew. While we sat in silence, she struck again. The quiet became deafening as I watched my parents glaring at each other. After my dad passed by the school, I realized he was heading for the police department. As he drew nearer to the station, the car behind veered off and sped away, and we circled back and dropped Ruth off for her practice. The ice cream was forgotten.

I suppose both of my parents felt that if it wasn't acknowledged, it didn't happen, and we would all forget about it, but I never forgot the crazy look on Brenda's face as she stepped on her accelerator.

LARRY DANIEL

CHAPTER 4

The following excerpt from my father's memoir details a strange event that came shortly after his and Tom's trip to the gambling hall and should have been enough for him to change direction. Unfortunately, it wasn't. Unlike much of what's preceded, I have some personal recollections of these events as well:

"Tom pulled into my driveway around dusk one evening in his new Oldsmobile and blew the horn. I went to the door clad only in pants. Tom hung his head out the window, and laughed a hideous laugh that gave me pause. My first instinct was to protect him, knowing an accident or worse loomed if I didn't intervene. Also, to save my wife and kids embarrassment, I felt like I had to do something. I stepped off my porch and moved swiftly toward the driver's side of the car, opened the door, and pushed Tom to the middle forcing his passenger to the other door. Tom was in top form, so drunk he hardly knew his own name.

"Wow, Lemus," Tom declared, "look what I've got here!"

She was the most homely and disoriented looking middle-aged female I had ever seen, with hair of straw and dirty legs, and just as stoned as Tom.

"Tom, what in the hell have you done?" I asked. "Why'd you come to my house like this?"

"I only wanted you to meet my new girlfriend, ain't she nice?"

She was incoherent and unhelpful, so I asked Tom where the woman lived so I could take her home. He opened a whiskey bottle and took a slug, then passed it to me. I took a healthy swallow, thinking it might ease the embarrassment I felt. I started the Olds, and backed out of the driveway."

My father, who was already malleable from several years of the fast lane with Tom Dawson, jumped into his role as sidekick and protector. But this mockery was merely a test of boundaries to see how far Dawson could take his friend, and what loyalties he could expect from him in the future. Slowly, but surely, Dad assumed the role of target in this bully's twisted game. My father was oblivious.

The story continues:

"Tom wanted me to take him to Don's liquor store on Highway 71 before I took his passenger home. I drove straight there and parked in front. Tom crawled over his companion and staggered into the liquor store. Don was there, and Tom talked for what seemed like an hour. I sat behind the wheel, half dressed and reluctant to go inside. I finished off the bottle that Tom left. Finally, Tom staggered back out of the store with two more bottles of whiskey. By this time, I was well on my way to catching up with him and his girlfriend.

The Dawson's money now fed many coffers in the local power structure, so I wasn't afraid to drive. Drunk or not, in Springdale, I was immune to arrest with a Dawson in the car. Even so, I knew it was in Tom's best interest, and mine, to take the woman home. After an hour of driving in circles due to a complete breakdown in communication, I found her shack some 100 yards off the Storey Road on the eastern outskirts of town. We left her standing by the side of the road and left.

By this time, I was feeling no pain, but still hadn't figured out what to do with Tom. I didn't want to take him home with me because I didn't want my children to see him this way, but I really wanted to go home, so I thought I would turn the situation around. As I pulled into my driveway, I parked and slumped over the steering wheel and pretended to pass out, thinking that Tom would then have to help me. After the porch light came on and my wife opened the door, Tom greeted her with, "Lemus has had too much to drink!"

They both helped me to my bed. I lay there thanking God that I was through with him for the night. As it turned out my gratitude was premature. Outside, I heard a scream.

"No! Stop, Tom. Please stop!"

I came out of the bedroom and saw Dawson pulling on my wife's arm.

"Let her go!" I ordered. "Get out of here! You're drunk!"

He staggered away back to the car, suddenly more impaired, muttering he was just kidding around.

Doris confided in me later that Tom had demanded sex before leaving and put his hand on her.

He left, weaving in and out of traffic down Emerald and over to Ruby Drive, somehow managing the short distance home."

Remembering that my father's girlfriend had attacked us with her car, I don't think Tom Dawson's exploits were so repulsive that Dad couldn't laugh them off and move past them. But for Dawson to be grabbing my mother and him not slapping him around for it was evidence of his selective passivity based on what he thought Dawson could still do for him. Dawson was boorish, but his influence over the town softened my father's concern enough for him to keep playing along. For whatever reason, my dad wasn't against getting in deeper. He was in the big leagues now, and sometimes that meant looking the other way:

"My home on Emerald Avenue was next door to another home I built the previous year, and was now occupied by Sherman Katz. Sherman was a partner with Jim Dawson. The official name of the company was Dawson-Katz Produce, and Jim owned 60% of the company and Sherman, 40%. Tom Dawson was not a major stockholder at the time, even though his influence in the company since his university graduation accelerated rapidly.

Sherman could not be considered a suit-and-tie man in the company. He was a field man who oversaw the operations of the truckers and the chicken catchers. He and his wife, Pamela, were down-to-earth people, but strange things can happen even to down-to-earth people.

On a rainy afternoon, I was sitting in my office on Hunt Street with Tom, my brother Sam, and Kim Roche, an architect from Ft. Smith. I'd just opened our second bottle of Wild Turkey. That particular bottle had been delivered to us by way of taxi cab, at Tom's request, from one of Don's liquor stores. Tom had a way of making people forget about his outrageous behavior. As we were pouring the whiskey, the telephone rang. When I answered, I heard Joan Dawson's voice asking if Tom was in my office.

"Yes, he's here," I said.

"Let me talk to him quick," she said. "Pamela's just shot Sherman!"

I handed the phone to Tom. He asked his wife if she was with Pamela, then began instructing her to keep Pamela calm and not allow her to speak to anyone until he could get there. Tom hung up, and with a somber voice said, "Sherman's been shot. I'll see you all later."

Having been the Katz neighbor for several years, I was aware that Pamela had a boyfriend, a traveling salesman. That afternoon, my brother and I drove north into Springdale and both noticed Pamela driving south out of Springdale with what appeared to be some of her wardrobe hanging in the back seat of her car. I remember commenting to Sam, "There goes some trouble," as we passed.

After Tom left, Sam and Kim inquired about my conversation with Joan and I repeated what Joan said to me. Needless to say, Sam, Ken, and I were surprised upon reading the Friday evening news headlines, "Local Businessman Commits Murder-Suicide."

Sherman's shooting provided Tom with the opportunity to cash in on one of his promised favors from the upper echelons of Arkansas state government. After a few early morning calls, it was decided that poor Sherman had partied with his wife and the salesman, and after a few drinks, unexpectedly pulled a gun and opened fire on the salesman, killing him, then shooting himself between the eyes. During those early morning phone calls, it was not only determined who held the gun that killed Sherman, but also who would benefit from the unfortunate circumstances of Sherman's death. Sherman's share of the Dawson-Katz organization, after all, was worth a good deal to some people. All of this took place before Sherman Katz' body was even cold.

In those few minutes that followed Sherman's death, Tom Dawson became the judge and jury, and when the verdict came in, the Dawsons owned all of the Katz stock in the Dawson-Katz Corporation. He had purchased the stock from Pamela at the ridiculously low price of five cents on the dollar and perhaps the assurance to Pamela that there would be no criminal investigation into Sherman's apparent suicide. The Dawsons lost no time in dropping the Katz name from their company, either. They did it the same day.

Within a couple of days, I was in the office of the director of the First Commercial Bank in Springdale. Like everyone else in town, he was discussing Sherman's death. Since I was the Katz' next door neighbor, he confided in me that Sherman's death was a real shame, but what was happening to Pamela as a result was also tragic.

Talk was rampant after Sherman Katz' death, and there was much speculation about who pulled the trigger. The death weapon was a .22 caliber pistol that Sherman borrowed from Wilson Todd, a local broker. Mr. Todd told me in the course of a conversation, many days later, that two days before the shooting, Sherman borrowed the gun with the explanation that he needed to kill a rat. To my knowledge, no rats were killed that evening.

Lovers' triangles very rarely have happy endings, but Tom confided in me a few days after Sherman's funeral that the arrangements he had made with Pamela following Sherman's death constituted the deal of a lifetime for him. He told me everything and seemed quite proud.

Apparently, Jim was pleased with Tom's deal, and it made him realize how capable and crafty Tom was. After that incident, Jim backed off and let Tom run the business the way he saw fit."

On occasion, my father and I took drives around town in his car, him jawing about point spreads, the over and under, and parlay odds. He'd stop by small businesses, beer joints, and people's houses to press the flesh. He operated as a bookie during the football season, and we dropped by the various places after games to pay or collect. Dad looked sharp in his lucky tan slacks and loafers.

Dad was a highly visible player in town. Wherever he went, people noticed him and made him the center of attention, he didn't have to try. He flashed hundreds for me to see and would often drive by large parcels of land that he'd bought, saying that someday it would all be mine. His business opportunities blossomed, and he used those opportunities to help others get their starts in business. He was generous and popular, but only later would I realize that the whole time, he was tangling himself further with Dawson and his cronies, too:

"The Dawson poultry business was becoming very influential and a major player in the region thanks to Tom and Jim's shrewd thinking. Tom began to expand his assets to things other than chickens. My development business expanded beyond residential and commercial construction, and grew to include a concrete delivery business and part of a lumber yard. My contacts were extensive, and my name was recognized.

I was approached by Frank Mooney to enter into the shopping center business. Frank had formerly been a football bookie and in green stamp sales (green stamps were a rewards program at grocery stores, and originated in the 1930s) but found his way into the Dawson organization and later became Tom's right-hand man. Frank knew his way around the grocery business through his contacts in the trading stamp sales promotions. At that time, I owned an ideal tract of land zoned for a shopping center. The property laid smack dab in the middle of a residential development I just completed. I planned to build a shopping center myself and honestly, I'm not certain why I allowed Frank and Tom to become partners in the project.

Upon completion of the shopping center on Hunt Avenue, I found myself a 60% owner of the shopping center, and a 40% owner of a grocery retail business that operated within the shopping center. I became more and more entangled with Tom, and now Frank, and thought it might serve my interests because Tom was making a lot of money.

Having discovered new ways to make and spend money, Frank and Tom decided to buy another property, a motor hotel—the Mountain Inn, located in downtown Fayetteville. The new hotel was originally a community project that was under-financed and a losing proposition for the city, so Tom and Frank went to the Teamsters' Union and obtained a loan that was inflated to twice the hotel's actual worth. These kinds of loans were handed out by the Teamsters Union to buyers of many of the large hotel-casinos in Las Vegas. In turn, they gave kickbacks to the union. This was the kind of stuff that Jimmy Hoffa was known for before he disappeared in 1975.

The inflated loan allowed Tom and Frank to pocket some of the money and at the same time, float their hotel project until they could find an unsuspecting buyer to dump it on.

When they took ownership, one of the first things Frank and Tom did was to convert the basement into the Gaslight Club. The fourth floor would be set apart as their own personal playpen.

Frank and Tom kept several rooms overlooking the pool off-limits to paying guests. Most of Dawson's special friends, including me, were given keys to these rooms. Becoming one of Dawson's special friends involved providing him with some favors in return. Politicians, lawyers, musicians, and long-time acquaintances made up the bulk of the exclusive key-holders.

By this time, Tom and I had a mutual friend who was making it big as a musician, and we both rubbed elbows with some of the biggest names in the business, including Ray Charles, who frequented the Mountain Inn in those days. Tom was able to further seduce his guest with the glamour of people they would have otherwise never encountered, tempting the star-struck crowd with sexual favors that were provided on the fourth floor. Hidden cameras were set up in certain rooms.

Archibald Fleeman, the 38-year-old counsel for Dawson Produce, could often be found on the fourth floor, mingling and providing advice for the specific set of problems the key-holding crowd faced. Fleeman, from Kansas City, had worked his way up the ladder and into Dawson's good graces, and eventually became Tom's top advisor. It was rumored that he was an inside trader and netting Dawson large profits.

The assessor had a key as well, and provided low-ball estimates on the vast properties the Dawson's held, and saved them a small fortune in taxes. Everyone there had something Tom wanted and expected in return for a key to the fourth floor.

Most of the activities that took place of the fourth floor involved private parties between key-holders and a steady stream of young women. Tom himself was bald and unattractive, but he placed a young man named Phil Davis, who had no trouble attracting women, in a strategic position at his poultry plant and offices. Phil had once traveled with a rock group, increasing his allure. His job was to screen and procure as many attractive and willing ladies for the fourth floor as possible from the poultry plant and offices. Many times, money changed hands, but I never had to pay for the services that the Mountain Inn and Tom Dawson offered me.

During the Mountain Inn days, a famous musician friend of mine and Tom's extended a special invitation to us to attend one of his performances with his well-known band in nearby Tulsa, Oklahoma. I had a very nice woman with whom I kept regular company, but Tom was unable to find any female to accompany him. It became my task to find a date for him, so I called a friend of mine, a pretty airline stewardess named Patricia. I stretched the truth about Tom's looks, and she agreed to be his date.

Tom and I traveled separately to Tulsa. He wanted to make the two-hour drive, and I wanted to fly my plane. So, I left early with my lady friend and flew to Oklahoma City to pick up Patricia. We flew to Tulsa, where we were to meet Tom at the Trade-Winds Motel. When Patricia laid eyes on him, it was apparent that she was disappointed, but she tried to be a good sport, and we went to the concert.

After the show, we returned to the motel, where we planned to party with members of the band. Patti wanted no part of the party and demanded to be taken home to Oklahoma City. I told her it was unsafe for me to fly the plane after the drinking I had done. Tom said he would drive her home, which was about 90 minutes away.

I didn't see Tom again that evening or for the next few days, but I did hear from a very angry and humiliated Patricia. She told me the story of her ride to Oklahoma City that took on nightmarish proportions. Tom got into a fist-fight with the poor girl so she would submit to his sexual demands. He was lucky to evade being arrested, and needless to say, I knew better than to ever call her number again."

My father was pointing a finger, but he was barely above the accusation he leveled at Dawson. The fairness he wished for blacks didn't apply to women. Dawson on the other hand, was too powerful, rather than lucky, to have been arrested.

"Eventually, Jim found Phil wandering around inside the plant. He did not recognize him and asked what his job was. When Phil couldn't explain sufficiently, Jim fired him. No matter how much power Tom gained, he still had to step around a troublesome Jim from time to time.

The fourth floor of the Mountain Inn remained Tom's playground until an unsuspecting buyer from Little Rock arrived, and we all turned in our keys. Around this time, Jim wanted a position on the board of the First Commercial Bank of Springdale, so he started buying all of the available stock he could get his hands on. When Fred Comstock died and left a large portion *of his stock to a daughter (who lived in Denver), Jim was made aware of the inheritance and made a hurried trip to Colorado where he successfully bought her stock. The purchase gave him enough leverage to demand a seat on the eight-member board.*

On the night of the first meeting after Jim's acquisition, the first item on the agenda for business at hand was the matter of reducing the board from eight members to four. This was carried immediately by four members who volunteered to resign rather than let Jim have a seat on the board. This is what the majority of the citizens of Springdale thought of Jim Dawson."

In the drinking establishments we often visited, there was a pool table, and Dad taught me to play while he chased beers between runs of nine-ball. He'd pass me the can and the proprietors never cared. If it had a little salt on the top of it, I liked it better, but my favorite became mixing in tomato juice to make what was known as a red beer. While George Jones whined on the juke box, we whined right along with him.

Between lyrics, he'd whistle while he shot and made remarks guaranteed to make me blush. He'd humorously contort his face and say cryptic things like, "strap it on" or, "skin it back." Occasionally, we'd drive to Fayetteville to see his black friends. I observed money changing hands from side wagers and a few bucks getting dropped on anyone deemed down on their luck.

I'd become an even bigger Razorback football fan after I met some of the players and my father got some autographs for me. He picked me up one afternoon in late '66 and we headed to Razorback Stadium for a game against the SMU Mustangs. That year, the Hogs—as they were affectionately called—had a good team and were favored to win easily. He told me that we had a stopover before the game, so we cut across town using a shortcut he knew about to avoid the heavy traffic surrounding the affair. Before long, we crested a hill, and took in the vast football complex that sat inside its cavernous bowl. The bleachers were stacked up one by one to a press box that spread across the top of the west side. Our destination was an upscale apartment on a hill, overlooking it all, and we pulled into the driveway.

He walked in and signaled for me to follow. The apartment was neatly kept with large windows that looked out over the stadium. A young woman walked out of the bedroom and Dad greeted her casually. He then motioned for me to sit on the couch while he changed his clothes from a closet that was filled with his belongings. The woman was tall, blond, and beautiful, and her powerful perfume filled the air. She ignored me and followed him into the bedroom. I waited a few anxious moments, putting two and two together, and gathered that Dad was cozy with the young lady. He soon emerged and we proceeded to walk across the street to the game.

Our seats were on the 50-yard line amongst the other old timers surrounded by billowing cigar smoke and upward-facing whiskey flasks. I got a unique sight and smell of a college football game in the mid 1960s.

The Hogs got out to a good lead and maintained it throughout the game, and my seat offered an ideal vantage point of the quarterback throwing perfect spirals to his receivers as the crowd of 44,000 went wild. We called the hogs by raising then shaking our hands and yelling, *woo-pig-sooie*, the team's official cheer.

The defense was stellar that day, and pitched a shutout behind All-American lineman Logan Phipps, who many years later would thank me on national television

THE RUINING OF LEMUS DANIEL

for my role in saving his son's life. He would define it as a miracle.

With three minutes to play and a score of 22-0, victory was assured. Dad pulled on my arm and we made a mad dash for the exit to beat the crowd. We walked back across the street to the house on the hill and retrieved our car, but before we left, my father poked his head inside the door and spoke to the young woman. I heard him call her Angel.

LARRY DANIEL

CHAPTER 5

I turned 12 years old in the summer of 1967, "The Summer of Love."

The school year had been a good one but was drawing to an end. I tried to emulate my father's big personality and had gained a little more confidence. Still, I was stoic about the other women in his life.

A month before school ended, my mother informed me that Dad was picking me up and taking me to California. The news was unexpected, but at my mother's request, the school had granted me permission to leave early. She would miss me, she said, but I'd be just fine. I'd spent time away at camp before, but this was different. It would be just the two of us.

He pulled up in his new, white Cadillac El Dorado that sported a fancy black top, and loaded my suitcase in the trunk. He talked about the saloons that filled the old town, preserved to replicate the wild West of the old cowboy days, as we drove towards Dodge City, Kansas. He talked about bridges, cranes, and truck hauling capacity, and was keen on the details regarding the composition of the road we drove on. I tried to hang on every word and nodded "yes" when it was appropriate. We were headed to California, and although I was excited, I was also anxious.

After leaving the saloons of Dodge City, we drove up Pike's Peak and then visited an establishment in the Rocky Mountains where a pool table sat almost on its side. When you struck the cue ball, it would defy gravity and seemingly roll uphill into the corner pocket. The background had been altered to create the illusion.

I took in the fresh air and the bracing scent of pine while we weaved through the towering peaks of the Rockies on our way to Wyoming and Yellowstone. After entering Wyoming, a raging river raced alongside us on the highway. We got out along the way and took some pictures with my dad's Polaroid camera and made Casper, Wyoming, by nightfall.

We reached the south gate of Yellowstone the next day, and encountered some black bears by the side of the road. A crowd of cars were stopped with their windows down to observe the white-collared adult bears. Some people threw food out of the window, and the fat, well-fed animals seemed almost picky. My dad took a quick picture of me after I got out of the car about thirty yards from the scene. He clicked the photo and I watched it develop in the car, fanning it to make it dry quicker. I favored this particular picture above all the others.

Our room was at The Old Faithful Inn in the heart of Yellowstone. It was a magnificent structure of lodgepole pine and rhyolite stone that had been completed in 1904, the largest log building in the world, with huge open beams overhead and a giant, 85-foot long fireplace made from 500 tons of stone. Many of the original articles of the time of its construction hung from every rafter, and made me feel like I had gone back as a trapper or a hunter. Old Faithful geyser was just across the parking lot.

The geysers spewed and the waterfalls raged as wildlife blended in perfectly with the setting, and stoked my young imagination. Buffalo, elk, and more black bears, wandered unafraid out in the open. My father seemed pleased with himself when I told him that this might have been the best day of my life. After another night at the Lodge, we set off for our next destination on the west coast.

After crossing into Nevada, he began showing me how well the car performed by letting go of the steering wheel while traveling west on Interstate 80. Traffic was absent, speed limits were absent, and he was going over 80 mph with no hands on the wheel. After a long minute, he suggested that I drive. I thought he was joking, but after he pulled over, it was clear that he wasn't. I was just big enough to reach the gas pedal with the seat pulled all the way up, so I pulled out onto the barren highway just beyond the Bonneville Salt Flats. My eyes widened as I peered over the top of the steering wheel at a highway as straight as a string, and I gained courage as I increased my speed.

"Let go of the wheel," my dad dared me. I balked, but he insisted, so I let my fingertips cautiously hover ever so close to the wheel and slowly pressed the accelerator with my foot. I finally put my hands by my side as I reached around 60 mph on the desolate highway. After a quick minute, he reclaimed the wheel. I sat in the passenger seat, basking in glory. I would have run through a brick wall for him. Similar to catching a just out-of-reach football, or fly a plane, driving a car without any hands was another example of my dad pushing my limits, and me wanting only to please him.

Nevada was empty and dry and I couldn't wait to get through it to California where relatives I'd never met awaited us. By late evening, we arrived in the small town of Weimar, which sat off Interstate 80 about an hour east of Sacramento. The house was a short distance from the highway, and was surrounded by woods and secluded. I was relieved to get out of the car and my aunt Caroline made me feel welcome. After she came out and embraced my dad and me, I could sense that their relationship was one of deep rooted acceptance. She was the oldest of my dad's sisters and looked a lot like my grandmother Daniel. Her husband, Uncle Willy, struck me as a friendly, but odd man who'd stockpiled an underground bunker with food and water in case of apocalypse. The next morning we said goodbye with hugs, promises to keep up, and a reminder that Caroline was my favorite aunt now.

Within the hour, we were pulled over a few cars back from a barricade. The police were stationed at intersections off a main square in downtown Sacramento, stopping traffic for an impending spectacle. My dad somehow knew, but hadn't mentioned it, and let it unfold for me. Suddenly, I heard the rumble and roar of a never-ending stream of Harley Davidson motorcycles parading by and carrying a notorious looking motorcycle gang. The Hells Angels emblem stitched boldly across their leather vests tipped me off to who they were. They were on their way to San Francisco, the hub of their organization, and our destination as well.

Once we reached "The City," we made Union Station our headquarters for the couple of days we stayed. We caught a baseball game at Candlestick Park that night and watched Willie Mays, the "Say Hey Kid," play centerfield in a winning 7-5 effort. After the game, we drove back, parked a few blocks from the hotel, and walked toward our room. An occasional street light showed the way and, before long, illuminated a man and a woman standing in a dark alleyway across the street. The scant clothing of the young woman looked suspicious, yet my father strolled over to them and started talking. I stayed put across the street as he bargained with the pair, and after he quit talking to them, rejoined me for the rest of the walk to our hotel. He'd be right back, he told me, and for me to go on to bed for the night.

The next morning, we strolled into Haight-Ashbury, the headquarters for the Summer of Love movement that had taken over the nation that year. Free love, psychedelic music, and drugs were the primary themes, and any kid from Springdale, Arkansas, would have been quite amused by what was going on here. We walked by quaint little row houses, shops, and record stores. I saw long-haired anti-war soldiers in full uniform, wearing frayed blue jeans with patches, beaded necklaces, and head bands with paisley designs. There was a constant gesturing of the two-fingered peace sign, like an easy-to-guess password, that caused them to nod their heads in approval whenever I flashed it back playfully.

Just west of the Haight, a few war protestors loitered among the masses of barefoot and un-bathed young adults on the beautiful grounds of Golden Gate Park, the site of the Human Be-In, where Timothy Leary told the throng to turn on, tune in, and drop-out just months earlier. People dragged around blankets, played music, and sang songs. I thought I smelled straw burning. In a few short years, I'd be dragging a blanket around and sleeping in a park, just like these youngsters.

We finished our tour the next day by seeing Chinatown and the Wharf, and prepared for the drive south to Los Angeles, which invited conversation about what I had witnessed in San Francisco.

"What about all those kids?" he asked.

I ventured, "Different, I guess." Everyone's hair was long, and the clothes, colorful, but I wasn't prepared for a deep conversation with my dad about what was going on at Haight-Ashbury. I briefly thought of how dangerous it felt, and how strange it was, to watch him walk into a dark alley to solicit a working girl. It was great to see Willie Mays play centerfield. I'm not sure what he'd hoped to hear.

The war in Vietnam was also on his mind, and now mine as he stated his anti-war stance while he drove. He voiced his distaste for the military because of his own experience in World War II, which he described as miserable, though he saw no action. He promised that by the time I was old enough to be drafted, he'd take me to Canada.

After three hours of driving, we detoured towards the coast so I could see some big houses near the ocean before we entered the greater Los Angeles area. I saw spectacular homes with panoramic views that could only be described as paradise. Palm trees, sunshine, and the smell of the nearby ocean, wafted over my senses, my window rolled down. "It takes a lot of money to live here," he said.

We missed the undeniable crush of traffic he promised would soon arrive, and several freeway exchanges later we arrived at my aunt Florence's house in Duarte, a small town near Pasadena. At Florence's feet, two yapping Chihuahuas greeted us at the door, giving me every indication they wanted to bite my ankles, though they refrained. Florence cooked a table full of food and insisted that I gorge myself into a coma, to which I complied. I had a well-established tendency now of not saying "no."

Florence, like Caroline, adored her brother, but Dad held a special affection for Florence, who'd gone through a teenage pregnancy. My father never judged her and maintained close ties with her.

"Tell your Aunt Caroline that I'm your favorite aunt now," she insisted over dinner.

After sleeping off the excess, we traveled the short distance to Garden Grove in Orange County and our headquarters for the remaining time of my stay in sunny southern California.

We turned off Beach Boulevard, a four-lane highway in Orange County, and arrived at an apartment complex, not far from Disneyland Amusement Park. I noticed a Jack-in-the-Box hamburger place next door where a person could talk to a plastic clown outside—a Pop goes the Weasel lookalike— to order a meal, something I'd never seen in Arkansas. My dad promised a day at Disneyland as soon as we got settled, and I looked forward to never ending days at Huntington Beach, just a few miles south on Beach Blvd.

When I walked into the apartment, I was greeted by Brenda, the dark haired and heavily made-up woman who'd rammed our car back in Springdale, with a fake smile that knocked the air right out of my sails. Dad seemed unfazed. He'd been providing wonderful experiences for me, but now I faced the brick wall I'd thought of after driving in Nevada. I wasn't sure why she was there, or how much time I'd have to spend with her, and after I discovered that she lived there, I started to shrink. I couldn't confront him, couldn't say anything. He acted so nonchalant about it that I finally took a cue from him when he offered it.

"There's nothing to worry about," he insisted. "There's a basketball goal out back and I'm pretty sure you'll find a ball out there. Why don't you go shoot a little?" Sucker punched, I found the ball and started pumping shots. I leaned hard on that basketball and orange rim, hoping that I could manage to stay out of her way.

My father had arranged for me to work mornings on an ice cream truck with a distant cousin. The next morning, I walked the few blocks to the job and arrived by 8:00 a.m. to prepare for the day with 16-year-old Rusty, Linda's son, who was related to somebody somewhere. Linda was reserved and didn't smother me with food or attention, and I was more than okay with that. I'm not sure what my father was doing with his time while I peddled ice cream, but after a few days, I stopped thinking about him. I was adjusting and Disneyland could wait.

Rusty drove a converted van with small refrigerators in the back that held a variety of frozen treats that we couldn't eat ourselves until the day was over, and then, only one. We slowly rolled by neighborhoods playing jingle music while kids raced out to the curb to hand over their silver coins. Rusty treated me well and didn't mock the southern drawl that always drew immediate attention from the kids on the route.

By early afternoon, I was finished working and left to spend the rest of the day however I wanted. Most days, I just shot hoops at the apartment. I wanted to go to the beach, and Rusty told me that he often hitchhiked there, and that if I wanted, I could go with him the next time he went. I admitted that I did, so after another morning on the route, we found ourselves standing at the busy intersection of Beach Boulevard and Garden Grove with our thumbs out. The pavement was scorching hot, and I regretted going barefoot, dancing to shady spots whenever possible.

Before long, a middle-aged woman pulled over, and we flopped into the back seat of her car. She joked about taking us home to feed us before dropping us off. We declined and soon found ourselves enjoying the salty aroma and ocean scenery of Huntington Beach. Getting to the beach by way of thumb proved far easier than I thought it would be.

The beaches of California differed from what I'd experienced in Florida when I was younger. The water was much colder, and the waves more powerful. Rusty showed me around the surf shops and hot dog stands that he frequented and confided in me that he wanted to be a professional surfer someday. After a couple of hours, we returned the same way we came.

When I finally told Dad about hitchhiking to the beach, he said that it sounded like a good idea as long as Rusty was with me. Rusty didn't always want to go to the beach, but I did, so every so often, after the ice cream route, I defied my father and walked over to the corner, stuck my thumb out, and caught a ride.

I looked terribly out of place among the long haired, shirtless youths of southern California in my outdated attire. The SoCal beach version of free love was expressed openly via boundary-free groping and pot-smoking on the beach, and I watched all of it, curious, yet puzzled. I saw the same types of youngsters I'd witnessed in San Francisco, but at closer quarters now. I sat just out of view on the brown sand of Huntington Beach and wondered what some of my friends back home would have thought about what I was witnessing. These spectacles would play a big role in forming my perspective as an adult. The budding identity of my generation was blooming here.

After a month in Orange County, I caught on. I ditched the Beatles bowl haircut for an all-out assault on length and bought a pair of up-to-date surfer shorts. I wanted to surf but couldn't get a board, so I body surfed instead and became pretty good; plus, I was working on a killer tan.

My dad and I hadn't done much together since we'd arrived, but we finally took in a baseball game at the new Anaheim Stadium, and watched Mickey Mantle knock one out against Anaheim's new expansion team, the Angels. On the way home, he said he had a surprise for me the next day and to be ready to get up early.

It was still dark outside as we drove to Long Beach harbor the next morning and hopped aboard a large fishing boat. We were headed out to sea. For a couple of hours, the choppy waters had me curled up on a bunk down below and trying not to throw up, but when the boat finally stopped, I recovered quickly and had the time of my life. Right away, I began reeling in large sea bass. Dad was having terrible luck when suddenly, a huge tug on his pole caught his attention. The pole bent dramatically and we all gathered around to watch him reel in the monster. As his catch neared the boat, one of the crew pulled out some scissors to cut the line. I thought my father was going to clock him. He shot him a menacing look as the crew member explained that he'd hooked a six-foot long shark and there was no way it could come on board. As we drove home, we found it remarkable and had a good laugh about it. It was just us for that brief moment, and in spite of everything else, I could still look up to my dad. Things would never be the same.

He let me know we'd be leaving in a few days, so I started thinking about my friends back home, and was excited to share everything I'd seen. While I lounged around the apartment the next day, Brenda walked in and said she needed me to go with her to pick up my dad. She'd stayed out of my way during my time there and I'd witnessed only one confrontation with Dad, so far. I dropped my guard a little. We drove for miles and I didn't recognize any of the places we passed. After a half hour or so, she pulled into a liquor store parking lot. A phone booth stood in the back corner of the lot. She told me to get out and wait for her there. She was going down the street to pick him up, and then they'd come back to get me. "You can't go where he is," she'd said. "I'll be right back." I don't know why, but I believed her.

I sat on the small seat inside the phone booth and waited. I had no idea where I was. After an hour passed, I began to smell a rat. Time crept toward two hours, and even though the phone booth was somewhat obscured from the liquor store, some patrons were beginning to notice me. But before anyone came out to check on me, Dad and Brenda pulled up.

He looked mad, and she stayed quiet. She wasn't happy about him going back to Arkansas, and she'd shown him how far she was willing to go. I didn't say a word and my father offered no explanation.

A few days later, the road trip home was unrelenting. The stopovers and vacation atmosphere were gone. We took the much shorter southern route, and my father drove without stopping except for gas while I slept through the night. My mother was waiting on me when he dropped me off on Emerald Avenue, and after a pat on the back from him, and a squeeze from Mom, I was transported back to my former life, a little older and more experienced. After my father left, I got the sense I might not see him for a while. School would be in session soon and I looked forward to catching up with my friends.

I had little inkling then why my father had taken me to California. At best, I'd deduced, it was a chance for us to bond; at worst, an opportunity for him to indulge in his affair with Brenda. Years later, he would document the real reasons for the trip in his tell-all:

"*Tom had taken over the helm of the Dawson organization and Jim was in the picture less and less. Jim needed other things to occupy his time, so Tom decided that Jim should oversee the building of an elaborate resort home to be used by both of the*

Dawson families. It was to be built on the shores of the newly-formed Beaver Lake, and promised a nice payday for me.

I agreed to be the contractor. The plans had been drawn up by John Vine, a Fayetteville architect. He had entered into an oral contract with Jim to provide the plans and render onsite consultation for 10% of the total cost of the home. My fees would be the same.

Construction hardly began when Jim called me to his home on Emerald Avenue to review the plans. I arrived at 8:00 one evening to find Jim with his young son, Tom's half brother Terry, whom he had with his new wife, Ellen. As we went over the plans, Jim asked me if I could complete the task without the architect. I didn't feel there was anything too complicated in home construction for me to handle without an architect's consultation, so I said I could.

Early the next morning, I learned why Jim called me over. I was readying my personnel for the work day when Jim called from his office and said he needed to see me immediately. I dropped everything. When I arrived, I found Jim sitting behind his desk with Terry beside him and John Vine in the corner. Jim, without even saying hello to me, barked, "John, we don't need you anymore! Tell him Lemus, you can build this house without any help. Ain't that right, Terry?"

I remained silent, as did 13-year-old Terry.

Finally, John said softly: "Jim, pay me what you think is right, and I will leave."

Jim instructed his secretary to draft a check for John in the amount of $500, which was $5,000 less than what he had already earned, and $25,000 less than what he was entitled to upon completion of the house.

Poor Terry stood there shaking, and I, feeling like a sheep-killing dog, said nothing.

During the construction of the lake house, Tom pretty much insisted that Jim stay on the building site—not so much to oversee the progress, but to keep him out of the way while Tom ran the family business. This made things much easier for Tom, but put a burden on me. It was hard to babysit the old man and keep my many jobs running smoothly. As the construction neared completion, Jim brainstormed to bring about fifteen young men from the chicken catching crew out to the job site. "Lemus, these men are going to help you speed this job up," he crowed. "We're going to finish in record time."

What a mess it turned out to be. There was not a skilled man in the bunch. Jim had brought them from the company and reasoned he could pay them from the Dawson payroll. I kept telling him that they were impeding progress and that my men could not work around them, but Jim brought them anyway.

After two weeks of chaos, Jim couldn't understand why the home was not completed. He showed up one morning in a huff, telling his office personnel that he was going to the lake house and "fire the first person he saw on the job who was not producing." He happened to see two young men standing around when he arrived and shouted, "You, and you, go to the office and get your checks. You're fired! Go on. . .get out of here!"

One of the men replied, "We're from the telephone company, sir, and we're trying to figure out the wire layout for the telephone outlets. Don't you want phones in your house?" Jim Dawson, void of shame, did not apologize, but telephones were installed in the home nevertheless.

By the time the lake house was completed, I was at my wit's end. I submitted my final statement to Jim, who, as was his custom, found reason to discount the amount by half. I accepted it without argument because I was thankful to get away from the crazy old man. Little did I know that Jim Dawson was not through with me, and the big show was just around the corner.

I managed to evade Jim Dawson for the better part of a year, but in the summer of 1966, he appeared in my office. He said he'd found the best deal yet: A 40-acre tract of land was for sale in the southwest part of town. I had my own successful land development and construction business, and did not really care to become partners with Jim Dawson in any type of project, but after discussing the matter with Tom and deciding to keep my relationship with him on good terms, I agreed to be a part of the deal.

I wrote a check for my part of the purchase price and told him to buy the land. I got my mind back on the various projects I had going, and assumed Jim was handling the details of the escrow and picking out names for the "nice, little curved streets" he intended to build.

About four months later, having not heard from Jim Dawson, I asked him how the escrow was going. He told me that escrow had closed two months earlier and that he had already sold 20 acres of the land to the School District. It was the first I'd heard of the transaction, and I asked for the selling price. He told me that since the land went to the school, he had sold it for the same price we had paid. I asked him if I should not have been informed about the sale and reimbursed for my part.

"You have children," Jim said. "Don't you want to help the public schools?"

I investigated the matter myself and found that he made a tidy profit on the sale. He also demanded that the school be named for him, which the school board refused to do.

Prior to the land agreement, Jim bought an insurance company. When we partnered on the 40 acres, he insisted that I change all of my insurance coverage to his new company. I complied and soon after, suffered a loss of $8,000. The claim was appraised, and the check, issued in Georgia, was sent to Jim to give to me. Jim refused to give me the check.

One morning I ran into him at the Coffee Cup Café and demanded he give me the check. He invited me to his office to discuss the matter, and I rode with him in his car.

The work day had already begun as Jim and I entered his glass-walled office. Once again, I demanded the check and, once again, he refused. I also tried to discuss the property we had purchased and the remaining 20 acres, which, I argued, belonged to me. Jim refused to discuss that as well, and signaled his secretary to call the police.

When Jerome Gray, a Springdale policeman, walked into Jim's office, I thought it was on a social call. I spoke to him and Jerome said, "Lemus, come with me."

I said, "Jerome, in a minute—I have some business to settle with Jim first."

Jerome then insisted. I turned to him and asked, "What's the problem? What's going on?" Jerome replied, "I am here to remove you from Jim's office, Lemus."

I left without my check or resolution to the 20 acres, and Jerome drove me to my parked car at the Coffee Cup. From there, I went straight to my attorney's office. My attorney, Bob Monday, called the insurance office in Atlanta and asked them to stop payment on the check that Jim had, and issue me a new check. They sent the new check directly to me.

I still had the 20 acres to worry about, but fate solved that worry, when Jim and his wife were killed at a railroad crossing on Super Bowl Sunday, 1967, on their way to their lake house. The train plowed into their car and killed them instantly. I imagine that Jim still had that useless $8,000 insurance check in his pocket.

Upon learning of the accident, several of my associates asked, "What's the matter, wouldn't the train stop for Jim?"

I'd been at the Golf Club on that Super Bowl Sunday. After Jim and his wife had lunch, Jim invited everyone he thought was worthy to join them at the lake house to watch the game. Not one person had accepted the invitation. No one wanted to be around the old fool.

It was make or break time with Tom, and the squabbles I'd had with Jim caused my relationship with Tom to sour. I thought I could manage it, but first wanted to resolve the issue of the 20 acres. So, through a friend who was executive director of the local savings and loan that handled the paper work—and where Tom sat on the Board of Directors—I had the title of the remaining 20 acres transferred to me, its rightful owner, without involving Tom.

After Jim's death and those two business resolutions, an incident occurred that changed my relationship with Tom for good. My business dealings with Jim, along with Tom's need to control everything and everybody in town, brought us to the point of no return.

I was separated from my wife and took up residency with a stunning beauty named Angelique, a coed in Fayetteville. As I was financially able to do pretty much whatever I wanted, I provided her with a new automobile, a nice apartment, and a comfortable lifestyle as my mistress. I came and went at the home on Emerald and continued to provide financially for my wife and kids.

My relationship with Angel—a nickname given Angelique by our friends on the Razorback football team—made me the envy of many men. After recalling that Tom had propositioned my wife, I was not surprised to learn that he harassed Angel as well, and tried to lure her with extravagant promises. She told me he was becoming a nuisance by calling her and making advances.

Tom called one day while I was there. I told her to answer the phone in the living room while I listened in on the extension in the other room.

"Hi Babe," he began. "When are you going to see the light and ditch that jerk you're living with? You just say the word and there'll be a new Lincoln in the driveway of a new apartment for you, and a bank account." Angelique kept the conversation alive with a few well placed "oohs" and "ahhs." Tom went on to say, "I'm making a trip to New York in a couple of days. You can make the trip with me and it'll be a good chance to make your break with him. You know, Lemus is washed up. . .he's through. . .he's broke. It's just a matter of weeks before it's over for him. . ."

"You ugly little swine," I interrupted. "You couldn't screw your own dog without bribery!" Tom was caught off guard and pretended he was joking, making the excuse that he knew I was on the other line all along.

My relationship with Angelique ended a short time later—as had been my experience with these kind of arrangements—but Tom Dawson didn't have anything to do with that. I had my own apartment that I kept, while I visited the house on Emerald often to see the kids and keep up with Doris. Doris and I were still on speaking terms and she understood what was happening in my relationship with Jim and Tom, when it seemed that no one else did. I started to consider a move back home.

Doris and I were dining at the Springdale Golf Club early one evening when Tom Dawson and Tiny Henson entered the club. Tiny had just returned from a stay at a federal prison in Oklahoma after being busted for his gambling operation near Ft. Smith. They chose a table near us even though the dining room was practically empty.

Midway through our meals, I noticed Tom was drinking more and turning up the volume on his irritating laugh. I asked Doris to call it quits on our meal so we could avoid a confrontation. When I stood up, he got even louder and I heard my name, then Doris'. I walked straight to his table, picked up his chair with him still in it, and turned it upside down, slamming him to the floor as Tiny Henson looked on. I signed my dinner check and we left.

I will remember that incident until the day I die.

Tom Dawson would unleash his "dogs" on me and I would find out over the next year what living in a company-owned town was like when you're on the outs with the owner.

One of the dogs I worried most about was Clyde Winston, the Chief of Police. This man's bite was equal to his bark, and he had been standing in the wings and waiting to fulfill a promise he'd made to me in 1959.

I remembered what happened to David Allen and wondered what would happen to me. As a one-time friend of Tom Dawson, I was safe from harassment. But it wasn't 1959, it was 1967, and I just turned Dawson upside down in his chair. I had also bypassed his authority in the savings and loan, had difficulties with his now-deceased father, and humiliated him in front of Angelique. Tom was angry, and when it was passed down that I was no longer under his protection, Chief Winston immediately let me know what I was in for.

One evening, I went to the Holiday Café for dinner and drinks. After a while, I left the café and started home. Almost immediately after exiting Highway 71, I noticed a Springdale police car tailing me. Because of recent events, I was sure I was about to be pulled over, so I slowed down, and sure enough, the red lights came on. I was approached by Officer Husk Karman and another officer, and he said, "You have no license plate."

I looked at the rear of my car and he was right. I looked at Karman and said, "I'm sure it was there when I left the office this evening." He asked for my license and registration. As I got my license out of my pocket, he flashed his flashlight all around

*inside my car and inside my glove box as I reached for my regis-
tration. He wrote me a ticket and let me go.*

*The next morning, I received a call from the police depart-
ment, telling me that they had found my license plate. I went to
the station and picked it up, wondering who would pick up a lost
license plate in the middle of the night and get it to the police
station by early morning. They tore up the ticket, but it was a
statement that I heard loud and clear: Dawson certainly had the
power, leverage, and motivation, to encourage Winston to cause
trouble for me. I decided to leave town for a while. After all, I
had seven sisters in California."*

Dad was getting too big for his britches in Tom's envious eyes
and casting too big of a shadow. Dawson had resorted to calling his girlfriend, itching for a fight. In response, Dad called
him an ugly little swine, while Angel listened in and giggled.

My father, who'd been trying to stay on good terms with
Tom Dawson by agreeing to a land deal with Jim Dawson,
learned it was all in bad faith, and the way he got his acreage
back turned out to be another slap to Tom's egotistical face.
Dad's mixture of temper and righteous indignation came to
a head, and he'd forgotten his place in the Dawson hierarchy.
Things like that had never sat well with him. After finally
provoking my father into doing something foolish, like turn
him upside down in his chair, Tom was poised to strike. It
gave Dawson the go-ahead to retaliate in earnest.

The time in California was merely to cool Tom Dawson's
temper and lessen the chances of Clyde Winston's retaliation
by the considerable means he possessed. It didn't work. Legs
up on a recliner in my living room, I remember the first time
I read the following section of his manuscript. I couldn't put it
down while I remembered the madness and the misery:

"I could see the gleam in Chief Winston's eyes the first time I was arrested. I experienced nine arrests before the year was out. I was also stopped and my car searched five times. The arrests included an unlabeled drug, speeding, improper head lamp, improper license display, (again), trash burning, a building code violation, an assault, and drunk driving.

John Peterson, the Springdale News reporter, was the one responsible for keeping my name in the public eye. Newspaper and radio accounts of my arrests were overblown, and my character was called into question. I had become public enemy No. 1. I ran with a fast crowd, and now it wanted to consume me.

In spite of the physical abuse I received from the arrests— which including attacks with gloved fists, night sticks, tight handcuffs, and a pistol whipping—the most embarrassing part of the ordeal was the shame and shunning of my wife and four small children. My children were between the ages of nine and 15 at the time, and very sensitive to the remarks from classmates after my name appeared in the paper after each arrest.

I have never laid a hand on a woman in anger. The arrest for assault stemmed from a party at my apartment. Present were another building contractor, two of my employees, and a law student I knew at the time. Several young ladies were present as well, including Brenda, who followed me from California.

I spent some time with her before, and she thought she had a chance to become my next wife, should Doris and I split for good. She became intoxicated and high strung enough at the party that I didn't want anything to do with her. During the course of the evening, she decided that I was not paying enough attention to her and became violent—throwing objects and running wildly around the apartment. I was not even in the room when she tripped and fell head first into a brick planter. Her head wound required stitches, so two of the young men present loaded her into the car and rushed her to the hospital. Not wanting to hear her drunken, jealous accusations upon her return, I left the apartment and went home to Emerald Avenue for the night.

Brenda returned to find that I was gone and realized she could not follow me home to continue her harassment, but she knew what troubles I was having with the police. She drove straight to the police station and announced that I had assaulted her.

Four police cars and eight officers, along with German shepherd police dogs, came to my house to arrest me without an arrest warrant at two-thirty in the morning.

I was sound asleep as two cars parked in my driveway and two parked at the curb with lights flashing. The first thing I heard was the bullhorn blaring, "Lemus Daniel, come out of your front door with your hands in the air, and no funny stuff!"

I peered out of my window to see the red flashing lights and the spotlights searching the exterior of my home. One by one, the lights came on in the upscale neighborhood that was home to my business associates and long-time friends.

Doris woke up frightened and began to cry. As I left, I instructed her to call my attorney, Bob Monday. I was handcuffed and slapped into the back seat of a car with a growling dog for a companion.

By 6:00 that morning, Brenda sobered up and had realized what she had done and refused to sign the arrest warrant. Chief Winston arrived at the time of my arrest, along with Mayor Slim Parkinson and City Attorney Monroe Bowman. The circus was in full swing.

My attorney threatened to call District Judge Hixson Moore, when the police decided to release me and instead jail Brenda until she agreed to sign the arrest warrant. Bob Monday got statements from the other occupants at the apartment that night that Brenda had injured herself, but the pressure was mounting from Winston, and Tom Dawson even sent his current girlfriend, Patsy

Smith, over with flowers to encourage Brenda to sign the warrant. But she held fast and, after two days, was released only after she agreed to leave town. They wanted her gone so badly that they paid her way, and she was put on a bus back to California.

The next day, I answered a knock on my apartment door, and there stood City Attorney, Monroe Bowman. He walked past me into my home, and waved a piece of paper under my nose saying it was a search warrant. He proceeded to instruct two officers with him to "Begin the search." They looked under the beds, in drawers, in the bathroom, and under furniture. I couldn't imagine what they were looking for, because I had never even owned a gun. Then Bowman opened a kitchen cabinet, reached in, and asked, "What's this?"

He picked up one white pill on the shelf next to a bottle of prescription pills identical to the one in his hand. The bottle label read "Take one as needed for pain, not to exceed six per day," and my family physician's name accompanied the instruction.

I was led from my apartment by this young, immature city attorney and his two Barney Fifes and taken to jail again. That meant another trip for Bob Monday as well. It was explained to Bob that the unlabeled pill would have to be sent to Little Rock to be analyzed before my case could be determined. Meanwhile, I was free on bond.

The pill matter lingered for a month. It seemed we couldn't get a court date, or the analysis results were late. There was always an excuse however the Springdale News didn't hesitate to keep this one pill in the papers.

I asked for and got a meeting with the three-member police commission, who agreed to a meeting so I could air my complaints. I addressed my concerns and without deliberation or study, said they could see no problem on the part of the police department.

I was confused, dismayed and disgusted. I didn't know how to stop the harassment I was receiving or where to start, although I knew Dawson was behind it all. I remembered a key-carrying attorney friend of mine, Douglas Dickson. He always told me that Tom Dawson was so jealous of me that he couldn't see straight. Money was certainly not at the center of it, because I had very little compared to him. He couldn't stand to see me with something that he couldn't have for himself—like an attractive and willing girlfriend—that he didn't have to pay or drug.

Police cars dogged me everywhere I went, but the straw that broke the camel's back happened on a cold November morning in 1967. As I approached the houses I had under construction on Glenda Street in Springdale, I saw a police car stopped in front of one of them. Red Donald, my construction foreman, was being interrogated by Officer Gray. I realized that I needed help, so I headed back to my office and called Bob Monday. I had him set up an appointment for me with the law firm Goodwin and Howell in Little Rock immediately. Bob suggested a few times that Goodwin and Howell would be the best firm to handle a case such as mine. I gathered up various news clippings concerning my arrests and some additional information Bob said they would need, as well as money. I called my employees to the office in the middle of the work day and divided the many work tools among them. I paid them their wages and tried to explain what was going down. My employees thought a lot of me and begged me to change my mind, but I knew I couldn't survive.

I headed to Little Rock. It was cash out front for me, and I signed an agreement with Goodwin and Howell to represent me in a personal libel suit against the Mayor, City Attorney, Chief of Police, patrolmen Husk Karmen, Jerome Gray, and Stephen White, who had beaten me during the drunk-driving arrest. The lawsuit was filed on a Monday in November, 1967, naming the six defendants in a conspiracy to violate my civil rights, for a half million dollars in damages. The war was now out in the open, but only a few realized it was actually between me and Dawson. It was the belief of most of Springdale that I had declared war on the town itself and it became very hard to win as public sentiment swung towards the city.

Bob Monday called me after news of the suit hit the papers and told me they had dropped the unlabeled drug charge and my $25 bond was being returned. I said, "Thanks a lot." All other pending charges were dropped soon thereafter.

I knew that even if I won the lawsuit, I would still be a loser because there was no way I could ever live in Springdale again after this kind of fight. I could hear Tom Dawson's voice: "Lemus is all washed up. He's broke. . . he's through in Springdale." Tom was making good on his word, and my little world was crumbling.

I knew my business would eventually wind up in the bankruptcy courts, so I immediately tried to liquidate without holding an auction.

By now, I was ready to leave town, and needed to be able to trust someone in order to recover as much as possible before I left. Harold Knox, an ex-classmate, gave me sympathy and support, and offered to help me as I attempted to liquidate my assets. I told him I feared bankruptcy, but wasn't quite ready to give up on everything. I mentioned that I had a prime 20-acre parcel of land with no encumbrances and no ready buyer for it.

Harold said, "Deed the land to me, and I'll be glad to hold it for you. Then, when the smoke clears, I'll return it to you." At the time, I thought he was the best friend I ever had, so I accepted his offer without the slightest reservation and deeded the land to him for $1. The ink was barely dry when he sold the property $50,000. I was devastated.

So, I sold the Emerald house and arranged for my family to relocate to a small three bedroom house in a low income neighborhood in Springdale. It was a big change for the kids. Two weeks after filing my lawsuit, I kissed my children goodbye, arranged an amicable divorce from my wife, and left for California, where my sisters lived. There, I waited for the trial that was to be held in Ft. Smith at the Arkansas District Federal Court with honorable judge Willis Paulson presiding. The trial was scheduled for September, 1968."

LARRY DANIEL

CHAPTER 6

My absence for a big part of the summer had me trying to catch up with my grade school friends and share my California experience, but nobody was around. They were either not at home or not available, according to their parents. After walking to Murphy Park, I noticed some kids playing organized baseball and decided to join. I missed sign-ups, so a team would have to pick me up even though their roster was already set. The next day, I did the sign-up myself and ended up on the Athletics, where I rode the bench. Basketball was still my passion.

The youth center became a refuge for me. I spent every day I could shooting hoops before school started up. A trampoline sat in the corner of the gym, and from it I could jump to a ledge high up on the wall wide enough to stand on. One day, I noticed that one of the flimsy panels on the outside wall was slightly ajar enough to slide my small frame through. The next day, the center was closed because it was a Sunday, but I walked the two miles to the park to see if anybody I knew was there. I found two of my new friends from the team, Andy Larson and Johnnie Mackey, looking for something to do, and told them that I knew how to get into the center even though it was closed.

We took the short walk to the center, and I climbed up the iron railing on the outside and up to the loosened panel above, slid through it, jumped down to the trampoline below, and opened one of the side doors for my friends. They were impressed. We shot hoops and played pool in the abandoned center, then grabbed a snack from the concession stand. I failed to acknowledge that eating the candy bar was stealing.

After an hour or so, we heard a car pull up and the main entrance door open and close. We scrambled to hide under the concession counter and listened anxiously for the footsteps of Danny Smith, the Director of the Youth Center, who found us, ordered us out from under the counter, and marched us into his office. After lecturing us sternly, he said that instead of calling the police, our punishment would be confessing to our parents. I was relieved, but feared my dad's reaction and hoped he wasn't home. When I told my mother, she defaulted to denial. She felt the pressure of my father's transgressions, and couldn't deal with mine as well.

I could feel the uncertainty of something greater swirling overhead. At first, I'd thought it might be because of the youth center escapade, but soon dominoes that I hadn't even known existed started to fall.

A couple of weeks before school started, I caught Mom chasing Dad around the kitchen with a frying pan and screaming at him. Not long after, my sisters and I watched the police come to take him away in the middle of the night in dramatic fashion. My hysterical mother gathered us in the bedroom, ordered us to keep quiet, and promised it would soon be over. That was followed by the local newspaper and radio beginning the smear campaign against my father, by making derogatory comments that swiftly became public opinion. Finally, Dad relocated us from the Emerald Avenue house into a small pen north of town. The cramped quarters required that I sleep in a converted garage so my younger sisters could share one small bedroom and Ruth could take another for herself. The plane was gone, and so was the boat. I didn't know what was going on. Nothing was explained to me or my sisters, and my new friends, Andy and Johnnie, informed me they could no longer associate with me.

Watching my father getting hauled away by the police was shocking. The artificial calm that followed wasn't any better. My mother's initial hysteria gave way to something resembling composure, and she tried to convince us everything would be alright. Somehow, I didn't believe her.

"Your dad is going through some stuff right now," was all she said. I looked forward to school and basketball. These were the only things on my horizon.

Before the seventh grade began, I asked for and was assigned athletics for the eighth and final period, meaning I was on the junior high basketball team. During the first practice, I flung long range bombs for the coach, emulating my hero, the LSU star Pistol Pete Maravich, with his long shaggy hair and floppy socks. Stanley Hayes was my coach, and I liked him instantly. He was tall with a flat-top haircut and a big, inviting smile. I felt lucky to have him, and he became someone I looked up to. Basketball was my salvation, at least for the time being, and I was able to periodically forget about what was happening around me.

Early in the season, behind by ten with seven seconds to play during a game against Fayetteville, Coach Hayes signaled for me to go back in. "When you catch it," he said, "shoot it." After the inbounds at mid-court, he intended for me to dribble as close as I could within the remaining seven seconds and attempt a reasonable game-ending shot, but I took him literally, and the second I touched it, I turned and heaved a half court prayer, luckily banking it in and scoring. I stole the following inbounds pass from our opponent, got fouled, and sank two free throws before the game ended. Hayes grinned as he mussed my hair before I ran off the court toward the locker room.

I pretended to be upset that we lost.

As the Christmas break drew near, Hayes did something for me that I would never forget. Johnnie Mackey, an older player and my partner in crime at the youth center break-in, was suspended from the varsity for breaking a rule. Hayes asked me to drop by his office for a talk. He wanted me, a seventh grader, to suit up for the predominately ninth grade varsity for our next game against Van Buren. I was a good player, but not that good.

Following a moment of skepticism, I finally believed when he handed me the bright red pullover I was to wear at school on game day. It was many sizes too big and reached my knees, but I hardly noticed. I strutted through school that day, my pride bubbling over, without considering that Hayes may have been deflecting my well-known troubles at home in a gesture of genuine empathy. I knew less about what was really going on in my family than most of the town.

That Friday night, my big moment finally arrived, doing pre-game drills with the varsity in front of the generous, 200-plus member crowd. When the game started, I sat at the end of the bench and watched our team fall behind quickly, unable to catch up over four quarters. With a little over a minute to play, Hayes called for me to enter the game. I nearly forgot to remove my sacred pullover before I walked onto the floor. In the background, I could hear my name from the cheer squad, "Yes he can, yes he can. . .if Larry can't do it, nobody can!" I was in heaven. The girls yelling my name were all ninth graders, the cutest and most popular in school.

Every time I touched the ball, my coach yelled for me to go ahead and shoot. I finally let one loose and narrowly missed my only attempt, and soon after, the game was over. Coach congratulated me on my effort in all three games, counting the seventh and eighth grade games I'd played in earlier that evening.

When the ball wasn't bouncing, it was a different story. After my shower, I walked home to four walls, flopped down on my bed in the garage, and acclimated to silence. My mother struggled and became inaccessible, while my dad remained invisible. They didn't want to be seen in public. My younger sisters coped by spending more time at my grandmother Daniel's, and Ruth stayed out more and more often with her boyfriend.

My father showed up out of the blue at the Christmas break and wanted to take us all to California during the couple of weeks that school was out. Mom wasn't interested, but my sisters and I always wanted to be with our dad whenever possible. He didn't offer anything about the arrests, radio reports, or the move to Glenda Street, but promised that we'd have fun. He acted as if he hadn't a care in the world and that we shouldn't, either. I only hoped that Brenda wouldn't make an appearance for the next two weeks.

After a flat tire in Oklahoma, we made good time because Dad drove straight through without stopping, except for gas. We finally rose to the top of the San Gabriel Mountains west of San Bernardino and saw the massive, smog-riddled Los Angeles basin for the first time. Coming from this direction, Los Angeles looked like a bowl full of yellow smoke. We met my aunt's Ellen and Millie in Whittier after traveling to Ellen's upscale home: Millie, quiet with a dry country wit that revealed her Arkansas roots; and Ellen considered social standing a priority. Neither of them fussed over meals like our aunt Florence. The next day, Dad dropped us off at Disneyland and let Ruth show us around.

Our father also planned for the four of us to attend the Rose Bowl parade in nearby Pasadena. On the way, we got some fried chicken at a drive-through. After placing the warm bucket of chicken on my lap while he drove, I stubbornly moved it to Hazel's lap because I didn't want to hold it. She moved it to Iris' lap while Ruth watched from the front seat. Dad, also watching all of this, snapped. His face turned beet red, and he asked, "Nobody wants to hold the fucking chicken?"

He snatched the bucket from Iris' lap and hurled it out of the moving car onto a four-lane Pasadena highway, scattering wings and legs along the asphalt. He yelled, "What about now? Are you hungry now?"

Our mouths were zipped tight and our eyes wide open as we sat motionless.

"That fucking chicken is long gone," he mumbled under his breath as he fought to compose himself.

We waited for it to blow over. We'd seen his temper before. It didn't arise often, but whenever it did, it always scared us. The pressure was getting to him. The worst part might have been the facade he'd been putting on for us. We remained unaware of the looming showdown in court.

The next day, my dad and I watched O.J. Simpson of the University of Southern California Trojans run a long touchdown in a losing effort against the Ohio State Buckeyes at the Rose Bowl game in front of 100,000 fans. He talked to me about moving here someday, finally broaching the situation in Arkansas.

It would be better if we were all here, he said, without mentioning Mom specifically. He didn't say it, but I suspect that he thought winning the lawsuit and cashing a $500,000 check would make everything alright in sunny southern California. There had been no sign of Brenda, and I pondered his vague offer before we made our way back to Arkansas for the remainder of the school year. After dropping us off at home, he disappeared again, and by the time my school year in Arkansas had wrapped up, the fantasy of living in southern California became a distant memory.

The hammer would soon fall on my father and whatever hope he had left, and we would all suffer the consequences of his poor decisions. He'd been an easy mark for the malignant Dawson, who sat back and pulled the strings of his destruction almost exclusively, because my father could get women whom Dawson couldn't. The hardest part was realizing that a large portion of the town I was from thought he had it coming. Maybe he did.

For all his faults, though, I have trouble accepting that he, or anyone, could deserve what happened to him during the lawsuit:

"Several hundred pages of depositions were taken from at least 15 people, and the trial stalled. I searched each deposition for Dawson's name but found none. Bob Monday informed me that after council meetings, the eight councilmen, along with Mayor Parkinson, City Attorney Bowman and Chief Winston, would go into closed door meetings, and discuss how the city would fund the attorney's fees and other expenses because they were being sued individually as private citizens, and not as city employees. It was never revealed in the news media how Archibald Fleeman, Dawson's chief counsel, and now lead attorney for the defendants, was paid.

Finally, I was called from California to Springdale to give my deposition. One call brought me to the mayor's office, where I found Mayor Parkinson and his attorney, Archibald Fleeman, with my attorney, Arnold Howell, along with a court reporter who sat quietly in the corner.

The session started abruptly with Fleeman using abusive language and calling me names. My lawyer spoke up and the two hassled back and forth. I finally said, "The hell with you people! I didn't come all the way from California to listen to this shit." I stood up. "I'm leaving."

The court reporter was going nuts trying to figure out what to record or not, everyone was talking at once, and even Mayor Parkinson—who was supposed to be a bystander—was trying to get a word in.

My attorney finally yelled, "Shut up! We'll start this thing over." The court reporter said that was illegal but after realizing she couldn't make heads or tails of the simultaneous conversations, she agreed to start over.

It went smoother the second time around, and Fleeman told my attorney off the record that if any money was to be made from this lawsuit, it would be in the form of a book.

I returned to California and waited for another call, which came at six in the morning about four weeks before my case was to be heard. My attorney seemed anxious and asked me if I could come to Arkansas right away. I didn't question it and booked a flight to Little Rock, where I arrived the next day.

I was shocked to see Officer Stephen White, a defendant, sitting in my attorney's office when I arrived. An opened bottle of Jack Daniels sat on Howell's desk and he offered me some and announced that White was there to help us. I was skeptical and frankly, scared to death of Officer White, the same man who'd pistol-whipped me. After a drink or two, I relaxed enough to listen to what he had to say.

White said he had no money and didn't want the burden of a lawsuit, and also mentioned that he was mistreated by Chief Winston and Mayor Parkinson and offered an apology of the mistreatment I suffered from him. He denied any knowledge of Dawson's involvement, but said Winston was behind the orders to get me.

White admitted that his orders included secretly searching my vehicles. He said that he and Chief Winston discussed planting illegal drugs in them. He went on to say that he had even been given the hair-raising orders to shoot me if the opportunity presented itself.

It was as if he were confiding in a priest. We were all sworn to secrecy and agreed that White would expose all he knew after he was seated on the witness stand. After White left, Howell told me the entire meeting had been recorded and that he'd also convinced White to sign a statement confirming his admissions. He assured me that this was our big break and that he would continue to work on my behalf. I visited my children and went back to California with new hopes of beating Dawson and the city of Springdale.

When the day finally arrived, it became worth the price of admission. My witnesses included Brenda, who had been incarcerated for two days for refusing to sign an arrest warrant on me, and a University student who had witnessed a clubbing I received on the head from Officer Karmen and Stephen White in the parking lot of my apartment.

But suddenly, witnesses for my behalf began to lose their memories and become scarce. They surely feared for their futures while living in Springdale after the trial. The witness that surprised me the most was Bob Monday, the attorney who had defended me during all the arrests, and in fact, helped bring us all to this point by suggesting I contact Goodwin and Howell.

On the opening day of the trial, Howell informed me that Bob was ill and would not be able to testify. I found that odd because Bob hadn't missed a day of work at his office in ten years. Bob Monday was able to get out of bed in the middle of the night to bail me out during the arrests but was sick today, of all days?

The jury was seated on the first day, and I took the stand on the second. I tried to explain to the jury the stops, arrests, beatings, and harassment I had received. Fleeman interrupted me no fewer than fifty times and yelled that I was a crazed man and should be caged on the spot. While Fleeman yelled, my eyes scanned the courtroom and I saw pictures of all the previous judges who'd sat on the bench in this same Federal Courtroom, stopping at Judge Parker's, the hanging judge. He had hanged more than 150 men, and six at one time, gleefully making a public spectacle of it.

After four hours of listening to Fleeman, Brenda took the stand and was somehow able to tell the story of her two-day lock-up and Winston's efforts to get my assault warrant signed. As expected, she was shaken and cried throughout her testimony.

The student was next on the stand. The first question Fleeman asked was whether he saw Officer White and Karmen strike me on the head in the parking lot of my apartment.

"Damn right, I did see two policemen strike Lemus Daniel on the head!" Judge Paulson interrupted the young man by saying, "Hold everything." He then took the young man into his chambers alone and reprimanded him for having used the word, "damn." The young man had not spent more than three minutes on the stand and did not return after his visit with the judge while my attorney curiously said nothing. My case was weakening, but I still had Stephen White, my ace in the hole. White's testimony itself would win the case for me.

On the third day, Mayor Parkinson was the first to take the stand for the defense. He didn't have much to say about the case, but dwelled on the subject of how well he was loved by the people of Springdale, and how he'd won the election by a landslide. The facts were that he'd won 54% of a two-man race on a platform that boasted no black families within the city limits of Springdale.

Monroe Bowman, the fresh-out-of-law-school city attorney, was next. While Goodwin interrogated Bowman, I asked Howell where Jerome Gray was, since he was one of the six defendants being sued. He told me that Fleeman wouldn't let him show since he was aware of a rape conviction in California some years earlier. Howell said that Fleeman wouldn't want that information brought out in the courtroom.

I accepted that, but I had also noticed that Stephen White was missing. Howell said that he would be there when we needed him. I turned back to hear Goodwin finish questioning Monroe Bowman. Bowman, a young and inexperienced liar, was having trouble with his answers and his testimony brought an end to another day.

The last day was to be the big one, the explosion. Stephen White was scheduled to take the stand.

Chief Winston was up first. He boasted of "master-minding the arrest of Lemus Daniel," and thought he should be commended for it. Winston talked for about an hour.

As Husk Karmen took the stand, I asked Howell where White was. I nearly fell out of my chair when he said, "He won't be here. He's had a nervous breakdown." As Gardner questioned Karmen, my whispers began to draw attention as I demanded to see the statement White was supposed to have signed, and asked where the tape of our conversation was. He looked at me calmly, and said, "What statement? What tapes are you talking about?"

The air went out of me like a pricked balloon. At that moment, I remembered being told that Goodwin and Howell was the only law firm to handle my case because they were not afraid of Tom Dawson. They had opened a divorce suit against Tom for his wife, Joan. But now, I was beginning to see why Joan's suit had failed.

Tom Dawson was right. My life's work, my family, and my future were gone. I could never again live in a town that I had worked so hard to help build.

As my attorney helped Officer Karmen select the proper answers to his questions, I gathered up the few papers in front of me, pushed my chair back, and walked out of the courtroom, never to return. I got in my car and headed towards Springdale to tell my ex-wife, my mother, and my children that I wouldn't be back. That evening, I heard the news of my defeat on the radio."

My behavior became "irresponsible and erratic."

My father admits that once banished to California, he became "irresponsible" and "erratic." As I recall, "dangerous" and "unstable," might be better descriptions. Post-traumatic stress, extreme paranoia, and alcohol ravaged his soul and burned deep inside him. He headed for the west coast and plotted his revenge while I kept my head down and set about the long task of coming to terms with my new reality as the son of public enemy No.1.

PART II

BAD COMPANY

LARRY DANIEL

CHAPTER 7

Race riots and Martin Luther King's assassination dominated the headlines in 1968, casting fear and uncertainty on a nation, and my little world in Springdale felt just as perilous. Before he left, my father attempted to explain our predicament by saying he'd been set up and the cops were after him for something he didn't do. He had to leave now and his last words were "you can't trust anyone."

After the baseball season had ended, I happened upon a couple of kids that were my age from the poorer side of the tracks. I met Greg and Lenny shooting hoops at an east side park in Springdale and we quickly hit it off. They lived next door to each other near the chicken plant, and even though I hadn't seen them around the school gym during my seventh grade year, they weren't new to town. They were good players with the potential of being major contributors for the team and before long I was beating a path to Greg's house to play basketball almost every day. We played games like twenty-one and horse and it kept me at his primitive goal and dusty back yard until dark. I'd been skirting the youth center with its more sophisticated goal anyway because of the break-in incident the previous summer. Even if they didn't hold it against me, it was still embarrassing.

Greg was muscular for his age and hard to stop when he was determined to score. Lenny was taller, a good shooter, and could rebound. I could shoot as well, with better ball handling skills, and envisioned myself as a point guard. They were going to sign up and we all looked forward to the upcoming season.

Greg and Lenny accepted me without reservation. I was still skinny and easy to push around, so it was good to have bigger friends to protect me. After long afternoons of practicing, we often visited a small convenience store near Greg's house. On one of those trips to the store, Lenny suggested we shoplift something small to see if we could get away with it. Greg confessed he'd done this with Lenny before and they convinced me that we wouldn't get caught. I feared losing their companionship if I didn't go along.

Once inside, I anxiously walked the aisles and finally settled on a pack of five different colored bubble gum balls in an elongated plastic package about three inches long. I turned my body away from the front counter and slyly slipped them in my pocket. When I noticed Greg and Lenny were already waiting outside, my heart rate spiked, and I assumed it was time to complete the caper. As I moved for the door, I heard a deep voice from the distance, bellowing, "Hold it right there!"

I caught a glimpse of Greg and Lenny disappearing as the manager marched me to his office and ordered me to empty my pockets. Out came the package of gum, worth all of five cents. "How much money do you have?" he asked, before I pulled out four red pennies and laid them on the desk. I was at his mercy, and his look of contempt slowly softened. After a brief lecture, he added a penny and let me go with a warning to not come back. I walked out thinking it was a good thing I didn't have five red pennies. I discovered Greg and Lenny waiting around the corner and I replayed the story to them while they laughed and playfully pushed me back and forth.

They hadn't shoplifted anything and admitted they'd never had the guts to try.

In the fall of 1968, I started the eighth grade, and once again, I had athletics scheduled for the final period. Boys that played on the seventh grade or junior varsity team the prior year were all assigned athletics, and newcomers with ability, like Greg and Lenny, were added. We'd been waiting all summer for this, but before the first practice, I discovered Coach Foreman would be coaching the JV basketball team instead of Coach Hayes. Coach Foreman was there to put me in my place.

Around this time, my dad had lost his lawsuit against the city and the newspapers covered the front page with biased details, making me even more leprous. It was out in the open now and the public sentiment leaned heavily against him. While my father high-tailed it to California for good, I was getting familiar with stigma for reasons I couldn't comprehend.

Foreman was a short man with a constant, bulldog-looking scowl, and had a reputation for intimidation and scorn. His shoulders slumped as he stalked the court and slung criticisms toward any player that he deemed unimportant. I may have considered myself a preseason starter, but Foreman took five minutes to replace me during the first practice. Basketball was my life, but that year, a lot of it was spent on his bench. Whenever I saw Hayes at the gym, he always talked with me and encouraged me to stick with it.

Greg and Lenny were great players but terrible students and I soon understood why I hadn't seen them on the team the year before. By the end of the first semester, their failing grades forced Foreman to dismiss them from the team. My grades were adequate, so I gained more playing time, even though I knew Foreman hated sending me in. After the season was over, I was without a clue what my next move should be. I fell through the cracks and became susceptible to making bad decisions.

I started hanging out with Rory, Jonas and Trey, a trio of acne-fearing teenagers, just like me. Rory Davidson was a short, hyperactive and banty rooster-looking kid with round glasses that lived on Butler Street in Springdale with his dad, Jack, and stepmom, Georgia. Rory's dad was a rounder, so Rory's stepmom moved in and out frequently. We'd occasionally gather in Jack's small living room and he would prattle on about how to satisfy a woman, which sparked our curiosity about a woman's anatomy.

Jonas Strickland lived a couple of blocks away from my house, and when we weren't listening to Jack, we spent most of our time there. Jonas' parents were elderly and therefore disinterested in our hormone-fueled impulses, so we knew we wouldn't be hassled much. Jonas was a soft-spoken, teddy bear kind of kid, who normally wouldn't hurt a fly, but was big and able enough if provoked.

Trey Watson lived only four blocks from Jonas, so everyone could meet there at a moment's notice. Trey was what we called book-smart but a good fit for this unusual group. I'd enjoyed a modest-sized circle of friends in grade school, but that was no longer true.

We'd all had beers before, but we couldn't wait to turn 21 and buy it legally, so in the meantime, we conspired to beat the system. While passing by a liquor store one day on Highway 71, I noticed they'd left wine bottles on an outside shelf protruding from a cinder block building, advertising to passers-by. I knew a large field existed behind the liquor store that required an approximate mile walk through a field to get to the back of the building. I reported this to Rory and figured I might get big points if we could pull it off.

A few days later, Rory, Jonas, and I walked through the pasture with a few trees and some brush to conceal us in places. As we approached the back of the building, we split up and duck-walked up the sides within striking distance of the bottles; Rory was ready on the right corner, and Jonas and me on the left. When Rory signaled, we moved quickly, reaching up from our crouched positions, grabbing a bottle apiece, and sprinting as if our lives depended on it. I grabbed two. With wine in hand, we scurried down the hillside until we were a safe distance from the scene of the crime. Back at Jonas' house, we stashed the loot and decided that we would drink it that night. I told my mother I was staying over at Jonas,' and as usual, she didn't object.

"Did they see you?" asked Trey, who'd been the least willing to do the dirty deed.

"Nah, I don't think so," Jonas bragged. "It doesn't matter they would've never caught us."

"Let's get drunk," Rory crowed.

We waited for Jonas' parents to go to bed for the night, which was earlier than most. We glanced at the label before opening the first bottle. The alcohol volume read 20% and we all shrugged it off, grossly underestimating what it could do to us. After the first few swigs, we drank freely, and by midnight, we found ourselves in Jonas' front yard feeling rowdy, and drunk wrestling, before each of us paused to vomit a purplish gush. The next morning, back in Jonas' bedroom and amnesiac to any further details, my mouth and clothes reeked of the puke. I felt proud, the unforeseen hangover becoming another feather in my "growing up" cap. We recuperated in Jonas' room for a short while trying to recall and match the last thing we remembered before retreating to our homes. I snuck in unnoticed and changed my clothes and brushed my teeth.

During the summer of 1969 I performed more stunts, like stealing a bicycle from a store front in broad daylight. Rory and I spray painted it black and I rode it for the remainder of the summer, keeping it at Rory's. I was trending downward, so from this point on, I'd taunt death a couple of times before my high school class graduated.

The summer of love was now over but the revolution continued, with drugs, sex, and rock and roll as the battle cry. That fall, an enormous music festival got the attention of America—and a few lost kids in Springdale—and drew them into the fire. The poster read, "An Aquarian exposition: Three days of peace and music" at the Woodstock music festival happening at Max Yasgur's farm, near Bethel, New York.

The hair, clothes, music, protesters, and drugs weren't just on television.

CHAPTER 8

My relationship with my mother and sisters continued to evaporate. I struggled internally, isolated myself more, and got stuck in my own cramped version of hell. There'd been no call–to-arms meeting about our circumstance and the place on Glenda Street was a house, but not a home.

When school started, basketball was back in play, but I hadn't prepared as I had the previous summer. As the football season wrapped up, I did a few drills and practiced my free throw shooting, once making eleven in a row in front of Hayes and Principal Rich, who was a decent player himself. Still, my mind was elsewhere most of the time, and I wasn't close to any of the kids on the team, except for a country kid named Jimmy Vernon that had ridden the bench with me the previous season.

Coach Hayes reminded me that he was making no promises after he saw me getting pushed around easily by the bigger kids in practice. Their bodies were filling out and mine wasn't, but I still had an unrivaled outside shot. By the time the season started, I'd earned the sixth man spot, meaning I was the first guy off the bench whenever a substitution was made, and that was okay with me. After a few games, I'd gotten plenty of playing time and was staying out of trouble. My friendship with the gang took a back seat to basketball, but they occasionally reminded me that I was still one of them.

Halfway through the school year, Rory and Jonas suggested that we skip school. I fell for it. It turns out, we had nowhere to go and walked around aimlessly for hours, finally finding an obscure field near my house, where we ended up sitting around a tree smoking cigarettes. No one was immune to my dad's new reputation.

"What's the deal with your dad, anyway? Rory asked. "My dad says the cops were after him."

I felt my face reddening, and said, "I don't want to talk about it."

"Jack told me about it," he continued. "He heard it on the radio that your dad's a bad guy. He met him once and didn't think he was such a bad guy. He said he gets a lot of girls."

"Do you think he can get us some girls?" Jonas asked. He'd regretted it after seeing my expression, offering, "I was kidding. Sorry."

It was touchy subject matter. I knew about the women but couldn't identify my father as a criminal. I didn't understand my own place in this drama and felt flawed and ashamed. I knew at some point I was going to have to learn how to explain what had happened to my family.

The next day, Hayes showed me that he was still paying attention. Perhaps he could sense my guilt and with just two carefully worded questions, we both discovered that I was a terrible liar. He was suspicious and asked, "Where were you yesterday, Larry?"

"Sick at home," I replied.

"Are you sure?"

I started stuttering something when our eyes met, then stopped, unable to go through with it. Not to him. "This'll be between you and me," he assured me, and made my punishment running up and down the bleachers in the gym 500 times. It took five days to complete.

I ended up having a good season, and cracked the starting line-up for the last few games. My mom even attended the last one, the first time she'd seen me play. I was elated but secretly wished my dad was there, too. But it was too little, too late, because when the school year ended, there was no more Coach Hayes and nothing could stand in the way of me expressing my rebellion.

That summer, the gang and I took up where we left off and I came and went, using the house to eat and sleep. Discipline was out of the question. Rory scored some pot and we were all eager to try it. I knew a little about marijuana from my time In California a few years earlier, but had no real experience. Our first joint wasn't very potent. It was wrapped in yellow zig-zag papers, deeply inhaled and held in, then ceremoniously exhaled. We acted more stoned than we were, but the weed eventually got stronger and we didn't have to act. I stepped willingly into the drug culture, but still had a friend or two that just liked to drink.

While sitting on the bench the prior basketball season, Jimmy Vernon repeatedly reminded me that his older brother, Kermit, could get us into the Rockwood Club if I ever wanted to go. I took him up on it one evening and again, told my mother I was spending the night with a friend.

The Rockwood Club was a notorious honky-tonk on the southern outskirts of Fayetteville. It was dingy and run down, and I was woefully unaware of its nasty reputation for testy cowboys and fights in the parking lot. Kermit drove a tricked-up red Dodge, wore his hair slicked back, and chain-smoked filter cigarettes.

We took turns drinking from a pint of cherry vodka as Kermit slid around corners in his hot rod, and by the time we arrived, it was dark and I was a little tipsy. Jimmy and I found a booth and somehow scored another bottle while Kermit roamed the honky-tonk. We lost track of him when the country band started. Nobody said a word about our age.

The booth allowed me to lean against the wall once the noise and the syrupy alcohol got to be too much, which was around 2:00 a.m. by my estimation. Small skirmishes broke out that were getting escorted to the parking lot, and my apprehension spiked. I asked when we could leave. Jimmy said he'd go ask Kermit and wandered into the melee of rowdies. A minute later, he reappeared with Kermit in tow.

"What?" Kermit asked.

"When can we go home?"

He punched me straight in the face and bloodied my nose. "Shut the fuck up," he said, and walked away.

I retreated to my booth, stunned. The music pounded and my head swam.

Just before daybreak, an unapologetic and extremely intoxicated Kermit signaled for Jimmy and me to load up. I felt lucky he wasn't leaving me there, but pretty soon, I'd wished he had. I got in the back seat and kept my eyes closed and head down as he sped in and out of dirt road ditches bellowing, "Yee-haw!" Suddenly, the car whipped side to side and I heard the back tire blow. I was puzzled by Jimmy's calm demeanor while Kermit ignored the flat and hit the gas. The tire flapped furiously for almost a mile before Kermit had to concede and stop to change the tire.

The time with the lug wrench seemed to calm him down and only when I recognized a street sign near my house at daybreak, did I dare to raise my head.

I was ready to lay low for a while, so I kept to myself in my converted garage bedroom and read a magazine during a muggy spring evening in the wake of a storm. When the hangers in my closet started rattling, the windows followed suit and shuddered as if a freight train were passing just outside. A minute later, my mother poked her head in and said the radio had announced that a tornado just passed. Outside, I could smell the unfamiliar swampy odor that a twister leaves behind. The radio said it had hit two blocks north of Glenda Street, and I instantly thought of Jonas, who lived directly in its path. I headed that way, bracing myself for whatever I might find.

I found Jonas standing in his unblemished yard. "Did you hear that roar when it passed by?" he asked.

I nodded, "Man, you were lucky." To the west lay a row of houses that my dad built years before, trees uprooted and roofs torn off, symbolic of the builder's current life. We agreed to get together the following evening to plan our next caper.

The following evening at Jonas' house, Rory, mentioned a party at the Blue Springs recreation area at Beaver Lake. After we got a ride from Jack, we were promised a ride home with one of Rory's friends. Once there, we grabbed a beer and strolled among the older crowd. I glanced over at a group of people and noticed a hot blond smiling at me. She walked toward me and introduced herself. "I'm Jackie and you're cute," she said. "What's your name?"

I tried to play it cool, but I didn't know what to say, barely managing, "Larry." In those days, I lacked confidence around girls. Rory's dad, Jack, routinely spouted a variety of adult rated instruction after downing a few beers which could be boiled down to, "Just grab 'em." I took whatever he said with a grain of salt.

She did all the talking and got around to asking me if I wanted to see a movie with her, *Yellow Submarine*, by the Beatles. It was playing at a nearby outdoor theatre the next evening and I said "sure." It was free, but if it had cost anything I would have wrangled the money somehow.

I kept my hands to myself and enjoyed the show, as did Jackie, who was a year and a half older than me. Full-figured for her age, she was out of my league and maybe just toying with me, but I was smitten. We agreed to meet again and a few nights later we found ourselves with the gang at Jonas' house smoking some pot. Afterwards she asked me to walk her the few blocks to her parents' home. Half way there, we stopped at a hidden corner of an elementary school building and Jackie took control, leading me to the ground. While we kissed, she expertly unbuttoned my jeans, slipped her hand onto my undefiled boner and began stroking me. Following her lead, I reached into her shorts. After a few minutes of this, I wasn't sure how to proceed, revealing to her that she'd wandered upon a bona-fide virgin. Afterwards, I remained chaste, but couldn't have cared less. I was on cloud nine confident that I had a girlfriend to call my own.

Later on, the gang was full of questions about her, but I refrained from divulging too much about the experience. I answered them by saying that I liked her a lot and hoped she could be my steady girlfriend. I couldn't figure out why she was attracted to me in the first place, but I tried to not ruminate too much. My shoulders were squarer and my head was higher when I thought of her. A few days later, having not heard from her, I decided to drop by her house. I asked her mom if she was home.

"Jackie's gone," her mother announced. "She's hitchhiking to California with Donnie." She'd said it without a hint of concern that her 16-year-old daughter was on the road west with her thumb out. I didn't ask who Donnie was. I acted nonchalant, but quickly surmised that I was just another dumb kid with nothing to offer. It was just two dates but I didn't like it. Instead of feeling macho over our little moment, I felt foolish.

The record player from the living room finally made its way to my bedroom and I retreated more and more often to listen to rock 'n roll, loudly, spinning my vinyl records over and over, and pausing only to sneak out to my back yard to smoke pot.

Days later, while Trey and I were sitting around Jonas' house, Rory came in and pulled out a pill bottle from his pocket and displayed a dozen small white tablets, handing each of us one. "They're white crosses and they'll make you feel great," he announced.

We all swallowed the pills without delay. After thirty minutes, the rush of energy that the illicit drug provided made up for a missing Jackie. As the euphoria washed over me and the others, we chattered non-stop for hours about anything and everything in a race to get a word in edgewise. I ran my mouth about her, and while I blabbered on, they sat in wonder.

Jonas marveled, "She did what?"

Buzzed on meth, I felt confident, energetic, and free of my circumstances. I wanted more, as did Jonas, and Rory said he could get lots of it. It was easy to get because his dad, Jack, had it hidden in his closet. Trey was hesitant and pulled away after the first time and no longer wanted any part of it.

As it drew nearer, my sophomore year of high school upped my anxiety. The day I registered, I learned that I didn't have any classes with Rory or Jonas, and it unsettled me. I had just one class with Trey and we weren't that close after he began to avoid the group. I also noticed that I had athletics scheduled for the final period, meaning I was expected to play on the high school basketball team. I hadn't even thought about it, and sure as hell hadn't prepared for it.

The high school coach, Timothy North, was a balding, middle-age man with thick glasses, a noticeable waistline, and a reputation for being even-handed. He scouted the younger kids during their prior basketball seasons so he would know who was coming down the pike. I'd been a starter by the end of the season but hadn't practiced a lick since then and didn't think I cared anymore, but when the time came, I suited up, ran drills, long hair and Pistol Pete floppy socks and all. I still had the skills to make it.

The coach blew his whistle and yelled while I struggled during wind sprints at the second practice. Jimmy Dawson, a former friend, Tom Dawson's son, and current teammate, yelled along with him for me to try and keep up. Out of shape and severely gassed, I glared over at him, stared at the wooden floor, and decided that after the second practice, I would quit. Who did I think I was anyway? These kids weren't my friends. I was a Daniel, and my dad had been run out of town. I didn't belong.

The next day, I went to the school registrar and asked to be placed in a PE class instead of athletics, and my miniscule high school basketball career was over. Now I was free to continue my free-fall. I maintained my association with Rory but found that I didn't always need him to provide me with drugs. It was 1970, and it was abundantly clear that finding any substance in my high school was not going to be a problem.

CHAPTER 9

I made a habit of cutting classes with veteran truants and visiting an old three-story-house in nearby Fayetteville. It was called the Gray House because of its faded gray paint job and it sat next to a creepy old cemetery. Drugs were regularly bought and sold or sometimes just given away by the young adult occupants. The Gray House rented rooms by the week or the month, but was used mainly as a flop house. Those that didn't have a room there and were friends of the occupants flopped at the house until they were ready to leave. There were always people lounging around or sleeping something off.

I kept up with Rory after school even though we didn't have any classes together and continued taking the speed he offered, sometimes mixing it with weed. I was a regular insomniac now, and unable to pay attention during my classes. The high school teachers weren't as attentive either, and I could fade into the background for the most part by handing in the occasional paper or completing a pop quiz to fend off a full scale inquiry as to my lack of interest. I hated school and began seeking out my school-skipping buddies more and more as the first semester rolled on.

The designated cigarette smoking area located around the corner of the gym was now crawling with high school kids smoking pot, who quickly stashed it when teachers came around. The smell of it permeated the air, as did the adult's willful ignorance, misunderstanding random giggling, and red eyes even while they sat in class. I did that too, and before the semester was over, I did other things more ghastly.

Sitting on Jonas' unmade bed in his dingy bedroom, Rory pulled out three syringes and set them on the counter. He placed two white meth pills in a spoon before adding a small amount of water to them. As the pills dissolved, he struck a match and held it under the spoon, until the mixture boiled. He then dropped a tiny cotton ball into the spoon and with the syringe, drew up the now-purified liquid through the cotton, and filtered it into the syringe. He attached a small-gauge needle onto the syringe and flicked the air bubbles up to the top and pushed them out. Rory continued, "It works quicker this way." He fixed a belt around his arm and injected it.

Following the initial shock, I became curious, asking, "Does it hurt?"

Rory responded, "No, man. It's easy and I'll do it for you guys. The rush is magic."

I glanced at Jonas and his eyes widened. We both liked the drug and decided we didn't have a problem with it if it didn't hurt. Trey wasn't anywhere around for this.

I went first and Rory fixed the belt around my arm, prompting a large vein to show itself on my right arm. He swabbed some alcohol he'd brought around the now swollen vein and told me to hold still. He continually tapped the tiny needle into my vein without much discomfort and released the belt from my arm. Pulling back slightly on the syringe plunger, traces of blood flowed back into the syringe confirming the sure placement of the needle in my vein. He slowly pushed the drug into my circulation and I immediately felt the rush of the substance take over my brain. My spine tingled and my heart raced. Jonas went next but Rory missed his vein, creating a purple bruise. Jonas grimaced but endured while I ground my teeth and watched Rory dig around in Jonas' meaty forearm. Rory reassured Jonas, withdrew, and tried again higher up on his arm. Afterwards, the three of us sat bug-eyed in a circle while our skin crawled. Any boundaries I had left had been bulldozed to the ground.

As the school year dragged on, I'd missed as many classes as I'd attended. Finally, my mother and I were summoned to the school principal's office. Mr. Clem, the stern disciplinarian high school principal, started the meeting with, "Mrs. Daniel, your son has missed so much school that he can't possibly advance even if he doesn't miss another day. His grades are all Ds and Fs," before sanctimoniously adding, "I think he has an attitude problem." My mother agreed.

"That's what his dad says," she said.

That stung me. My blood boiled as I wondered when my father had offered this grand wisdom. It was obviously true, but coming from Principal Clem and my absent dad by way of my bewildered mother, I rejected it with prejudice. Had my mother been talking to him about me? Where was he now? I hadn't seen him for almost two years. I looked right through Mr. Clem as if he weren't there. Sitting in my little bubble, I was tuned out. I didn't hear another word.

My mother and I drove home in a communal daze and I wondered what was next. There was no reason for me to continue going to school, and Clem expelled me for the remainder of the school year. I sat in my room void of any conversation, and after a while, I convinced her to take me to a friend's house across town. I knew that my friend, Michael, had been suspended from school himself for a couple of weeks and maybe I could unload on him. After sitting around at Michael's for an hour or so, we rummaged around in his mom's medicine cabinet and I found some diet pills and put them in my pocket. After another hour or two of lounging around, my mother returned to take me home.

Later that night, I abused the amphetamine that turned out to be much more potent than I anticipated. I became ill. My chest got tight, my face pale, and sweat rolled off my forehead. The vomiting alerted my mother that something was terribly wrong and I finally admitted that I had swallowed some diet pills that I'd found at my friend Michael's house. She immediately called the doctor. As we readied to drive to the physician's home as he directed, I threw on a long-sleeve shirt to conceal the tracks on my arm.

When we arrived at the physician's house, I overheard him telling her that I was having a heart attack while he prepared a shot to my hip to counter the amphetamine. Within a few minutes, the chest pains ceased and my color improved. She'd saved my life, but remained none the wiser about the extent of my drug use. We didn't know what to say to each other. She talked to somebody else about it.

CHAPTER 10

My dad pulled up in his Cadillac El Dorado as if he'd never left, walked in the front door, and told me, "Come on, we're going for a ride."

I was apprehensive and felt inexplicably guilty. I got in the passenger seat and basked in the wintery airstream coming in my window. He left it down deliberately and silently dared me to raise it. After all this time, he was still trying to toughen me up. This felt nothing like the cruising we did when my world was right, me with my long hair, and my slumped shoulders. The irritation coming off him was palpable as he drove toward downtown Springdale. Without a word, he pulled into a small barber shop near the high school and announced that I was getting a haircut. I sat in silence, more afraid now, but still defiant. My hair was past my shoulders and I liked it that way.

He demanded, "Get your ass out of the car right now!"

I sat clenched and furious, and thought, *this is how you come to me?*

He came around to my side of the car, flung the door open, slapped me across the face and dragged me out by my long hair. While I protested, he hauled me into the shop, which had a only few customers. I finally gave up and sat defeated on the barber seat. My dad asked me, "How do you want it cut?"

"You tell me," I snapped, earning a look from him that promised another round of physical abuse.

The barber knew my dad and tried to soften the situation by offering different ways to cut it but my father was having none of it. "Just cut it," he ordered.

My buzzed head mirrored my earlier years when we got our haircuts together. My locks were shorn and my dignity stomped on. His hair was longer than mine now.

I returned to the car and seethed as we drove back to Glenda Street, trying to look like I was ignoring his monologue. He would be back in Arkansas for a while, even though it was under threat of arrest by Clyde Winston. He wasn't calling the shots anymore, but he had some work lined up repairing the recent tornado damage. Because I wasn't in school anymore, he would pick me up in the morning.

That night, I replayed the day over and over and decided that I wasn't going to be picked up or go anywhere with my father. I lifted my bedroom window and, with nothing but $2 and the clothes on my back, slipped out and headed towards Jonas' house. I spent the night on his couch aware that my mother would tell my dad to look for me there, so I rose early and continued on to my friend Chuck's before he could arrive on Glenda Street. I told Chuck of my ordeal and he assured me I could hang out there for the time being.

Chuck was good-natured, but spacy. He resembled Ferdinand the Bull of cartoon lore, and always sported a goofy grin and smelled the flowers. He used pot frequently and I didn't know if his demeanor was a bug or a feature.

He told me he wanted to go to a rock concert in Little Rock that night but couldn't figure out how to pull it off. The rock group, Mountain, was playing and he knew some people that were going. It was fantasy talk at first, but I convinced him that even though we only had a few bucks between us, and no tickets or ride, it would work out if we got an early start by hitchhiking Highway 71 down to Interstate 40. Once in Little Rock, we could hook up with his friends, get tickets, and enjoy the show. Afterwards, someone there could give us a ride home. We anticipated it would take around four or five hours to cover the 200-plus miles, and with my experience with hitchhiking in California, I assured him it would be a breeze.

We made the short distance to Highway 71 and stood with our thumbs out by mid-morning ready for adventure. We caught our first ride within thirty minutes and covered around twenty-five miles far enough away that the current adventure was more real than yesterday's drama. But it soon became clear this wasn't like hitching on the busy boulevards of California. The traffic was light, so we sat for over two hours before anyone else stopped for us. Our next ride took us to the town of Mulberry on Interstate 40, a half hour closer to Little Rock. Mulberry offered us a busier hub of traffic, so we figured the rides would come quicker, but we were wrong.

"Do you think this was a bad idea?" Chuck asked while we sat watching the time and cars pass. "Maybe we could turn back."

"Nope, we'll get a ride soon," I said. "There's still plenty of time." I may have been deceiving Chuck. My real interest was staying away from Springdale while my dad looked for me.

Cars and semi-trucks continued to rumble by. We stood with pleading eyes and thumbs turned upward, but we failed to convey our trustworthiness, or I'd confused the attitudes of Arkansan motorists with those on the west coast. Finally, a semi-truck piloted by a balding old-timer in a grimy ball cap stopped and let us in. He rolled his eyes when we said we were going to a rock concert and carried on a steady dialogue about his son, a boy about our age who liked to hunt and fish.

In Little Rock, the trucker informed us that he was continuing to Memphis and let us off at the hectic interchange of I-40 and I-30, apologizing that he had no choice. We crossed the busy freeway on foot and headed into downtown Little Rock. There, as darkness fell, we stopped at a gas station and asked where the auditorium hosting the Mountain concert was located. We had a few miles yet to go, and started walking south. We were losing precious time.

A little after 9:00 p.m., we finally reached the massive music venue that rose like a mountain from the dangerous and violent neighborhoods of south Little Rock. We saw a parking lot full of cars, but none that we knew, presumably everyone already inside the sold-out show. We didn't have enough money to buy a ticket even if it was available. Dejected and devoid of a plan, we kept walking westward and I tried to remember that I just wanted to remain hidden from my dad.

The predominately black citizens of south Little Rock looked at us like we were touched in the head. They sat on their dilapidated porches, shaking their heads at the pair of displaced white boys. We finally asked a couple where we might spend the night.

The woman asked, "Boy, don't you know where you are?" Then she tipped us on our circumstance, saying, "This is a dangerous place for you."

We continued walking and at the next block, we asked an elderly man the same question. He mentioned a rescue mission just a couple of blocks ahead that would take us for the night. Relieved, we hastened our pace, found the shelter, and entered.

Inside sat several cots inhabited by a host of vagabonds. They were people you might see sitting on a sidewalk and asking for spare change: unshaven, disheveled, or disabled with dirty clothes. They kept to themselves, which seemed like a pretty good idea to me. The people running the shelter asked me for identification and all I could find was an old library card, which was enough.

When morning came, we broke our fast with shit on a shingle. After the cheap gravy with hamburger meat on a slice of bread went down, we set out for Springdale thumbs out on the same interstate where we'd arrived. Chuck stood unfazed, still with that goofy grin, while I noticed one of the older men from the shelter sitting on the other side of the freeway, headed east towards Memphis. I wondered if I could live his life if I had to.

Another trucker picked us up and took us all the way to Alma, only an hour shy of Springdale. I supplemented the SOS from that morning with a candy bar and a Coke from the only dollar I had left. When we reached the intersection that led to either Springdale or Fayetteville, I left Chuck and headed towards the Fayetteville Gray House. I didn't walk through the front door of my mother's house on Glenda Street for another seven months.

CHAPTER 11

I got to the Gray House by late evening and walked in without hesitation. I was greeted by some of the residents that had remembered me and made arrangements to sleep on an old couch on the second floor. I wouldn't be able to use the shower. Spring was coming and the nicer weather would make a roof over my head less of a priority, but for now, I had shelter when I really needed it. Now I needed money, and an older Vietnam veteran named Willie offered me some advice.

The next day, I took Willie's advice and found the rock ledge on Dickson Street, one of the main drags in the modest-sized college town. To the east, lay the entertainment district and a few bars, including the popular Swinging Door Saloon, to the west, the entrance to the sprawling university campus. The rock wall ran about 35 feet and stood nearly four feet tall at the apex, tapering down to three feet at its end in keeping with the grade of the sloped road. The apex allowed for me to dangle my feet while I bothered passers-by for spare change. It was also known as a meeting place for drug transactions, so you never knew what the people hanging out there were up to.

It was hard at first and the insults from the pedestrians initially discouraged me, but after a woman forked over a dollar, I decided to stick with it. A few hours later, I had more than four dollars and considered myself in the chips.

"Get a job," came at me most often, followed by questions as to why I wasn't in school, all of it, falling on deaf ears. Instead, I studied what worked and what didn't. I was young and helpless-looking and that worked to my advantage. I wasn't the only one at the wall panhandling and sometimes this caused conflict so I learned to spread out a bit or just give up when bigger, older kids showed up. The local culture in 1971 mimicked what I'd witnessed in Golden Gate Park in 1967, where homeless hippies were an accepted thread of the social fabric. The cops were never called on us.

After a couple of days of this routine and loitering at the Gray House, one of my school-skipping buddies, Curtis, showed up. I filled him in on the happenings of the prior week and he took me with him to his parent's house to feed me and let me shower. I wanted to see some of my former classmates and let them know what I was up to, so Curtis took me with him to school that Monday morning. I visited with friends before class in the parking lot area and let them know I'd been expelled, ducking out of sight when I noticed one of my former teachers walking by. After arranging to meet another friend, Eric, to go to the bowling alley after school, I napped in the back of Curtis' car waiting for the bell to ring at 3:00 p.m.

The bowling alley in Springdale offered hamburgers and fries for only $1.25, and I could come up with that much in an hour of panhandling. I never bowled but there was a pinball machine that cost a quarter that I liked to play.

For the remaining school year from which I'd been expelled, I hopped from car to car and house to house, trying to stay hidden, and bouncing around until I felt like I no longer had to hide. Even though no one seemed to suspect that I was missing or a runaway, I never stayed in one place too long. Where my friends went, I went, out of town, sleeping on floors, park benches, the ground, and the back seats of cars. I borrowed or stole clothes and panhandled at every opportunity. In my spare time, I took up LSD.

I didn't always eat well and remained thin, so in the wee hours of dawn, when I stayed at the Gray House, I stole freshly-baked bread left out to cool at a bakery on Dickson Street. They made the doughy delight every morning, and the sweet smell enticed me from over a block away.

Eventually, I began stealing unattended lawnmowers with friends who drove trucks, pawning them for $20 a pop. While casing an upscale neighborhood one day, Curtis and I loaded an over-sized lawn mower into the still-open trunk of his compact car and sped away in broad daylight with the grass-stained blades sticking out. After a payday, I frequented all-you-can-eat buffets and stayed for hours to get my money's worth.

Vending machines were also easy targets. I came across a row of them one day and reached my skinny, malnourished arm up a drop slot to see if I could snag something edible. Instead, I felt a switch, tripped it, and coins began raining into the bottom tray, clattering like a slot machine. I scored more than $30 in quarters, dimes, and nickels.

After I'd survived the summer, I sat on the wall one evening, listening to a distant radio play the Beatles' *The Long and Winding Road*. As it grew darker, a large shirtless man approached. He seemed impaired, which didn't surprise me at first, but when he got close enough for me to smell him I realized no one else was around. He demanded my T-shirt that wouldn't come close to covering his body. I said "no." He grabbed me, and in a moment wrestled the shirt off me and onto himself. He looked ridiculous, standing there with the fabric stretched taut across the upper half of his bloated stomach.

Just then, two men—Vietnam veterans I presumed—with long hair, bandanas, and green Army issue shirts and boots, appeared. They'd seen what had just gone down. One of them brandished a large knife and told the man to return my shirt. He removed the shirt, which was by now distended and reeking, handed it back, and shuffled away. I returned to the Gray House to lick my wounds. Somehow, I'd avoided being seriously harmed during my homeless stretch, but knew I couldn't count on my luck to continue. It was just a matter of time before thugs or the cops would reel me in. *Then what?*

The answer came the following morning, delivered by the "baddest thug," as the papers would have it, in all of Springdale. I met a couple of new guys from out of town that were looking to score when we were interrupted by a disturbance outside.

"Send him out or I'll burn this fucking place to the ground!" someone hollered.

"I mean it! Larry Daniel is in there and if you don't send him out right now, I'll set this fucking place on fire!"

Soon, Willie and a couple of other guys that ran the flop house came pounding up the stairs. "Who is that?" Willie asked, and I just shook my head and headed for the door.

Lemus Daniel stood in the street in front of his Cadillac El Dorado. It was older now, but still pearly. My bare feet, oily hair, stained jeans, and smelly T-shirt said everything. His expression told me he meant business and wasn't interested in my side of the story.

On the ride home to Glenda Street, I surrendered and listened while he talked of being forced to leave town soon after our incident at the barber shop, where he'd returned from California to straighten me out after a call from my mother nearly seven months prior. He added that he'd been looking for me for a while.

He also mentioned that I was going back to school and would talk to the principal about keeping me with my class as a junior. This time, he insisted, he was here to stay, occupying an apartment and preparing to build a large residential subdivision on a property that he used to own, the police, Dawson, and all the rest be damned. I didn't trust a word of it. I never would.

Growing up, I saw him as a flawed, but well-intentioned man, far from the criminal he'd been made out to be. Now, he'd become something else entirely.

LARRY DANIEL

CHAPTER 12

My mother eyed me like a feral cat that wandered into her kitchen, unsure of what it might do next, but relaxed after a few minutes of observing me and gave me a simple hug. She'd found some Woodstock-themed wallpaper to put up in my old bedroom and at least I had the decency to keep my mouth shut about it. These days, I didn't give a damn about any Woodstock-themed wall paper.

I was pissed off, but even more wary of my father who, an hour earlier, threatened to set fire to a structure full of people. On instinct and dumb luck I'd been living day to day, on my own, with a lot of those days altered or impaired. Repressed anger had taken root, and it expressed itself with a mixture of ambivalence and impulsivity, not to mention poor self-image. I was also conflicted. I may have been afraid of my father, but I knew he'd come to get me and I'd never be able to forget it.

I returned to school, managed decent grades in math because of a teacher that tried to reach me, maintained a few friendships with oddballs like me, but still occasionally walked the halls high on something. My dad's gift of an old white Pontiac was more welcome but came with strings. I had to work as a laborer at a subdivision site on weekends in repayment. Occasionally, I spotted my sisters on campus, but we never had much to say to each other. They stuck together and had a mixed crowd they were busy fitting in with.

After school let out in 1972, I started working full time with my dad and got to know his crew. Bobby, Jake, Ricky, Riley, and Tripp, all had criminal records, and all of them were dead or in prison by the time I was able to legally drink. They said things about women that made Rory's dad, Jack, sound like a choir boy, and after some playful but humiliating prodding let my father know I'd never been all the way with a girl before. He promised to remedy the situation.

Riley and Tripp were always together and always in trouble. I viewed Riley as especially dangerous. He'd been to jail for a variety of offenses—including assault and burglary—and Tripp was his sidekick. Tripp was gullible and worshipped Riley, who used him for whatever purposes he saw fit. If Riley demanded something; anything, Tripp would do it and feel grateful for the opportunity.

Jake was big and gruff looking, but likable. He was the bald-headed, black sheep son of a prominent businessman in Springdale and was born tragically without any impulse control.

Ricky was a trigger-happy thief with a thick head of blond hair and a penchant for fast cars. He scared me as well, even though none of these guys would ever raise a hand to me because my father turned out to be the biggest gangster of them all.

Truth was, these roughnecks had my back if it ever came down to it, and there would be no more picking on little Larry Daniel, unless you were Lemus Daniel. For starters, any one of these guys would have put burning cigarettes out on Kermit's forehead for punching me at the Rockwood Club. In this crew, I was *amico nostra*, a "friend of theirs."

And finally, there was Bobby. He quickly became my favorite. He was a towering ladies' man with a good tan and curly hair, more likely to break out in dance to a Creedence Clearwater Revival song than to get in a fight. He was charismatic and impossible to dislike, even though he was one of the biggest drug dealers in Northwest Arkansas. I took his word as gospel.

It was clear to see that my father was in his element with these characters. During the day, I watched him rule his gang of misfits with a steely fist, tolerating no questions, and at night, get up to no good as they all got staggeringly drunk. On the first job I worked with him that summer, he swore revenge and exhibited his hatred of the police in a short ceremony with the men. Just before the cement dried on a large street drainage for all to see on West Emerald Avenue, he inscribed these words with a nail:

"Dedicated to Fuhrer Parkinson and the Springdale Gestapo"

Our long days in the subdividing ditches usually ended at Wayne's beer joint on Highway 71. Wayne's was a hole-in-the-wall that was inhabited by mostly construction workers or the unemployed, chain-smokers in between drinks. It was one of a dozen beer joints within a few miles that sold cold beer, pickled eggs, peanuts, and nothing more. We had to be careful when driving through town because the police still fancied a Lemus Daniel arrest, but three years on, we hoped they'd moved on to ruining other people's lives. Anytime our crew walked in, the juke box played and cold Pabst Blue Ribbons sat in front of each seat. We drank for hours. I usually kept mine to a few because I didn't like beer that much, but Dad always kept them coming. After a few beers the playful gibberish would start up. "What you boys think?" Dad hollered.

"I don't know, what you think?" echoed from any one of the men.

"I'm just a boll weevil looking for a home," my father crowed. They all laughed dutifully and took another swig.

Once properly intoxicated, paranoia set in and he'd tap me on the knee and begin slipping $100 bills to me under the table. He'd become worried his own men might mug him if they got the chance. When he was drunk, I became the only person on earth that he trusted. I would always return the money—sometimes up to a couple of grand—the following morning without a word.

By the middle of summer 1972, I'd become an accepted part of the crew and available for other duties. I didn't hesitate when my father told me to hop in his car for a drive to a country home on the outskirts of Avoca, where a little old lady lived. He'd sold her a car, and she hadn't made a payment, so it had to be repossessed.

A doughy, goofy-looking, middle-age deputy waited as we arrived. My job was to drive the car away after the deputy made it legal. I got in, started the car, and out the old lady came, with a twelve gauge shotgun leveled at my head. She jammed it in the open window and cocked the trigger. I heard the click and sat motionless, prompting the deputy to enforce the law with a stammering stream of uh-oh's and oh-my's.

"I'll blow his brains plumb across this car," the woman dared.

The deputy was pleading now: "No, no. No. Take it easy, Mrs. Conners. We'll leave, isn't that right, Lemus?"

My dad gave me the nod, "Turn it off, Larry."

I shut down the engine of the old model Ford, which was worth less than $1,000, got out of the car and retreated at gunpoint. I could sense that my father thought he could've wrestled the gun away from her, and I half expected him to try, but the deputy folded from the bluff and was done for the day. Without his support, it wasn't worth the risk.

"Disorganized as a dog fight," Dad mumbled about the deputy.

Back on the job, we cut streets with bulldozers and dug water and sewer lines with backhoes. Sometimes, we used dynamite to blast stubborn rock out of the way. We laid clay sewer pipe after lubing the end and thumping it in, a sound distinct from any other. The water mainline was interrupted by fire hydrants we set along the way at prescribed intervals, and we carried shovels to shield the pipe while covering it with fine chat from the front end loader. After both lines were in and covered, we formed street curbs and followed a truck while it slowly poured concrete into the forms. We leveled and worked it until it dried in the sweltering summer heat. We worked without shirts and sweat buckets, unable to wash the day's work from our hands, and smelled to high heaven for days. It was a physical, no-joke job.

On one of those summer days, after bulldozing a new street on a subdivision in Springdale, Bobby asked me to get in the car with him and Dad. We were going for a ride on the newly formed dirt road that would become an asphalt street in the coming weeks. Cruising slowly I smelled the pungent odor of marijuana. Bobby passed the fat joint back to me from the passenger seat while Dad drove. I took a toke and passed it back to Bobby, who passed it to my father, who drew deeply and passed it back to Bobby. After this initiation, we would smoke only after the day's work was done. If we needed a boost while digging the ditches and laying the pipe, we drank wine from bottles that were cloudy with amphetamines after Bobby dumped in a handful of mini-whites and shook the bottles.

Over the coming months, I discovered that Dad knew a lot about pot, including how to move copious amounts of it for profit, which helped explain how he suddenly had so much money.

Just before my seventeenth birthday, Dad and his friend, Truman, announced that we were going to Tulsa. My father was never in the habit of explaining much of anything, and I wasn't in the habit of asking questions. We arrived at the Trade Winds motel in Tulsa by early afternoon and met a man named Cleveland who worked not only as a bell hop, but a pimp.

"All set, Lemus," Cleveland announced. He expressed a Cheshire grin and rubbed his chin, then asked, "Is this the young man?" My dad nodded, belying the fact that he hadn't said a word to me, and I was sent in to see her on the bed.

Her name was Monique. She was dark-skinned and obviously once beautiful, but now looked weathered. She lay naked on the bed. This was the first I knew of any plan for me to lose my virginity and I was extremely uncomfortable from the start. I still didn't know where to begin. I closed the door behind me, removed my pants, and lay down beside her. My dad and his friend waited outside. I pretended to be interested but she couldn't help but notice that I wasn't aroused by her.

She didn't seem terribly interested in sex after that. Instead she showed me her watch and informed me that it was broken. She wanted to know if I could fix it. I took it from her and inspected it, doing my best to act cool and savvy about watches. Lying on the motel bed in my white briefs with the naked pro, I was studying the watch when Dad poked his head in the door to check on my progress. He surveyed the scene and shook his head, finding nothing had happened. He quickly summoned Cleveland to complain. Cleveland came in and the argument ensued.

"What are you doing, Monique?" Cleveland demanded. "You know Lemus is a good customer and you treat him like this?"

Monique was immediately repentant and acknowledged her variance from the routine. She promised to earn her money without further delay. Everyone seemed satisfied, except for me and I began shaking my head, no. I said that I wasn't going through with it. Dad shot me a look and told me to wait in the car. He and Truman stayed inside with Monique while I sat in the back seat thinking there must be something wrong with me.

LARRY DANIEL

CHAPTER 13

The primitive milieu of the crew was sometimes off-set by lunch at Grandma Daniel's beautiful sandstone abode. She served as a surrogate mother of sorts to these shady characters, feeding and fussing over these men of questionable morals, giving them something they could get nowhere else. They were putty in her hands whenever they sat around her spacious table, helping themselves to her homemade dishes, these men that only a mother could love.

Late in August of 1972, Dad decided to host a party at his apartment before he lost me to my senior year of high school. Brenda was back in town after a stint in California with her parents, and I wasn't too happy about it. Bobby was there with a girlfriend along with a local musician who played guitar and sang. Others that I didn't recognize drank and mingled. Everybody felt good, and I thought we might escape a scene, until Brenda finally started in, announcing, "Who do you think you are, anyway, Daddy's little pet?" before adding a little extra sauce, declaring, "I'm going to be your new momma."

Bobby could hear this and instinctively wagged his head "no" at me over her shoulder, but I ignored him and informed Brenda that she was a fucking bitch. She didn't take kindly to this revelation. Her right hand came around and connected with my left ear, and it rang. My father was on her at once and dragged her into the bedroom. I could feel my face burning. I was old enough to defend myself now and considered slapping her back. But maybe we both underestimated Brenda. She and my father hadn't even emerged from the bedroom when we heard sirens in the driveway. She'd planned ahead and called the cops before provoking me, knowing she would get a rise out of Dad.

He came out of the bedroom and stood in the front doorway, screaming for them to either come inside and arrest him or get the hell off his property. I knew what he'd suffered at the hands of law enforcement and what could still be done to him, but he seemed wholly unaware of the peril. He'd gone off the rails and was cursing them. I thought that they might come in and arrest him, or worse, but they didn't get out of their cars, and after more verbal abuse from my father, drove away in retreat.

Brenda came out and sat by herself like a petulant child, with her arms crossed and a pouty expression on her face. She was a professional-grade troublemaker. I was very aware of the devastation she'd helped bring down on my father. After that, the party didn't take long to break up. I rode there with my dad, but rather than driving back with him, I opted to walk the mile home to my mother's house.

It was dark and balmy, but now and then street lights illuminated my shoes, one replacing the other in quick succession as I fumed. *What hold did this woman have over my dad? Why had he thrown everything away? What was wrong with him?*

I'd been constantly reminded that Tom Dawson set the wheels of punishment in motion, but I believed he could have recovered to some degree, had he collected himself and resisted this poisonous relationship. But no, Brenda was there to finish the job. My father blamed Dawson and Winston for his troubles, but now I blamed her. I wasn't strong enough to blame him yet.

While the school year progressed, the motivation I'd somehow mustered to complete my junior year of high school went missing. In fewer than two months, my attendance record raised another red flag with the school administration, and it prompted another meeting with the principal. This time, it was just me and neither of my parents.

In contrast to my meeting with Principal Clem as a sophomore, he was cordial and suggested that I enroll at the West Campus of Fayetteville High where building trades were taught and marginal students sometimes did well. I knew that troublemakers and truants were often offered West Campus, and agreed to give it a try.

I told Dad about it and he said if it was up to him, I would stop wasting my time and just come back to work. Instead, I started classes at West Campus after semester break, but after only one month, I took his advice and said goodbye to high school forever. I'd never attended a prom or belonged to a group of any kind in the short time I'd spent in high school.

Dad was happy when I reported that I was ready to take up where we'd left off and he described the planned work ahead. He explained we had a small subdivision to do before building new homes at a different location. The new homes would be constructed from the ground up by digging foundations, laying blocks, and pouring concrete floors. Ruth's husband, Marty, would also be involved, and we'd be learning how to rough frame, hang drywall, and paint. It would be hard work, he said, but I was no stranger to that. After the small subdivision job, I'd start on the houses when he returned from a quick trip to California. I was excited for the money and to be doing it with him again. I was a working man now.

My first day started at the Sunrise Café, Dad's favorite place for early morning coffee. He paid for breakfast, and after that, I ate what I could. While I sipped on some coffee, he laid out his ground rules, informing me that Harold Knox was soon going to regret taking advantage of him and I'd better be on board with whatever that entailed. He would pay dearly for ripping him off when Tom Dawson put blood in the water in 1967. Knox, posing as a friend and kicking him when he was down, would stand in as a whipping boy for his wrath instead of the impossible–to reach Dawson.

"A couple of my boys brought two rattlesnakes from one of those desert shops in New Mexico on I-40 last week and put them in Knox's unlocked car at his house," he boasted.

I hadn't heard anything about a prominent man in Springdale being bitten by a rattlesnake in his car, so I assumed that Knox noticed them before it was too late. I wondered who the boys that Dad mentioned might be. The message to Knox was made clear, and I was also now aware of the seriousness of my father's intent. None of this persuaded me to break off from him, and I figured I could pretend I was all in on the hatred. My father wanted revenge and I could never speak to the contrary. His rage lay just beneath the surface, ready to spew out at a moment's notice.

We did the small residential water and sewer line for Mr. Patton, a man he'd known for years and owned a small hamburger place next to Dad's office before he was banished. We finished it after several weeks of digging and laying line with the crew, but before we covered it up, Dad and I took a drive to see Patton about getting paid. I waited in the car while my father went inside. Within a few minutes, he came storming out and sped back to the job site, jaw clenched and eyes betraying his bad intentions. After jerking to a screeching halt, he hopped on the backhoe that sat off to the side, started it up, positioned it, and started jabbing holes in the water and sewer lines with the jagged end of the bucket.

"He didn't have my fucking money," he growled. "They all think they can get away with screwing with me!"

The pipe cracked and caved as he raised and then violently stabbed the teeth of the bucket onto the pipe, then moved to another position down the line and repeated the process. He didn't stop until he'd destroyed most of it and left it buried under several feet of soil. I knew to step aside and kept my mouth shut. If I hadn't, I felt he might have hurt me. He drove me home in complete silence while his ears smoked. He left for California soon after, and in his absence, I prepared to launch my new career in house construction. I was short on options and bracing myself for more outrageous behavior.

Following his promised trip to California, he encountered the police about the car bombing of someone that was a defendant in the lawsuit he filed against the city four years prior. The police officer had gotten into his patrol car then fought for his life after the explosion.

This was my father's detailed description of the circumstances surrounding the car bombing:

"I tied up some loose ends in Los Angeles and headed back to Springdale. My son was eager for me to get back to start some houses.

After driving non-stop from Los Angeles to Springdale and arriving late in the afternoon, I went directly to my mother's house. After saying hello, I went directly to bed and slept until six the next morning. The smells of coffee and sizzling bacon along with the radio (set at a high volume because my mother didn't hear so well anymore) awoke me. It also let me know my mom wanted me up to hear what was being said.

With the bedroom door ajar, I distinctly heard the news bulletin on the radio, which announced, "Husk Karmen, a local police officer, was blown up by a car bomb last night and is in critical condition."

I sprang to my feet and went to the kitchen while my mom poured me a cup of coffee. She asked, "Lemus, what could that be all about?"

I replied, "Well Mom, someone else must hate the idiot as much as I do."

Husk Karmen was one of the six defendants in the lawsuit I filed four years earlier, but I didn't think much about the bombing. My mind was on getting over to my ex-wife's house to see my children, including Larry, who was going to be working for me. By mid-morning, I sat in Doris' home with my children, and I peered out the open front door to see an unmarked police car pull up into the driveway. When the first plain clothes cop got out of the car, I knew what was about to happen.

The cop asked, "Are you Lemus Daniel?"

"That's right," I said.

"We'd like to talk to you."

As the other cop got out of the car, I stood between the two of them and asked, "Who sent you? Tom Dawson?"

The two cops acted as if they didn't hear me. They were a special task force sent from Little Rock and they wanted to know how long I had been in town, and if I had heard about the police bombing.

I told them I'd heard of it and also mentioned that I felt no sorrow for Karmen. They asked me if I would accompany them to the police station to answer a few questions.

"No way," I said, "Unless you want to put me under arrest."

Then they started to bargain with me and asked me if I would submit to a lie detector test.

"Why?" I asked.

"We're aware of your problems with the local police, and you are a suspect in the police car bombing." They looked at each other, and added, "You will be under surveillance until the guilty person is caught, but if you take our lie detector test and pass, we won't bother you again."

I said, "Set up your equipment anywhere besides the Springdale police station, and I will oblige you."

With my agreement, they jumped on their two-way radios and told their men to move the equipment to the Holiday Inn in Springdale and they would administer the test there. The cops then looked at me, opened their car door, and told me to get in.

"I know the way," I said. "I'll see you there."

"Oh no, you ride with us."

"No," I replied, "You can ride with me if you like, but I'm not getting in that car with you. Go ahead and arrest me if you like."

They agreed to follow me to the room at the Holiday Inn, which they did bumper to bumper style. As our parade reached the hotel, the other detectives arrived with their equipment. We entered a room and while the men were setting up, I had about 30 minutes to talk to my captors. They asked me some off-the-wall questions and I started to talk.

I said, "If wishing for something like this to happen would make me guilty, you can put that machine away and take me straight to prison. I think it's the greatest thing that could happen in this town. Too bad it didn't happen to them all."

They asked me if I knew of any suspects that could be responsible for the bombing.

"Yes, I do, about 75% of the population of this town. There are few people who have escaped the brutality of the police." Then I began to toy with the cops. "Okay, I'll tell you everything *if you'll call the newspaper and get me the front page." I had plenty to say and was ready to expose them all.*

By the time they got the machine set up and I finished my speech, one of the cops said, "We're wasting our time, Lemus Daniel had nothing to do with the bombing." They went ahead with the polygraph anyway and then dismissed me without arresting me."

Husk Karmen lived and was assigned to desk duty after a lengthy recovery. I had to consider if my father was capable of doing something like this, or getting somebody to do it for him. When I wondered aloud about it, he denied it, cursed Karmen, and there was never another word spoken. I went through the ordeal of reading the headline news and listening to the radio echo the suspicion that my father was somehow a part of the attack on Officer Karmen. Of course he was a suspect because he'd been pistol-whipped by Karmen, and retaliated with a lawsuit that he'd lost.

But Karmen got around and there were other suspects. My dad mentioned to the investigators that he knew a lot of people that might have done the dirty deed. I don't know what kind of explosive that was used, but I hadn't forgotten the random sticks of dynamite I was used to seeing on my dad's subdivision job sites.

Dealing with my father's notoriety was something I'd done before as an innocent 12-year-old boy, so now as a 17-year-old henchman-in-training, I thought I should be tough enough to handle it. But I wasn't tough, and one look from my father was all it took for me to cower in the corner to prove it. I remained woefully unprepared for whatever the next crazy thing might be. It would eventually come and make this incident pale in comparison.

Ruth and her husband, Marty, who'd completed a military stint in Germany, had returned to Arkansas with his wife and young daughter and was looking for work. Ruth was a daddy's girl and held a special bond with her father, who tried to help her and her husband get a foothold in the building business. In order to build the houses that my father had mentioned to me, a deal was made for him to get construction loans through a friend of his by the name of Robert Allenby, the manager at the local savings and loan. Tom Dawson sat on the Board, so my dad and his friend had to maneuver around him. My father's story described getting us started on the houses:

"I kept the road hot between California and Northwest Arkansas. I was also trying to establish my son-in-law in the construction business in Springdale. When I first went to see Bob about approving loans to Marty, Bob said, 'You know you're through in Springdale, Tom won't let me help you.' "

Bob knew how well I knew Dawson. I had been a direct partner with Bob on several land deals where I could carry the cash to Bob, back-door style, all done covertly through his sister-in-law's name. Bob agreed to make loans to Marty as long as I stayed completely out of the picture."

I signed on as a laborer and kept busy during my initial workdays. Before I could blink, we had the foundation squared, the footing dug, blocks laid, and concrete poured. As expected, it was hard work, but void of the characters of the past year, even though I still saw Bobby every so often. Ricky had recently been arrested for stealing a backhoe and was now in jail.

Working with my father again revealed that regardless of his rollercoaster behavior, he never compromised his old-school work ethic. He was out of bed before daybreak and at the Sunrise Café for biscuits and gravy without fail, no matter how drunk he became the night before. I stayed at his apartment some nights, and when I didn't, he was at my mother's doorstep while it was still dark. He continued to keep the window on my side rolled down while we drove through the outside chill. He was a concentrated task master and almost normal, but after three in the afternoon, he started drinking and usually consumed at least one case of beer. He would get so obnoxious that he was hard to be around.

The more I actually learned about what Knox did, the more I genuinely came to hate him, too, which made things so much easier now that they were OUR enemies. But I could only handle so much of this, so after the work was done and the evening approached, I tried to make myself scarce.

I had my own hell to raise.

CHAPTER 14

Dad took me aside and rewarded me with the keys to a Porsche 914 that he'd been driving for the past few months. It was a couple of years old, had a black convertible top, a Volkswagen engine, and a sexy Porsche body. It was painted orange but it was pure gold to me. It kept me motivated and loyal to him while I hit the road in that five-speed cube of sugar.

Circling a popular hot spot in Springdale became something I could do proudly now and I never missed an opportunity. The 'Vic-Mon' was a drive-in burger place with booths for the cars to pull into and order after circling to locate friends. I spotted Jackie there one day with a friend she'd brought back from the west coast. She introduced herself as Patti and they invited me for a get together at Jackie's boyfriend's apartment in Fayetteville. I had forgotten all about Jackie, liked what I saw in Patti, and told them I would follow them.

Jackie's boyfriend, Robert, had a small apartment with a swimming pool near the university campus. After arriving, Jackie and Robert went inside and Patti and I hit the pool, and it was there that the monkey was finally off my back regarding my virginity. After that, I quickly made up for lost time with the ladies. The car helped and I took advantage, getting invitations and making new friends.

A new friend of mine, Harris, bought tickets to see the rock band Cactus in concert in Tulsa. He invited Wayne, another new friend of mine, and me. Wayne and I drove over in the Porsche and enjoyed the show, then met some other friends at an after-party. The place was full of people from all over town and we were introduced to the occupants and a couple of guys from Springdale, Earl and Brandon. The vibe seemed good when Harris told us all to come into the kitchen because he had something to show us. He pulled out a baggie with the dusty remnants of a hundred hits of LSD, laid it on the table, and dumped the contents into a cup of beer. There was no way to know for sure the strength of the concoction, but we didn't hesitate taking turns drinking it. Earl and Brandon declined. Our calculations turned out to be way off.

Within the hour, I regretted my flippant impulsiveness. I felt confused and anxious, and wandered outside to look for my car. I suddenly realized I didn't know where I was and couldn't drive the car anyway, so I headed back to the party. After finally finding the right door, I went inside and discovered the crowd still more than I could handle. I found a closet, entered it, and closed the door behind me. That didn't last long, so I came out and found a corner of the kitchen floor, laid down, and closed my eyes. I felt my head sink beneath the surface. Now concerned that I could be sucked into the underworld, I quickly arose and somehow made it to the living room, where a young woman approached me and started talking. As she spoke, I stood slack-jawed and muted, watching the walls breathe in and out. I made my way to a back bedroom where I found my fellow terrorized trippers and waited out the lingering overdose with them. The following weekend, I met Earl and Brandon at the Vic-Mon and we rehashed the Tulsa fiasco.

"Dude, you were messed up, Earl joked. "Are you an acid head?"

"Never again," I groaned. "That was enough for me." It was funny now even though it wasn't at the time.

Earl was originally from northern California, and moved to Tulsa, before ending up in Springdale with his folks. Springdale is where he met Brandon, and I liked them both, even though Brandon seemed a little rough around the edges. I figured the three of us could hang out some. Leaving the Vic-Mon, Brandon spun the tires of his Mustang Mach I and left a big cloud of smoke in the parking lot. He'd gotten the car from an insurance settlement after an accident that left his leg badly burned. I didn't know it at the time, but I just doubled down on bad company.

Earl and I found ourselves together again and headed north towards the popular hangout when I stopped at the last red light before the Vic-Mon. While waiting for the light to change, a shiny black Mach I, just like Brandon's, pulled up and revved its engine. The quarterback of the high school football team, Brewer McDonald, peered over at me and smiled.

"This Porsche can take that Mach I," Earl declared.

I didn't know if it could but was caught up in the idea of it. When the light changed, we were off. McDonald pushed ahead with his automatic transmission and I patiently went through the paces of first, second, and third. I began to catch him when I hit fourth and with less than fifty yards to go, I pushed it into fifth and skidded ahead of him into the hot spot. Earl was jubilant.

"I told you so!"

"Damn right!" I howled.

Earl invited me over to Brandon's pad to hang out that night, giving me the location and telling me to come around 7:00 p.m. "We'll drink some beers and smoke some weed," he promised.

That evening, I pulled into the gravel driveway of a modest-looking home with white vinyl siding and red trim. It was on the outskirts of town, and in the back yard sat a small building about twelve feet wide and sixteen feet long with old unpainted wooden lap siding and weathered shingles. I walked around and approached it, knocked on the door and heard, "Come on in."

The party pad was equipped with a fridge full of beer and a large sofa arranged efficiently enough for a small gathering to lounge after hours. The music playing told me we could be good friends. Earl and Brandon greeted me with a Thai stick joint that one of Earl's brothers brought back from Vietnam.

"Ever do any smack?" Earl asked. "My brother brought some heroin over with the Thai stick." Earl pulled out a baggie full of red capsules instead and handed me a couple.

"It's not heroin, they're reds. Take one," Brandon encouraged. I swallowed one and chased it with a beer. Soon, I was melted into the sofa listening to *Kiln House* from Fleetwood Mac and taking long draws on the sticky Asian marijuana. Brandon bragged about his car and sexual conquests while I took it all in. Brandon had curly blond hair that sat on top of a big-nosed face, and he limped slightly when he walked. He had three sisters—just like me—and one of them would figure prominently into my future.

Earl was a smooth-talking, persuasive guy who kept an even keel that concealed a rebellious soul. His brown, shoulder-length hair lay perfectly in proportion to his ready smile and easy tone of voice. Earl usually got whatever he wanted.

After a month on the job, Dad opened the back doors of his work van and revealed a stack of bricks in red wrapping paper. They were secured with tape, weighed a kilogram, and smelled of fresh Mexican pot. He told me to grab a few

to see what I could do with it. I thought of the many characters I'd encountered in my ever-widening circle that might
be interested. I knew Cowboy, who was my age and had a
speech impediment, would be. I'd never seen him without a
shiny red electric guitar. He couldn't play it, but never hesitated to pretend that he could. He'd throw it into the air and
catch it during any song from the Stones, and finish it off
with a raucous pretend solo. I knew very well what to do
with it. I was in now, all the way.

I let Earl in on my source and we started making trips to
Oklahoma. I sold to the manager of a fast food restaurant in
Muskogee, which always meant bedroom eyes from a tall
brunette that worked there, but unfortunately never materi-
alized into anything more. Afterwards, a drive to the town
square to see Superman–an elderly but muscular gentleman
who walked around in a superhero costume–was our last stop
before heading home. He was off his bean, but harmless and
it made for some good clean fun after completing the various
deals. I went often enough to afford my own apartment in
Fayetteville.

Earl and Brandon loitered at my new apartment and the
three of us became inseparable. They brought lots of wandering types and many of my mornings were spent stepping
over the random dopers that slept on my floor. The parties
got wilder and the drug use more dangerous. I dabbled in all
of the debauchery but was somehow able to keep showing up
for work.

That summer, I decided to attend a music festival in southern Arkansas. ZZ Top, a favorite group of mine, was playing
and would provide a perfect opportunity to turn a tidy profit.
Earl and Brandon were in Tulsa that weekend and wouldn't
attend, but I knew people that were. I looked forward to a

weekend of music, money-making, and perhaps a young lady could be convinced to see the layout of my small tent.

The night before the festival, I stayed in a cheap motel outside the tiny town of Sheridan, Arkansas, and prepared for the weekend. I filled baggies with 'lids' and double checked the tent, pillows, and blankets that I would need to sit around with friends before and after the music acts, Woodstock style. I wanted my camp to be a popular meeting place to maximize my profits.

The big show was slated for Saturday night after some lesser known bands played to the several thousands of fans that had shown up for the festival. The venue was a sprawling pasture with a small lake in the middle of it that provided the backdrop for the main stage in a picturesque setting. There was a nice breeze and the weather was perfect with low humidity, a rarity in southern Arkansas during the summer.

Right away, I made new friends as I displayed my wares and others displayed theirs like a trade show for mind-altering substances. The laid-back atmosphere had most of the attendees getting high as soon as they arrived, if they hadn't done so before. My camp was frequented by many, and it lured a girl from Mississippi that stayed with me the first night. A dealer came around on the second day and offered me what he said was pure THC paste, which was a concentrated form of the psychoactive component in marijuana. "I've done THC before but it wasn't a paste. Are you sure this is legit?" I asked.

"It's good," he replied then asked. "What about your weed?" He wanted me to light up one of my joints in a show and tell before he went to watch one of the opening acts, so I did.

I'd already sold out but had just enough to trade with him, so I said, "I'll trade you this small bag for your hit," and he agreed. I swallowed it and anticipated the effect, knowing the feature band would be taking the stage in a couple of hours. Within the half hour, I started to feel the full-bodied heaviness of something other than THC, but wasn't too concerned. I still didn't know that I would be fighting to survive the big mistake of consuming horse tranquilizer that was passed off as THC.

One by one, my friends left me in the tent for the stage and I informed them I would be along soon, still unaware that my condition would render me incapacitated. After a couple of hours, I lay alone in the tent and pondered not making it. At one point, it felt as if I had left my body, and looked down on myself from above. I was on the brink, and I couldn't move.

My friends started returning much later after the show. I was motionless, non-verbal, and they knew something was wrong. They poured ice and cold water over me, slapped my face, and repeated the sequence until I came around. I nearly died. Somebody else did.

By morning, I was finally able to get up and walk around while the drug finally phased out. While people mingled and talked about the night before, a bystander mentioned that another attendee at a different campsite made the same mistake as I did. That person died from the same horse tranquilizer I'd taken. Nobody knew who or where the dealer was.

Before driving home late the following day, I counted the big wad of cash that had somehow remained in my pocket while I lay paralyzed in the tent. I still felt weak, but didn't say a word about it when I showed up for work that Monday, where I endured a brutal day of forming for a concrete floor that we later poured. Dad showed no mercy whenever it came to work.

My father had a smile on his face that day. Clyde Winston had gotten fired. The following is my father's description of the termination of the Chief of Police:

"It was July 1, 1973, making it the 28th annual Springdale Rodeo, a community event led by a committee chaired by Truman 'Tubby' Parsley. The committee included the most civic-minded citizens of town and Parsley Stadium was where the rodeo was held. The stadium was named after Tubby.

Claude Madden, a former rodeo announcer and now an Oklahoma congressman, owned and provided all the livestock involved in the four-day event. Claude knew most all the rodeo contestants and their families personally, since they followed his shows wherever they went.

On the first evening of the event, a young lady left the spectator stand and went to her pick-up in the parking area. As she entered her truck, one of Clyde Winston's policemen approached her and began pointing a finger at an empty beer can lying on the ground beside her truck and said, 'You're drinking in public and you're drunk. Come on, you're going to jail,' and placed her in handcuffs. The young lady was not permitted to identify herself, or state that her young child was still in the stands, or that her husband was riding or trying to ride a wild bronc to make a living.

It was not until the bronc-riding cowboy finished his event that he discovered his wife was missing. It was suggested by someone who knew of the arrest that he should check the city jail and when he found his wife there and paid her fine, he noticed that the cops were marching a lot of attendees from the rodeo into the same situation as his wife.

The young cowboy became incensed and called Claude Madden, who was still in Tulsa. Claude hadn't intended to attend the rodeo until the final day but the phone call from the cowboy brought him flying into Springdale in his private jet that very night, where he arrived around 1:00 a.m. Within an hour, Truman Parsley, Mayor Parkinson, and Chief Clyde Winston were in conference with Congressman Claude Madden and he made things clear from the start, stating, 'Police Chief Clyde Winston will resign before 6:00 a.m. this morning or my livestock and all performers will vacate Springdale at that time.' This would leave some 40,000 ticket holders highly irritated. The rodeo went on, and the next day's paper stated, 'Chief Winston resigns, no reason given.' "

The fact that Chief Winston was no longer with the police department meant my father didn't have to look over his shoulder anymore.

LARRY DANIEL

After the concrete floor dried, we chalked the lines where the walls would go and nailed in so many "spikes" that my forearm muscles squeaked. After the walls were raised and braced, we ran two-by-six joists every two feet along the top of the walls and then cut roof rafters to length and connected them before they were decked with four-by-eight sheets of half-inch thick plywood. After we braced it, the rough frame roof was complete. We rushed to dry it in with tar paper before it rained, which always caused problems with warping the plywood if it got wet. The roof deck was also hand nailed, and I got to be pretty good at it after my bruised thumb and bloodied hand healed from the learning curve. If I ever so much as looked at a stray cloud in hopes of not having to work because of the weather, Dad's favorite quip was always, "Don't worry about the mule going blind, just load the wagon."

He'd bought me a leather nail and tool pouch and it made me feel more like a carpenter even though I had a ton yet to learn. A heavy framing hammer completed the pouch, making my ego even happier, and had me looking more the part. I worked all day, dry or wet, hot or cold.

We finally took a Friday off, which was rare because we worked on a pretty tight schedule. Dad said we were going somewhere and it would be a longer than usual trip so I loaded up with him and his girlfriend, Phyllis. Phyllis and my father had become an item over the last couple of months and she seemed eager to get along with everybody. She was unlike the troubled and now long-gone Brenda, and she tried hard to be nice to me. I tolerated her, but kept my distance. She was 20 years younger than Dad and had a big rack, which surprised no one that knew my father. She catered to him, so it looked like she might be around for a while.

We traveled east towards Newton County, which was at least two hours away, to see an old friend of his, Lonnie English, whom I'd met several times before. No details were given to me about this drive other than we were going out to see him and I was coming along. Newton County was a desolate and sparsely populated wilderness that had a reputation as a growing area for pot farmers.

When we finally approached the property, we found the creeks en route to his home had risen from the recent rains. While crossing one of them, the water reached mid-door level, which made us nervous, but we pressed on. Once we arrived, Lonnie greeted us and invited us in. His wife, Gretchen, stood by and offered a shy "hello." I did my best to keep out of the way in a corner. Phyllis stood near my Dad while Lonnie seemed nervous.

"Do you have my money?" my father asked.

"Lemus, things haven't turned out so well and I don't have it yet," he replied. "I'll get it soon."

"I need the $5,000 right now," he demanded.

Lonnie turned his gaze downward. He knew my father outweighed him by 60 pounds, and it was just us with nobody else around for miles. I realized what my role was about the time Dad reached into Phyllis' purse and pulled out a loaded .38 caliber handgun that he pointed at Lonnie. He was waving the gun around and threatening to shoot if Lonnie didn't hand over the keys to the late model Ford Bronco that sat just outside. "Hand 'em over!" he demanded. His gun-holding hand became fixed as his voice grew more serious. He held the gun under Lonnie's nose, and taunted him. Gretchen began crying out loud. "Shut the hell up!" my father threatened.

Lonnie slowly dropped the keys on the kitchen table and Phyllis handed them to me while Dad aimed the gun at Lonnie's chest. Phyllis knew all along what was going to go down. I thought that he could have accomplished this without the gun.

Dad instructed me to get in and drive. I looked at Lonnie and Gretchen on my way out of the door, an acknowledgement of complicity. He shook his head and kept staring at the ground. I wondered what the hell just happened.

While my father followed me out of Lonnie's driveway in his van, I was more than apprehensive, but managed the Bronco across the two creek crossings without a hiccup and dutifully delivered the vehicle to a parking garage in Fayetteville, where a crooked lawyer waited to turn it into cash.

My father's anger was on a hair trigger toward anyone that did him wrong or owed him money. He wasn't asking people to treat him fairly anymore, he was demanding it, and apparently it was my job to accompany him when he needed backup or a driver. My father exposed me to situations that put me at risk and this wouldn't be the last time.

After we'd finally completed the house we'd been working on, I had a few personal days off, so I got a hold of Brandon about a party I'd heard about in town. Neither of us knew the host very well so we weren't counting on much. The night was young and we were up for just about anything. Once we arrived, though, it didn't take long for Brandon to hint at leaving. Luckily for us, a mutual friend at the party suggested that we go to a club in Fayetteville with him. Our friend, Buddy, said he'd follow us to Brandon's so we could park our cars and go with him to the Gaslight, the popular club at the Mountain Inn in Fayetteville. He added that he knew someone that would let us in even though we were still underage.

The Gaslight had a reputation for players and adventuresome ladies, and we were eager to check it out. Neither Brandon nor I had seen the inside of it. I hadn't had anything to drink so I offered to drive, but Buddy said no, he was going to drive his car and if we wanted to go, we had to go with him.

Buddy was a thick-necked, ex-football player, well over 21 years old and for some reason, trying hard to impress us with his connections at this club. While we got in line, he assured us everything was okay and took the lead with Brandon on his tail to provide support. I stood back to see how all of this was going to work out.

While I stood in the distance, I heard what seemed to be a disagreement brewing and leaned in to hear a little better. I reminded Buddy that it was okay if we couldn't get in, it was worth the try, but Buddy now felt as if his reputation was on the line. Brandon started chiming in with Buddy in a heated confrontation with the gate-keeping bouncers. Brandon was writing a check with his mouth that his ass could not cash.

Suddenly and swiftly, a long-handled flashlight cracked Buddy over the skull, with blood flowing instantly and dropping him face down on the floor. Brandon came next. It produced a thud and profuse bleeding, but Brandon was still upright. They weren't finished with Brandon when another bouncer emerged from behind the counter and restrained him as the original assailant punched him in the face.

In an instant, I was at the stairs that led out of the main lobby where all of this was taking place. I was unrestrained and free to leave even though I had no car there. I knew I could walk home if necessary, or run, which I was strongly considering. However, one last look was too much for my conscience to bear as I watched smart-assed and bloodied Brandon suffering the bouncers' work-over.

Buddy was out cold on the floor when I walked into the fray and pulled Brandon from the bouncer's grip. The bouncer promptly turned and punched me in one eye and then the other, so I decided that was enough empathy for Brandon. I turned to run up the stairs and out into the dark night, and looked back to find Brandon on my heels. He was barely recognizable.

We were exposed on the street when I noticed a narrow alleyway, so we decided to enter it. There was no time to talk about what happened, just time enough to get clear of the area and regroup a plan to get home. Brandon's face was red with drying blood, but he was still lucid. We traveled through a small maze of alleys and became disoriented, but eventually ended up back on Highway 71. We were now completely exposed to the police cars that arrived at the disturbance at the Gaslight Club. The first unit almost hit Brandon accidently as we crossed the street in front of them toward freedom. They noticed his bloodied face after we walked right out in front of them. Without having any reason to be running, we ran.

"Halt!" the officer commanded.

"Stop right there!" another ordered.

We continued running. I had a lead on Brandon and I was sprinting as fast as I could.

BOOOOOM!

At the deafening sound of the shot, Brandon dropped and surrendered. They quickly swooped down on him and cuffed him.

BOOOOOM!

Another shot rang out, and even though I had a pretty good jump on them, it scared me enough to make me stop and hide under a car in a crowded parking lot. I slid under one and waited, hoping they weren't mad enough to beat me up–or worse–if they found me. I imagined the worst when they pulled up right next to me. They ordered me out with my hands up, cuffed me, and gave me a short ride to the station. I was arrested for public drunkenness, even though I hadn't had anything to drink. Brandon was taken along with Buddy to the hospital and treated for his scalp wounds, and avoided the jailhouse.

I sat in jail, and waited for Marty to bail me out because I didn't want to call my father. The police brought in the bouncer that swung the flashlight. They walked him by my cell after they had processed him. He went crazy when he recognized me.

"How'd you like that, little boy?!" he screamed. Obviously tweaked, he added on his way past, "I'm going to get you too, you son-of-a-bitch!"

Finally, Marty arrived and rescued me from this horrific scene. I felt lucky that I hadn't ended up at the hospital. The hospital released Brandon the next day and I'd been given a fine for public intoxication.

"Where'd you get the shiner, Larry?" my father asked. Marty squealed, so he already knew. He reminded me of the Gaslight's reputation when it was a part of the Mountain Inn in the 1960s, and reminded me that it was a place to avoid.

"You need to be more careful, Larry. We've got too much going on for this," he warned, before adding something else that was on his mind. "That Brandon kid is trouble."

I learned that Brandon had been spotted earlier that week driving around town with my younger sister, Hazel, who was now a senior. The sighting was promptly reported to our father and he wasn't happy about it. It was news to me. On the rare occasion I'd bumped into her, she'd never said anything and Brandon had kept it to himself as well. The estrangement from the rest of my family was more evident than ever.

My father continued on about the Gaslight incident, "That's Jeremy Townsend, a convict and a Dawson hatchet man," he warned. "He's a killer. Those guys play for keeps."

Buddy was hospitalized for two weeks with a skull fracture before being discharged.

Dad had been working on some new deals and was ready for me to do some extra work for him. I readily accepted the opportunities and the cash they provided. He gave me $1,000 to see a man in Tulsa and make a small deal with him if I could. It was a practice run to see if we could do business in the future. When the man saw that I was alone, he seemed disappointed and asked, "Where's Lemus? Why didn't he show?"

"He couldn't make it, so he sent me. What's the problem?"

"Let me know when Lemus is available. No deal today," he decided.

Because I was already in Tulsa, I called Earl to let him know I was in town to party and had a grand. Instead of returning the money to my father, I was easily enticed to pick up a hundred downers with some of the money and meet some girls that my friend knew from a club in town. Earl and I got started on the pills and looked forward to a night in the city.

I was introduced to a couple of professional dancers at a local club that Earl frequented. As usual, Earl had his pick of companionship, and Betsy, a blond stripper, was Earl's current girlfriend. She brought along a friend for me, Rosie, who was a tall brunette. We caught a local blues band, drank some beers, and got more wasted as the night wore on. We eventually settled into a small motel, and later that night, Rosie left to go home. Around three that morning, someone started pounding on the door.

Bam, Bam, Bam. "Open up!"

The three of us, Betsy, Earl, and I, woke up groggy, looking to each other for explanations.

"What the hell?" Earl said, extricating himself from his bed sheets before heading for the door.

Again, *Bam, Bam, Bam!* "Open up, it's the police!"

A half-asleep Earl cracked open the door and found himself staring down a trio of armed Tulsa city police. Earl remembered the pills and ran to flush them. I watched from the bed as one of the cops grabbed him by the hair and snatched the evidence from him. We were all under arrest, and it had happened in a flash. Our rights were read and they handcuffed us, the three of us now headed towards the skyscraper jail in downtown Tulsa. I started smarting off, spouting something I must have seen on television, "I've got $700 and we'll be out in an hour. You pigs can't hold us."

The cops peeked back at me while Earl shook his head. Still groggy, I eventually picked up on Earl's body language and shut my mouth. It finally dawned on me that I was asking for it.

We were strip-searched before sitting for mug shots, finger printing, delousing, and further humiliation en route to our jail cell. We were charged with a felony intent to deliver, and sat sharing a cell with an attempted murderer and a host of other characters I knew better than to talk to. Betsy was taken away to a woman's cell, and after that, it was just Earl and me among the other law-breakers. Earl seemed to know what to expect, and I learned fast. "Don't talk to anyone," Earl advised. "They'll send a snitch in here to get you to talk to them. If they separate us, don't talk. They want to know where we got the pills."

Soon after, a young man about our age was escorted in and immediately tried to get close to us. He was obviously undercover and didn't spend much time in there after we wouldn't acknowledge him. No one else in the felony tank was wearing pressed jeans, a clean button-up shirt, and new cowboy boots, looking to score while sitting in a jail cell. They decided to let us sit over the weekend before arraigning us instead. Earl knew I had a lot of the money left and with his phone call was able to arrange for a lawyer for all three of us. He said it would be Monday, not the hour I had promised the arresting officer, before I got out.

That weekend, I lost track of time and space. Earl and I ate crappy food at designated intervals and sat around with seriously troubled individuals all day. At night, we slept on mattresses so thin that we might as well have been lying on the cement floor. We were forced by the authorities to give the mat up at five in the morning, the only instance I knew what the time actually was, with nary a clock on the wall and the dimmed lights never telling. A seasoned inmate, on his way to a stretch in a penitentiary in Texas, passed me a card after telling me I looked like someone he could trust, trying to get me to call a number for him when I got out as a part of some hare-brained scheme to spring him. I took it, nodded politely, but quickly discarded it. I vowed to myself I'd never go back.

When they finally let us out, I made my way back way to Springdale to tell my father about his money. He'd discovered the guy I was over there to meet in the first place was a cop, but couldn't reach me by phone to warn me. He didn't say anything else about the arrest, or his money, or my court date in another month or so. The lawyer we met with was pretty sure he could get me off because I hadn't touched the evidence when the cops busted in.

The arrest caused my fantasies about my lifestyle to be invaded by the harsh reality of a weekend in jail, including the hour I waited for Marty in the Fayetteville holding tank. I knew that I never wanted to go back and I began to think about making significant changes in my life.

Not long after my arrest and making the point even more obvious, the headlines read; *PAIR ARRESTED AT THE NORTHWEST MALL IN LARGEST METHAMPHETAMINE BUST IN THE HISTORY OF THE STATE.*

Riley and Tripp were set up, and local law enforcement orchestrated a dramatic bust. The police wanted a piece of Riley for a variety of reasons, including peddling mass quantities of meth. They were sentenced to 20 years in prison, but served fewer than 10 because of overcrowding. After his release, Tripp wised up and left the area, but Riley was just getting started. He spent more time in prison, going down again, his last arrest being described by someone who knew the story: "He was robbing a store when the cops sent a police dog after him. Once the dog attached itself to his leg, Riley snapped the animal's jaw and choked it to death with his bare hands. The cops charged in, shot him in the stomach, and loaded him in their cruiser. They drove around for about an hour while he bled, hoping he would die. When he didn't, they finally called for medical care. He'll be in prison for the rest of his life."

CHAPTER 16

After Marty found a buyer for his first home, it provided an opportunity for him to start two more, this time using more subcontractors. We still did a large portion of the work ourselves but could bring in other people to help us expedite the process. A man named Dennis Evans was hired to help frame one of the houses. Dennis was the fastest framer I'd ever seen and was able to pop in sixteen penny nails with one swing of the hammer. His knowledge of construction was impressive and he had a lot of experience, but he also had a drinking problem, as did most of the construction workers that I met. When Dennis drank, though, everyone was on notice. Blackouts, hit-and-run car wrecks, outrunning the police, and even sneaking into Marty's house late one night to avoid arrest, all served as evidence of Dennis and the bottle. He wore black because he liked Johnny Cash and played country music from his truck radio while he worked, which helped me to appreciate the art form. I remembered listening to the corny lyrics about truck drivers and rocky marriages with my dad at Wayne's Tavern, and began to enjoy the simplicity of the songs the more I was exposed to them by Dennis' radio.

Around this time, my father and I had another conversation about his plans. He intended to move my younger sisters to California as soon as they both finished high school and after getting Marty and Ruth set up in the building business. My youngest sister, Iris, was a junior, so less than a year remained for this to happen. "I don't want any of you to live in this hell-hole any longer than you have to," he declared. "You'll never get a fair shot here as long as you live." His plans were also meant to bring an end to Hazel's crush on Brandon.

Dad was set on reclaiming his bank account and trying to accumulate as much money as he could to get us all comfortably out of Springdale. He still dreamed of resettling us in southern California where many of my relatives lived, and where we could all start over. He rationalized that he was saving us from the town that had evicted him, and recovering his lifestyle by any means possible, which he thought was a small price to pay. I depended on him again, but he hadn't recovered from the tar and feathering he received from the city of Springdale, but instead spiraled further into a deeper hole. I was mired in my own impetuous and drug-riddled fog and unable to contribute anything to the contrary.

Later that week, after stating his intention of moving us all to California, I watched him mixing several five gallon buckets of cow feed with poison pellets. He wore rubber gloves and a troubled look as he integrated the lethal substance with the feed. The buckets were destined for a late night visit to Knox's farm full of cows in nearby Elkins, and after he informed me that he didn't need me for the deed, I was relieved. I perked up when he said he would be making another trip out to California soon and wanted me to come with him. I entertained the idea of a trip to the west coast and the possibility of one day taking up full time residency there.

"When do we leave?" I asked.

"In a couple of weeks," he said. "I've got a few things to do here first. We're going to stop off in Vegas."

I'd learned my way around my father's bizarre behavior from the past couple of years of being close to him. I'd learned what to say, what not to say, and how to go along for the ride. A solo trip with him wasn't like it was when I was a younger. Regardless, I loved going to the west coast.

I asked, "Can I gamble?" I'd played some poker with friends, but only a quarter limit and never winning or losing more than $10, tops.

"There's an age limit, but sometimes you can go down into the pits if you look old enough and nobody will bother you," he explained. "You'll lose your shirt if you try, but I won't stop you."

When the time came, we drove straight through to Las Vegas without stopping except for gas. We got a room for the night at the Circus Circus casino, and after he excused himself to the room, I wandered around the huge casino and took in the atmosphere. Wearing my best bell bottom slacks, turquoise inlaid belt buckle, and pearl snap shirt, I mustered up the courage to step into the pit and take a seat. It was still too early for the big crowds, so the place was sparse except for a few blackjack dealers standing around with their palms flat on their tables. The courteous dealer explained the game in the most basic terms. I had $10, so I laid the minimum of two dollars on the circle, and immediately started winning. Soon, I was making larger bets and hitting unlikely cards against the odds, assuming the money I was ahead was money I didn't have to begin with. Before long, I was making $100 bets, doubling down, and getting the right cards. It was true beginner's luck, and it had me up $1,000 after an hour.

When I returned to the room to show Dad, he grabbed all but $100 and told me it was for my own good. I proved him right when I returned to the table and gave back the hundred within a few minutes. Just before we left town, he gave me all the money back and I bought a nice piece of jewelry for a girl I was seeing in Fayetteville. She was my first real girlfriend and would eventually educate me on how little I understood about relationships.

The next day, we continued on to Aunt Florence's house in Duarte for a brief stopover, then onto Whittier, where my sisters would move the following year. Aunt Ellen recommended an apartment complex in a safe part of town, and she promised jobs for them after they arrived.

I saw a flyer for an upcoming performance from a music group that I liked, and the $800 dollars I had left started burning a hole in my pocket. John Mayall and the Bluesbreakers were playing that night in the historic Whisky-A-Go-Go in Hollywood and Dad wanted to come.

I could get used to living in L.A.

The drive into Hollywood that afternoon was dazzling. The sun was out and palm trees lined the Sunset Strip on the way to the Go-Go. I'd heard of the Whisky, and was familiar with the many headliners that had taken the stage at this modest but funky music auditorium, and I imagined what the inside must look like. We walked into a bar next door and ordered the local favorite, a Grasshopper, without a carding from the bartender. A young and shapely brunette sat on a stool next to us and started talking.

"Where are you guys from?" she asked, after hearing my accent.

"Arkansas. We're here to see Mayall play the Whisky tonight," I explained, cognizant of my drawl.

"That sounds fun. I like Mayall, too," she said with a bright smile and a wink, "and I like your accent."

My father knew the drill but I was slow to grasp it, unaware of a working girl's tactics. I offered to buy her a Grasshopper, which soon turned into a swarm of locusts. I was heading into uncharted territory, and Dad just smiled and went along with it. She offered to take us on a tour of the star's homes and we killed an hour doing that before the show. So, Hanna from Los Angeles, drove us by the mansions of Sonny and Cher and Tony Curtis in nearby Bel-Air and Beverly Hills.

We returned to the same bar for a few more drinks, and I started to get drunk and loose-tongued. I pulled out the money left from Vegas and made sure Hanna saw it, then bought her a ticket. Once we got inside, we found a dingy row of tables with cheap metal chairs close to the stage. I ordered a bottle of wine and spared no expense. I became more belligerent while my father sat by and enjoyed the show *I* was putting on more than the one we bought tickets for. He was anticipating me to work a deal with young Hanna, who was clearly waiting for the offer. When the band started, the Bluesbreakers made us all forget about any deals while the blind keyboard player worked his magic on the keys. John offered his version of blues music, and I kept drinking.

"You're acting like a fool," my father finally told me.

It didn't deter me and I kept getting louder and more obnoxious. He handed me the keys to the mid-size Toyota we'd driven to the show.

I noticed his absence after a few minutes and so did Hanna, who put the squeeze on me for $200. As John Mayall played his last song, I was shit-faced drunk and told her, "I don't pay for sex. I don't need to." I'd already spent half of that for her to sit with us.

Without delay, Hanna turned and walked out with another man. I was alone in Hollywood, well over the limit, and not sure how to get back to Whittier. It was 2:00 a.m. when I started driving east on Sunset Strip looking for an interchange that I might recognize. I needed to sober up quickly after I passed a police car that already pulled over some late night partygoers. After finally getting squared away on directions, I thought about what just happened.

Hanna was attractive, but I didn't care if I had sex with her or not. I wasn't sure if it was because I was seeing Jennifer back in Fayetteville, a girl I liked well enough to buy a bracelet for. I wondered why I paid for all those drinks? What about the ticket? As I drove around and sobered up, I pondered my ability to be loose with money as long as it wasn't specifically for sex. I figured it was a hang-up that I could live with. I assumed that I had some moral standards but couldn't say exactly what they were or where I got them. One thing was for sure; I'd never handled my liquor very well. I finally let it go. I continued driving and remembered that it had been a great show. At least I was going to have to gloat a little when I returned to Arkansas because Earl and Brandon were both big fans of Mayall.

After countless freeway interchanges and several wrong turns, I pulled into Ellen's driveway in Whittier and found Dad sitting in the kitchen waiting on me. He'd hailed a cab, and apologized for leaving me. He said he just couldn't stand watching me make such a fool of myself and had to get out of there before he lost it and delivered another ass-whipping.

"I'll never lay a hand on you again," he added.

"Making a fool of myself? Welcome to the club," I snorted. The opportunity to talk back to him was rare and possibly dangerous, but it had presented itself here and I was still drunk enough to take advantage of it. He hid a small grin and asked why I didn't take up with Hanna, softening the tension. It was the first time I can remember ever talking back to him.

"I don't know. I don't want to talk about it." I said, and again wondered what must be wrong with me. I was living Lemus' life, and not my own.

After visiting some of his friends and running a few remaining errands over the course of the next few days, we spent the night at Aunt Florence's in Duarte, and prepared to return to Arkansas. I thought of Jennifer and wondered if she would like the bracelet that I got for her.

CHAPTER 17

After returning from California, the first thing I did was to hurry over to Jennifer's place to show off the Vegas bracelet I'd picked up for her. The look on her face said we were finished. She thanked me for the bracelet then told me that I was getting too serious. There was a guy sitting in her living room who agreed with her. I took it hard, even though I knew this girl was promiscuous and always eyed my friends. I left the bracelet anyway.

I soon started seeing Lydia, the sister of one of the guys I'd met at the Gray House. Lydia was cute with an adorable smile and common sense, a real catch in many people's eyes. I'd grown taller and more solid because of all the heavy construction labor I'd done and had shoulder-length black hair that made me my womanizing father's son, if a bit more discriminate.

She loved the Porsche, but even after I wrapped it around a tree while showing off, she remained steadfast in her interest in me. No one was hurt in the wreck, but the car was never the same, and I ended up with a modest-looking yellow Vega hatchback instead. It came saddled with the same stipulations from my father.

Bad influences surrounded me except for Lydia, and I wasn't above infidelity, as the later part of my formative years were mired in acceptable examples of adultery. Jennifer was my first real attempt at a relationship with a woman since

Jackie, and after her rejection, I wasn't ready to care about another woman. Jennifer was a poor choice. When Lydia asked me to commit, I couldn't do it and was honest about it. Her parents even let me know they hoped I would become a part of the family. They had no idea what they were asking for. I bolted.

After waiting for several months, I finally got news from Earl that I'd been completely exonerated for the Tulsa arrest, but he received a year's probation. Because Earl grabbed the drugs, they pinned it on him. I felt bad and promised I'd buy him a beer, but he took it in stride and said he was glad there wasn't any jail time. He added that he'd been hanging out with a new friend in Tulsa and for Brandon and me to party with them whenever we got the chance. His good mood would be short lived. A couple of weeks later, disaster struck when his friend tried to kill him by shooting him in the chest.

Brandon called me with the news and I went to his house immediately. There, along with his sisters and mother, I learned that Earl had been shot the night before and was paralyzed from the chest down. Earl was considered a member of the family, so we readied ourselves for a quick trip to see him. He would live, but there was nothing that could be done about the use of his legs because the bullet had severed his spinal cord. At the hospital, we found him resting but obviously distressed. He was lucky to be alive, though he wasn't feeling it. On top of the paralysis, he was also recovering from a collapsed lung.

He'd met his friend and his wife in Tulsa earlier in the year, and not surprisingly, substances were a big part of their relationship. The man came home one day to find Earl with his wife. The husband jumped up on Earl's car, and kicked in his windshield. Earl fled on foot but was convinced to return by the wife, who wanted him to explain to the man that nothing adulterous had happened. The husband did not believe him, and shot Earl in the chest with a handgun.

The shooter was charged with attempted murder, and sat in the same jail cell Earl and I had shared just months before. We were all determined to help Earl overcome this and pledged to help him however we could, so after the hospital had released him, he returned to Springdale for rehabilitation. After he was fitted with a wheelchair, we were able to lift and move him around. He tried to make the best of his new situation, but his drug use increased.

Wendy, an old girlfriend of Earl's, Brandon, and I, became heavily involved as caretakers. Brandon and I were spending a lot of time together. His sister, Denise, and I began to take an interest in one another, which Brandon and his mother, Gloria, would come to hate. I did my best to play it straight around Lorene, Denise's four-year-old daughter and her ex, Fred. Their marriage was over, but Fred still figured into Lorene's life, and I tried to avoid her as much as I could.

The work continued with Marty as new projects began next to the newly built and sold properties. Dad showed up on the job with a couple of guys and said he would be out of town for the next few days. He introduced me to Roy and Lester, young men who were friendly but looked the part of dealers, and told me to do whatever Dennis instructed. I'd learned a lot from Dennis since he spent time teaching me what we were doing and why—something my father rarely bothered with. He was more interested in my work ethic.

As I listened to Dennis' radio a few days later, a breaking story came on;

"A small plane has crashed near the Mexican border shortly after takeoff this morning. There were no survivors, and

$30,000 was recovered in the wreckage. The plane was owned by Lemus Daniel of Springdale, Arkansas. We will provide more details as they become available."

Oh shit.

I quickly assumed the worst: That my father was on board and was now dead. My gut never seemed prepared for the rush of adrenaline that came with my association to him. I met with Marty and Ruth, who'd called my sisters, and we tried to make sense of the news. We waited for information to trickle in. I hadn't even known he'd owned a plane. Maybe he wasn't on it.

The three charred bodies were unidentifiable, and the FBI was called in to investigate the money found at the crash site. The older model, twin-engine plane evidently left the runway and quickly began sputtering. The pilot tried to return to the landing strip in nearby Pecos, Texas, a hundred miles or so from the border. Instead, they'd fallen from the sky and the fuel tank ignited on impact. The money survived because of a heavy duty container.

Few questioned the flight's purpose, but our dad was who mattered to us. The thought of losing him revealed the love I still had for him. We held onto a thread of hope that he hadn't been on board, but we all believed he had. I drove away from the job and started to think of what my life would be like without him. We all had to keep working on the houses because that was what he would have wanted. There was nothing else we could do but wait.

For two days, I was robotic and worked in a morbid funk, waiting on news from the radio because we had no contact with authorities. I continued to contemplate my future and realized I shouldn't have been surprised. He'd abandoned me, hit me, and emotionally abused me. His life was a reckless one. Accepting his death hurt me, and I was surprised by how much it hurt.

On the third day, I'd all but given up and just needed the authorities to make it official. I turned the corner on my way to work and saw someone who looked like my father in a car driving the other way. I couldn't believe my eyes and stopped in the middle of the intersection. The man who looked like my dad spotted me and grinned. He pulled over on the curb and stepped out. He looked like he hadn't slept and was haggard-looking.

"It's you!"

"We'll talk later," he said, meaning that we wouldn't talk about it at all.

"But what happened?"

"I said we'll talk later."

His fatherly instinct had to be in there somewhere. I didn't care, I was happy to see him. Seeing a parent come back from the dead is an education in and of itself.

Finally, the names were released: The pilot, Lester, and Roy. The crash left grieving family members in its wake. I could tell that my father was remorseful, but he refused to talk and I knew better than to keep asking. The plane crash served to strengthen my loyalties to my dad in spite of all the chaos that surrounded him. I still had him, and at the moment, that was all that I cared about.

I couldn't go a day without hearing about the drug kingpin, Lemus Daniel, and his $30,000 at the Mexican border from the radio, newspapers, and people on the street. It was 1967 all over again, 1973 all over again, and I didn't always keep my temper. The FBI held the money and came into town to interrogate him, where he evaded their questions and demanded the money be returned. They refused, held onto it, and prompted a grand jury to summon people to court to answer questions about drug dealing in our part of Arkansas. I learned from people that had been summoned that the questions involved me, too, along with my father. The price of poker went up and I knew that I would ultimately be held responsible for my actions.

Laying low became a priority after the plane crash and ongoing grand jury investigation, and it put an end to my steady flow of pocket money. Dad and Phyllis leased a place on Bull Shoals Lake while Marty, Dennis, and I continued to build houses. He brought the heat down on all of us. The screws were tightening and there was more to come.

CHAPTER 18

I started zeroing in on Brandon's sister, Denise, and finding ways to spend more time with her. She was nearly four years older than me and her young daughter, Lorene, had blond curls and an ornery smile. Denise was a beauty, full of curves and gorgeous brown hair. She'd married young under pressure from her domineering mother, and after five years, eventually wandered from her marriage to a school teacher. She had some attitude now, liked to be in control, and it looked good on her. When she wasn't working as a secretary, she could be found riding horses with friends. All that aside, the first time Brandon and I lit up with her, I noticed a twinkle in her eye that told me I had a chance.

Several days after Dad found a place to hide out in southern Missouri, he called me and asked me to visit, warning, "Make sure no one is following you." I drove up in a rental car, and met Phyllis and Bobby. Phyllis was a constant now, and I thought maybe they'd gotten married without telling me. There was after all, a cheap ring on her finger. I didn't ask or care.

The small place sat on a hillside with access to the lake. Dad obtained a small trolling boat and took Phyllis out on occasion, along with a black lab puppy that she'd convinced him to take in. He'd been adamant about not letting me have a pet when I was growing up, but Phyllis was trying to soften him up a bit and that was okay with me. She wanted it, he needed her, and they named the puppy, Lucy.

The secluded house had a small basement, and after he gave me a quick tour of the upstairs, we ended up there, where he showed me a pill press the size of a large washing machine. Bobby stood nearby while my father described the machine's ability to pump out thousands of pills a minute. Dad wasn't playing it cool at all. I realized, in spite of the FBI investigation, he was not giving up.

I was ready to leave after I saw the pill press and contemplated the implications in terms of a prison sentence, but Dad had an errand for me: Drive Bobby to Little Rock and return to Missouri as soon as I was done. I realized that this was why I'd been summoned in the first place— so Dad wouldn't have to do it. I reluctantly gave in and took the assignment.

Resentful though I was, I liked the thought of a drive with Bobby because I had always admired him and spent many days at work listening to his stories and sharing beers at parties. He was several years older than me and had served in Vietnam, and it changed him as it had so many others.

"I saw a lot of crazy shit, Larry," he said, as we curved through a small town on our way to Little Rock. "You should be glad you didn't have to go."

"I know. I'm lucky they stopped the draft in time. But I was 1H, so it wasn't for sure I would have gone," I surmised. "Dad said we'd move to Canada if they ever drafted me."

Bobby showed his great smile and patted me on the shoulder, and said, "Your dad may be a wild man, but he never stopped caring about you guys." I nodded, but my head spun as I remembered the ways he'd shown it.

"I was a pretty normal kid growing up," Bobby went on. "I played football and went to prom, then got sent to 'Nam. It messed me up some."

After a few more odd detours, I opened the window to reveal the barren pastures we drove alongside on dirt roads. "We're hiding out on back roads, Bobby. I'm getting afraid of the law. I mean, look at us. This is crazy," I confessed.

"Nobody's behind us," he said and offered nothing more.

As we drove, he talked about a girl named Peggy who'd done him wrong. She'd betrayed him, he said, and he was still distressed over it. He added that I needed to be on the lookout for such long-legged devils. I agreed and told him I'd experienced something similar and was learning to prefer older women. "That's the best kind," Bobby laughed. "They can teach you a thing or two."

I followed my father's orders and dropped Bobby off at an apartment in Little Rock. I remembered a small party at Brandon's that night, so against my father's wishes I drove to Springdale before heading back to Missouri the next day. I never saw Bobby again.

I partied with the guys at the pad and woke up around mid-morning before making quick time toward the hideout in Missouri. A steady drizzle turned into a downpour as I approached the small town of Hollister, just outside the quaint resort community of Branson. Assuming that my father was probably pacing the floor by now because I ignored his order to come right back, I pressed on the gas and approached a tight corner going too fast and lost control of the rental car. The sporty yellow Datsun slid sideways off the road and high centered a culvert in a ditch.

Uninjured, I extricated myself in the pouring rain and looked under the chassis to see if it was still drivable. Liquid poured from gashes in the oil and transmission pans. Not only was I soaked, but my hands were also now covered in motor oil. I was stranded miles away from my final destination. I approached a small house close by and knocked on the door. I needed to call my father, and the mild-mannered couple that lived there let me in. I called but there was no answer. As I tried again, I traced the couple's eyes to my feet and only then noticed the oily and muddy stains I'd left on their carpet. The look of regret on their faces convinced me to wrap it up after another call to my father went unanswered.

Before I left the house, I called the rental agency for the car to be towed and then stood on the side of the road, wet from head to toe. I stuck my thumb out and eventually a farmer driving a beat-up pick-up truck let me in the back. I sat silently as rain dripped from my nose and braced for the backlash for not coming right back and wrecking the rental car. Hours after I should have arrived, I finally found myself walking up the short dirt road to the house.

Dad stood on the front porch, his eyes as wide as saucers. He waved his arms frantically, howling something that sounded like, "Where were you? We've got to get out of here!" The rain subsided and only then did I notice the whirring sound of helicopters. I looked up to see two of them breaking through the clouds and circle above the house. The aircraft banked to the right to get a clear view, then swung wide out of sight for a moment.

I tried to explain my tardiness but he was having none of it. "Get in the fucking van, NOW!"

We drove down the dirt road and back out onto the two lane highway. His eyes were on fire, and his hypersensitive ears were wide open, listening for the helicopters.

The further we got from the hideout, the more apparent it became that the authorities weren't following us. I thought that his paranoia might have gotten the best of him. I'd seen it before and could never be sure what to believe. There were helicopters, alright, but no proof that they'd been circling because of the pill press. Or the police might, even then, have been ransacking the basement. You never knew for sure. My life was like walking through a minefield.

CHAPTER 19

The spring of 1975, Dad and I prepared to go to California again to keep the ball rolling for my sisters' relocation. I wasn't so sure about actually moving to California yet—I still had friends and Denise in Arkansas—but younger sisters were preparing for the move to Whittier. They were saying goodbye to their friends and our mother, with whom they had a good relationship. Secretarial jobs, arranged by our aunt Ellen in Whittier, were waiting for them as soon as Iris' high school finished, enabling their exodus from Springdale's judging eyes.

When I talked to them, they both described how excited they were. Dad convinced them that Springdale didn't offer any of the opportunities that California did. I thought we might be able to restore a relationship away from the bad memories because I traveled back and forth to California often and would see them whenever I was there. My sisters were unaware of most of their father's suspect behavior, even though they read the papers and heard the radio accuse him. They had no idea how much trouble he was really in.

My mother was melancholy about the move, but encouraged the girls. Mom had begun dating again and started attending the biggest church in town. She was reestablishing her life. When I finally went to see her before I left for the west coast with my dad, she seemed happy and asked me to go to church with her. I balked at the idea, but said I might when I got back from California. I knew it wasn't true. I shared a few things with her about my relationship with Denise.

"Bring her over sometime."

"I will, Mom."

"We can all go to church together," she persisted.

I informed Marty—who was busy with the construction company—that I would be traveling to California again with my dad, who was now completely out of the home building picture after the plane crash. I let him know I'd be ready to get back to work when I returned, but he suspected that we would all eventually relocate and was prepared for it. I told Denise I would be gone for a week or more, so she let her hair down and made sure I didn't have the energy to even look at another woman.

She was aware of the life I was living and heard unflattering stories from her brother. Even though Brandon and I associated with one another, he didn't like me sleeping with his oldest sister. Denise insisted that deep down she saw something else in me, and we decided that we would move in together when I returned from California. One of the small block houses near the main house that her mother, Gloria, and her stepdad, Carlton, lived in was now vacant and would cost next to nothing to rent.

I realized that four-year-old Lorene would be a challenge for me, but was sure I'd met my match in Denise and didn't want to let her go. If I'd been honest, I would have admitted that I lacked the courage to truly commit, but money was tight and I needed a place to stay. Perhaps she would help me escape the minefield before I was permanently maimed.

Dad and I set out on an early weekday morning, intent on driving straight through to Los Angeles, where we would see relatives, secure arrangements for my sisters, and visit some of Dad's friends. Before we left, we made a cautious return to the hideout to check on the pill press. There it sat, ready to be switched on.

Just outside of Oklahoma City, we picked up a couple of German hitchhikers. The pair started in Virginia, and they looked like it. I could see my father eyeing the girl's hairy armpits and unshaved legs after he pulled over, and he wasted no time in making arrangements with the 'boyfriend' Tomas, for Hilga to retreat with him to the back of the van. I could hear him banging away as I drove. Tomas asked if I wanted a turn, but I declined and kept driving. After my father had finished, we all settled in for the long drive. The boyfriend took a turn before we hit Arizona, and once again, I declined Hilga's offer. I couldn't wait to unload them.

As usual, our first stop was to Aunt Florence's house in Duarte, and naturally she fed us. She would have taken it personally if I wasn't ill from overeating by the time we left the driveway, so I played my part and gorged myself for her.

After surviving the smorgasbord, we set off to pay deposits to the complex where Hazel and Iris would live. My father would return for the move, but I was undecided about whether to make the return trip. I didn't have a job waiting for me, and even if I had, I was more than aware that it might not need to involve my father. I was leaning toward my relationship with Denise, hoping that she might help dictate my future decisions.

After meeting our obligations, we found ourselves with some time on our hands, so we headed west towards the beautiful coastline of Malibu on Pacific Coast Highway. Going north, we turned right off of PCH and drove up a steep, narrow road, and ended up at a funky looking studio that sat in an influential neighborhood overlooking the Pacific Ocean. Inside, I found a nice pool table with which I amused myself while Dad went to the back to let the occupants know that we'd arrived.

Rick Danko, the bassist for the popular group, The Band, and someone I recognized from the early days on Emerald Avenue, came out and started shooting pool with me. The sign hanging above the bar read "Shangri-La," where the group stayed and recorded. After the songs, *The Weight*, and *The Night They Drove Ole' Dixie Down* hit the mainstream, The Band became international stars.

Soon, Levon Helm, another member of the group, and my father joined Rick and me around the pool table and we broke out the beers. Other guests mingled with us. I was told we would take a drive into Hollywood and that I was supposed to go with Rick in his new Mercedes along with a manager. A cheerful dude with scraggly whiskers walked up and said, "Hi, I'm Gary, and I'm riding with you guys."

My father remained close to these guys over the years. I remembered Rick and Levon from my childhood, catching passes from Levon in my backyard during barbeques at our house. He was a big deal now. So was Rick, a kid at heart that went out his way to make me feel welcome.

Dad and Levon took a different vehicle, and I crawled into the front seat of Rick's car while Gary got in back. Soon, Rick had it up to ninety along the coastline highway that led to Brentwood. Gary brought out a small box from the back seat, and we all passed around a Panama Red joint. We were on our way to a rendezvous. That was all that I knew.

Driving through Bel-Air and Beverly Hills brought our speed down while we listened to artists on the radio and finished the joint. Rick gestured with a smile when Gordon Lightfoot, a good friend and fellow Canadian, came on. I noticed every woman on the sidewalk or in passing cars, turn their heads to look twice at Rick, Gary, and me, in the Mercedes. It was rock star status and it felt surreal.

We pulled up to Neil Diamond's condo in Hollywood, and Richard Manuel came out for us to take the rest of the way in. Richard, a singer and keyboard player in the group, was quiet but cordial during the short drive to the YMCA, our final destination. We parked across the street, and right on cue, Dad and Levon pulled up. We all said "hello," and a short, curly headed man with eyes like diamonds and a big smile approached with a hot dog in his hand from a nearby sidewalk stand. He seemed cocky and wore a perfect blue blazer.

"Larry, this is Bob Dylan," Levon said. I moved to shake Bob's hand.

"Nice to meet you," Dylan said as only he could say it. I was a little confused. Panama Red was swimming in my head and they're telling me that this was Bob Dylan. For a split second, I didn't believe them even though he looked just like him.

Bob laughed and looked at the others, personally aware of Panama Red's potency. We all went inside for the album cover shoot, the reason we were all there, for The Basement Tapes, a compilation from the early days at Big Pink. It sunk in as I walked side by side with Dylan the legend, knowing I would be spending the next couple of hours with him. My father really did it this time.

Once inside, we were met by the director of the photo shoot, and The Band and Dylan were instructed to go to a dressing room to select their outfits. The other two members of The Band, Robbie Robertson and Garth Hudson, came in later, as did several extras who were to be included in the picture. Dad and I were told to hang out by the railing in the back part of the basement where the pictures were taken.

Dylan's wife showed up and leaned against the rail next to us. The photographer suddenly called everyone to attention, disrupting the guys who were fooling around with the prop instruments. We stood directly behind while he called instructions, hoping for enough spontaneity to produce a memorable, circus-themed shot for the cover that included extras posing as clowns, sword swallowers, and strong men. The musicians had donned a variety of identities: Richard's commander outfit, and Levon, with a vest and jacket, as a southern gentleman. Dylan wore a south-of-the-border style red jacket and hat, and held an odd-shaped mandolin that he positioned like a violin under his chin. A pretty ballerina posing in the background didn't go unnoticed by Levon; and he approached her after the shoot and offered her a toke in the lobby. After we said goodbye, Dad and I headed back to Whittier for the night. I was looking forward to my return to Springdale and Denise now that I had a story worth telling. My father had made California look even better. Maybe she would want to come out.

We made a few more stops the next day and visited more of my father's friends. One friend, a guy known as "Fat Ted," owned several strip clubs in Orange County and was in deep with some shady people. He weighed more than 400 pounds and sang well enough to have appeared on the *Gong Show* a year earlier. He was nice to me, but I didn't know everything there was to know about him. Ronnie was another, a former Razorback football player in the late 1950s, who now lived in southern California.

I was torn between staying in California and distancing myself from my father to see where my relationship with Denise would take me. Escaping my old life wasn't going to be that easy after the experience I just had. My only prayer was that we didn't see any more hitchhikers on the way back.

CHAPTER 20

A fter Denise and I moved into the small block house just behind her mother, Gloria, and step-father, Carlton, I went back to work with Marty and Dennis. We furnished the house with all of Denise's things because I didn't have anything of value anyway. To celebrate my twentieth birthday, we went to Dallas and saw the Rolling Stones play in the Cotton Bowl, while my father returned to California to move my sisters out. I worried that Denise was too good for me, so I stayed on my toes and did my best to keep her interested, taking her to see Mick Jagger take the stage on top of an elephant before playing to more than 60,000 people. Soon after our trip to Dallas, Denise and I gathered in the living room of our tiny block house for a small party. Included were her sisters, Jenny and Crystal, along with Wendy and Earl, who were in from Tulsa, and Gloria, who brought her own whiskey. Brandon was out of town. As we sipped our way to tipsiness, I described the Stones' performance and bragged about the Mayall show in Hollywood. Gloria hated the fact Denise could take up with a guy like me.

"You're not as smart as you think you are," Gloria announced suddenly, interrupting my monologue. "As a matter of fact, I think you're a smartass, know-it-all."

I paused and glanced over at her. The others stopped and after seeing that Gloria was a little drunk, they looked at me to see if I would respond. I looked at her waiting for a punch line or some softening of the blow, but it didn't come.

"Maybe so," I retorted, "but I'm probably smarter than you." It wasn't much, but to this day, I wish I hadn't done that.

The room was filled with awkward laughter. Gloria got up quietly and exited the house. She walked up the fifty yards to her own place and went directly into her bedroom, where she removed a loaded .22 rifle from her closet, aimed it at her chest, and pulled the trigger.

Within a few minutes, Lorene pounded down to the tiny house where we were still drinking beers, shouting, "Grandma shot herself! Come quick, Grandpa says Grandma shot herself!"

In a flash we were all out the door and up the hill, with me in the lead and Denise right behind. We found Carlton sitting on a chair in the living room with his hands over his face, howling, "Why. . . Why? What have you done?" I turned the corner into the bedroom and found Gloria supine on the bed, blood pouring out of the bullet hole in her chest. Her blood-filled lungs gurgled their last as I looked on in shock. There was nothing anyone could do. We watched her die, silent.

"What have you done?" Carlton kept crying.

The decision was made to call the Sheriff's department, and eventually the coroner came. It was obvious that she was gone. As the authorities took control of the scene and questioned Carlton and the sisters, I left, retreating back to my now much more complicated life. Gloria was sick, Denise said, and wanted to forego a lengthy illness without being more specific. If she'd wanted to make a statement before doing what she intended to do anyway, she had succeeded.

After some time, Denise began to move past her mother's final gesture. Denise's brother, Brandon, remained bitter towards me and I tried to be respectful and stay away from the house as much as I could, but shortly after, Denise and I found our way back to each other, and our lives slowly resumed, more or less, as before.

We went to the lake, just the two of us, and found an isolated area to skinny dip. We swam out briefly then drew near each other. A storm approached as we made love in the shallow water, lightning charging the air around us. We laughed as we ran to the car through the rain. I hoped for the chance at a normal life. I didn't know that the final straw was coming.

Soon after, Dad called me and told me to meet him at Marty's office. There was something he needed to tell me. I told him I would be at Marty's most recent project and for him to drop by there instead, and he complied. As soon as I saw him, I knew something was wrong. I was getting tired of bad news.

"Bobby's dead," he said.

My head dropped. Shoulders slumped, the air left me.

"The cops in Little Rock killed him," he groaned, "rotten bastards."

Bobby had been inside a drugstore in the middle of the night and the police had been tipped off, surprising him while robbing it. After being told to freeze, Bobby ran for it and was shot in the head. He lingered in the hospital for a day before dying. The funeral was scheduled for the following week and we would both attend.

I couldn't breathe. I was devastated, and the chaos smothered me. I imagined Bobby rummaging with a flashlight looking for anything for the pill press. I felt betrayed that he died this way. He was like a big brother to me.

Over the years, basic locks and a lack of security systems had emboldened many a drug addict, but the pharmacies and police were getting tired of it and started cracking down. Bobby had nowhere to run.

The authorities were still focused on my father, and by association, me. After another acquaintance reminded me that they'd recently answered questions from the grand jury, I started plotting my escape. Earl was crippled, and Gloria and Bobby were dead. I had been to jail and didn't want to go back. I feared I was next. I had to get out.

My father and I joined the large gathering of mourners at Bobby's funeral. I cried my eyes out while my father scanned the crowd for undercover cops.

I was finished in Arkansas and left for California immediately after the funeral. Any hope of escaping my father seemed fleeting. His sister, Ellen, was building a new house on an upscale hillside in Whittier and said he could be the contractor in charge if he wanted. Now, he wanted. He promised me a job for a few months, and I figured that made me lucky. I could figure things out after I got there.

When I told Denise I had to leave town, she said she wanted to go, too. She revealed that her real dad lived about an hour from Whittier, and he told her she could live with him while she got resettled. It was decided that the five of us—Denise, Lorene, and I, along with my father and Phyllis—would depart within days for a permanent move away from the impending catastrophe of remaining in Arkansas. I traded my Vega for an older Ford pickup and fixed make-shift side boards on the truck bed so Denise and I could load as much stuff in the back as possible for the trip. I hoped the change in scenery would promote an end to the chaotic lifestyle I was trapped in. I was fearful, but new beginnings awaited me.

PART III

RUDE AWAKENING

CHAPTER 21

The white-line fevered drive to California was old hat for me, but for Denise and Lorene, an adventure was underway. We anticipated big changes as we covered the miles, soaking up the desert landscape of New Mexico and the fresh air of northern Arizona. Somewhere along the way, Denise contemplated the unknown of living with her real dad, with whom she'd had little contact over the last few years while Lorene conveyed the joy any five-year-old would from a promise to see Mickey Mouse. Denise calmed her by singing nursery rhymes and stroking her hair during the long drive, and I remembered how lucky I was to have escaped Arkansas before the law caught up with me.

We drove convoy style with Dad and Phyllis in the lead. The plywood sides on my truck bed held in some chairs, a table, and a few of Lorene's toys, and reminded me of pictures I'd seen of dust bowl refugees from the 1930s headed to California. A cheap blue tarp, secured with string and tape, covered our belongings and flapped furiously. We towed Denise's car behind the truck, and Dad's van pulled a small U-Haul trailer. We started out as refugees and were becoming migrants.

Even though Denise and I lived together in Springdale, there was no guarantee we would resume our co-habitation in California. There was a lot to sort out, and we couldn't afford a place anyway. After several years of knowing her father only through her mother's grim recollections, Denise planned to reconnect with him. Their phone conversation was promising, and he was eager to see Lorene. Denise had marketable skills and would be able to plug in quickly.

Southern California opened up like the Promised Land as we topped the San Bernardino mountains and began the descent into the arid, smoggy Los Angeles basin. Lorene's eyes were afire as I fed her embellished stories about amusement parks and beaches. When we reached the exit to Denise's dad's house, we separated from my father and headed into Fountain Valley, all flowers and neat rows of manicured homes with vibrant exteriors and clay tile roofs. As we pulled up, Douglas, Denise's father, met us in the driveway. My old truck with plywood sides failed to impress him and his body language told me he didn't care much for me. He invited us in for as long as it took to get a better look at me before I unhitched Denise's baby blue Gran Torino and unloaded some of her belongings into his garage.

"Thank you for bringing me my girls," he said tersely, and left me to the emptying out the truck bed.

My aunt Ellen, and her husband, Peter, were influential people in Whittier. They operated a credit union and started building a spacious new home on a hillside that overlooked a scenic valley. This prime piece of property would serve as my workplace for a few months as my father saw fit to employ me. I worked as a laborer, as I had in Springdale. I was given a stipend for living expenses along with a place to stay with Dad and Phyllis. It wasn't much, but I didn't complain.

That first night, I tucked my meager possessions in a corner bedroom at the apartment I now called home and got some sleep. The next evening, Dad and I set out for a nearby pool hall and I was introduced to Shorty White, a local hustler. Shorty was indeed height-challenged, had long stringy hair, and an arrogant strut. Shorty could set people up for big falls in nine-ball and had a jagged scar across his cheek, courtesy of a sore loser.

In the bar, Shorty was greeted by a half dozen patrons who recognized him. I heard the crack of pool balls, and we sat down and ordered beers. A pool table soon cleared for him and competitors began trickling in to kick off a long night of nine-ball at $100 a game. Under the table, my father showed me a wad of cash to bankroll his champion. Shorty started out slow and dropped a game, then another, and his oblivious rival agreed to up the stakes. Each time Shorty lost, Dad pulled out the cash. The crowd got bigger and rowdier when Shorty started running table after table with the game now at $200. When one player lost all he could afford, another took his place.

After a couple of hours, my father was piss-drunk, and handed me several thousand dollars before heading out to the van to sleep. I was on bankroll duty now and far from confident that I could avoid acquiring my own facial scar. All night long, at $250 a game and up to my neck in seedy characters, I gathered wadded up cash when Shorty won and grudgingly handed it back when he didn't. I was careful not to reveal the much larger bankroll in my pocket. Near dawn, Dad ambled back into the bar to claim his share of the money Shorty had won. Back at the apartment in Whittier, I fell asleep the minute I hit the lumpy twin bed.

That week, I visited with my sisters, something I'd rarely done in Arkansas. They'd made friends quickly since arriving in California. I told them about Denise and my job—staying in touch, going okay. We talked about Dad, but left plenty under the rug. None of us needed telling that his demons had followed him from Arkansas. My sisters were all grown up now, and their individual differences were more apparent to me. Hazel was more assertive and opinionated, and Iris, cheerful and welcoming. They grew up doing most everything together, and now that they were in California, they remained attached at the hip.

On the job, Dad was nearly still the man who'd dominated Springdale's building industry in his hey-day, even though he personally struggled to articulate what he wanted from me. He got impatient when I was slow to grasp something, which was often. He expected good work but didn't appreciate it, and "not good enough" seemed the norm. It had always been that way and I knew I didn't want to be a common laborer all my life. I was eager to learn more about framing, but most of my time was spent on a large landscaping project with ten-foot stacks of railroad tie timbers that bordered a towering garden. I carried timbers for days until my fingers bled and managed to rip a couple of finger nails off in the process, but it paid cash and I soldiered through.

In spite of the less-than-ideal father-son dynamic, things were going okay and I was getting acclimated. I'd been in California for a little over a month when things got sticky again. I walked into the apartment and was greeted by Phyllis. She asked, "Have you seen your dad?" I answered that I hadn't seen him. "The cops were here looking for him," she said, while casually peeking inside the fridge.

Momentarily stunned, I insisted, "For what?"

"Weed," she answered, straight-faced and apathetic. "Somebody he was supplying got busted and spilled the beans."

Phyllis couldn't appreciate my rising angst over this revelation. She knew the cost of her relationship with him and had no qualms about her main squeeze's lifestyle. She shrugged her shoulders, adding, "They came by about an hour ago." I had my eyes peeled for an exit.

I asked her, "Is there weed here now?"

"I don't think so."

The hair on the back of my neck spiked. I was a long way from Arkansas and had no desire to return or see anyone else who'd spell trouble. I got in my pick-up and drove straight to Fountain Valley to see Denise.

Douglas was in the garage when I arrived. He seemed a strange man to me, a real nitpicker, or because of his long nose and receding hairline, an evil genius. I found Denise in the living room of Douglas' beautifully decorated home adorned with expensive furniture. The spiral staircase and ornate dining room revealed a man with a few dollars and good taste. I was intimidated, and for what I had in mind, I couldn't afford intimidation. Denise hugged me and motioned for me to sit. I asked her how things were working out with Douglas and her step mom, Donna.

"Work is fun, but I'm not making that much money," she said. "They seem to like me, so it's good." She smiled and asked, "What about you?"

I was worked up but trying to play it cool. I mumbled that I was doing, "just fine," and looked around to see if Douglas was within ear shot, and when I saw he was not, I blurted out, "Please marry me. I need you. I want to be with you." I got down on one knee. "Take a chance on me," I pled.

She looked at me bashfully and gave me the feeling that she was thinking "yes" more than "no." We'd never mentioned marriage in Arkansas but had admitted that we had strong feelings for each other and could see ourselves together in the future. "Maybe," she offered. "Only one thing though, you'll need to ask for my hand."

I hadn't expected the old-fashioned protocol, especially involving a previously absent parent. I hesitated, swallowed hard, and was pretty sure how it would go. I walked into the garage where Douglas stood tinkering. I hemmed and hawed around a minute before I spit it out, announcing, "Sir, I want to marry your daughter."

Once again, he eyed my long hair and beat-up truck in the driveway. He could smell my desperation. "It would be a good idea if you guys waited for a year, and if you still feel like it's the right thing to do, you'll have my blessing," he reasoned.

I didn't have a year. I wasn't sure if I had another week. I believed that Denise and I had something, maybe not enough to commit to marriage, but something. I'd dropped out of high school, lived with my felonious father, and the odds of me being an adequate step-parent weren't good. Regardless, I was sure she wanted to marry me. I nodded to Douglas, and replied, "Yes sir."

Before I left, I told Denise that despite the absence of a blessing, I thought that we should at least live together, as we had in Arkansas. She confessed that she wasn't that fond of the atmosphere in Fountain Valley, and we agreed to find an apartment. I was ecstatic and kissed her hard. I resolved to keep this from my father, and drove back to Whittier and the tiny apartment I shared with him. Even though the police never returned, I was determined that things would be different.

We began thumbing through ads for apartments. She discovered a low-income complex in the tiny suburb of Midway City, between the more well-known towns of Westminster, Costa Mesa, and Huntington Beach in Orange County. It had two bedrooms and a swimming pool for Lorene, so we paid a deposit to start occupancy at the first of the month. Once we pulled that trigger, we went full steam ahead against the wishes of her dad, and most likely mine, and walked across the highway bridge to Westminster Mall to buy two cheap wedding bands. A friend at Denise's work agreed to watch Lorene and we set the date.

In October, 1975, we gathered whatever money we had and set off for Las Vegas. The goal was to have an inexpensive wedding at one of the many chapels I'd seen on my previous trip to Sin City. After expenses for a marriage license and humble accommodations, we figured we had around $200 left for the tables. I reminded Denise of my previous glory at blackjack and pointed out that nothing was preventing a repeat performance. I was ready to show her how a smooth operator does things in the heat of battle. We pulled into the most affordable motel I could find.

"I want a room for two nights," I announced to the desk clerk, adding that I was in town to get married.

"Congratulations! That'll be $60." the clerk said.

He laid several discount coupons for dinner on the counter and we left for the city clerk's office downtown. After paying $25 for a marriage license, and consuming a modest meal, we called it an early night. We had just enough left for the wedding the next day and to party on our wedding night.

Denise's beige dress was simple but her figure made it look expensive. Her long, flowing hair was made up in great detail and her toothy smile completed the masterpiece. I wore jeans because they were all I had, but at least they were clean.

I could smell liquor on the breath of the wobbly priest who presided over the vows. His nose glowed like Rudolph's as he read scripture through the ceremony, and we suppressed our snickers. In the end, she said "yes," and so did I. That night, we headed over to the Circus-Circus casino where I'd beaten the house a year before for $1,000. Denise stood behind me while I took a seat at the table, expecting me to rake in party money for the biggest night of our lives. I imagined throwing money in the air, naked in front of my brand-new wife, with champagne from the motel's minibar. The legend of my prowess at the blackjack table hung above us like a soap bubble, and the house set to popping it. I lost four straight hands then rallied briefly before dropping most of my cash within the hour. Denise, still radiant from our vows, suggested we call it an early night and return to the motel. I wasn't having it. I pushed the last $10 we had onto the circle in hopes of recovering at least enough to save some face in front of my biggest fan. The dealer dealt me two face cards and I held. I had twenty and was sure my luck was about to change. The dealer revealed twelve, and I turned to tell Denise that we would be sticking around a little while longer.

"Hang in there, babe. It's coming," I boldly predicted.

She leaned in, pushed her hair aside to whisper in my ear. The dealer turned over a nine for twenty-one and her proposition landed with a thud. Regrouping and eager to move to plan B, I raced back to the room, and discovered that my key didn't work. I reported my problem at the registrar's desk, and he informed me that I had only paid him for one night.

I claimed, "I said I wanted two nights," sure that the money I had laid on the counter the day before was for the whole amount.

The clerk responded, "You said you wanted two nights, but I only take the money for one at a time. I reserved tonight for you, but you haven't paid."

"It's my wedding night, whatever your name is." I protested, "Don't you care?"

"It's $60."

I'd lost all the money at the table. I had to go back to the car and tell Denise that we didn't have a room and would have to get on the road back toward southern California. She held her tongue. We headed south, four plus hours of highway between us and the apartment we now called home. I peeked at the gas gauge. At a little over a half tank, we weren't going to make it. I hadn't even thought about gas money.

Then Denise started talking. She said things were going to be different now and my dad wasn't going to be dragging me all over creation doing God knows what and I was going to get a real job and earn an honest wage. "You've got a family now," she kept saying.

I'd actually hoped she could stand between me and my father going forward. She seemed unaware of the gas gauge. After a while, Denise shut her eyes and slept, and soon, the dark silence of the road had me ruminating with the metro area on the horizon and the gas dial flat-lined. I fought back the impending feeling of doom and associated nausea. Soon, I would have to awaken her and announce that were stranded on the Interstate with our blinkers on. *Who would I call?* Surely not Lemus. Maybe Lemus, it all depended on who answered their phone first.

On fumes, we coasted into my sister's driveway in Whittier. I knocked on the door and Hazel answered in her bathrobe and slippers. It was 3:00 a.m. I explained the situation as briefly as possible and told her to go back to bed, and that we would be on our way later that morning if she could lend us a few bucks for gas. After she gave me a twenty and a blanket for the couch, she went back to bed, and Denise and I took the floor and got around to consummating our marriage on the carpet.

LARRY DANIEL

CHAPTER 22

We made ourselves at home in Midway City, and I took advantage of the swimming pool to bond with Lorene. She squealed when I threw her in the air and caught her. I tried to stay away from the difficult parts of parenting as much as possible and comforted myself by providing a bedroom where Lorene could sleep soundly. Dad didn't bat an eye when I stopped coming home with him in the evening, and I kept showing up for work without a word about the wedding. Hazel eventually told him what she knew from the explanation I gave her on our wedding night, and he brought it up while driving to a lumber yard for materials on Ellen's job. He casually mentioned, "So, you got married?"

I shrugged and looked out the window. *Better married with a step-daughter,* I wanted to say, *than in jail with you.* I needed the job.

When the transmission on my truck started slipping, I traded it in for an old Jeep mail truck with all the money Denise and I could muster. I wasn't bringing home a lot from Ellen's job, but Denise's job enabled us to pay rent and not starve. The unique Jeep was a faded pea green with the steering wheel on the right side. When I drove it, passing on the right on the highway, people gawked. I learned the hard way that the hood didn't latch while driving to Whittier from Midway City on Highway 39. As I approached an underpass going over 40 mph, a whoosh of air brought the heavy metal hood up onto my windshield and folded over the top, blinding me to oncoming traffic. I leaned out my driver's window and managed to maneuver safely to the shoulder, where I bent the hood back down, and secured it with my belt. At the job site, I replaced the belt with rope.

As Thanksgiving approached, Denise mentioned a trip back to Arkansas and wanted a favor. I owed it to her. After a phone call with Brandon, she asked me to make a trip back home to help him and Earl come out west. Brandon wrecked his car and needed a change of scenery. Denise painted a good picture of our life in southern California and assured Brandon that Douglas would help him resettle, even if only for a month or so. Earl's brothers in northern California told him that if he could get to southern California, they would retrieve him. Earl's brothers lived in Yuba City, California, where programs for the disabled would make life easier for Earl. It was a chance to redeem myself a little, so I agreed. I accumulated just enough money for the trip, and Earl and Brandon agreed to split gas expenses for the return. I thought I might visit my mother, too. I had less than a week to pull it off.

The funky Jeep performed adequately on the way out. It was slow, but not bad for a four-cylinder mail truck, and I reached Arkansas in 32 hours. I caught up on sleep at my mother's house and filled her in on the details of my marriage. It was sudden, I said, but I was happy, leaving out the events that led up to the rushed decision. Suddenly, I wanted her to be proud of me but knew I hadn't given her much reason.

My mother enjoyed her life as an empty nester. She cleaned out my old, converted garage bedroom and used the space to style her friends' hair. She also took up painting and used another bedroom to store her creations.

"It looks like you're staying busy," I said.

"I'm doing okay. Do you like my paintings?"

They looked good to me but I didn't know good art from bad. She explained that she had taken a few classes and planned to expand her hobby into ceramics. "They're nice," I answered.

She gave me a mood ring as a short-notice wedding gift. I put it on, and it turned orange, which meant "unsettled."

Later that day, I caught up with Earl and Brandon and we obtained a trailer and hitch for Brandon's belongings. Earl possessed little and traveled with less. He would depend on his brothers in Yuba City. Even with Earl's light load, the Jeep was barely a match for the U-Haul trailer, but we set off early on Thanksgiving Day, 1975, anyway, with a paraplegic wedged into the back seat and a blanket draped over him because the heater didn't function properly. Earl was elated, eager to see his brothers and to take advantage of California's welfare programs: Medical care, transportation fitted with lifts and steering mechanisms, and a job if he wanted. We were jovial and looking forward to being together. By the time we reached New Mexico, it had started to snow.

After passing through Albuquerque, the light snow turned to a blizzard. Sheets of ice soon covered the desolate interstate. Our woefully inadequate clothes were now supplemented by more blankets. We pressed on, now at 30 mph, dragged by the wind that careened against the trailer. The sun went down and the temperature followed, plunging from freezing toward five degrees. We passed a gas station, but it was closed for the holidays. As our mileage plummeted, I feared a night on the side of the road with a man who couldn't walk and no heat to warm us. Another closed gas station went by and the gas gauge hovered around empty. The lights of a third blossomed in the distance and we hoped it would save us. When we pulled in and saw the closed sign, we knew we were screwed. I wasn't a praying man, but it was appearing more and more like a plausible option. God saved me the trouble by sending a four wheel drive truck with an observant driver who spotted me waving my arms in the snow.

I shouted a summary of our predicament over the wind. For $5, he let us siphon enough gas to make it to Gallup, a mid-sized town about 40 miles west. Huddled in the Jeep while the hose ran, Earl, Brandon, and I agreed to stop once we got to Gallup. A room would take a bite from our budget, but we had no choice. In Gallup, we found the cheapest-looking place in town and I went in to negotiate.

"I'd like a room for one night, please," I requested, taking in the cheap western motif and inhaling the stale cigarette odor that stained the yellow ceiling. A thin man with a long black ponytail and a turquoise necklace stood across the counter.

"How many are in your party?"

"It's just me."

I knew that it would cost more for the two additional people. Every dollar counted.

"That'll be $25."

We hadn't budgeted for a room but I forked over the cash. I calculated how much it would take in gas and food to reach our final destination and figured we might have to go the rest of the way without much to eat.

The room was on the second floor in clear view of the office but I didn't dare return to request a different one. Brandon and I had to get Earl up the stairs and into the room without anyone see us do it. Since the shooting, Brandon and I had gotten pretty proficient at carrying Earl, but the icy conditions introduced new factors into the equation. We shivered with our backs to the snow, and each grabbed a leg with one arm and embraced Earl's back with the other. We made it upstairs all right, but found ourselves in plain view of the front desk. That's when Brandon slipped on some ice, and we dropped all 180 pounds of Earl's dead weight short of the door. He lay motionless while Brandon repeatedly apologized. While I scrambled for the room key, Brandon started pulling on Earl's paralyzed legs to get him closer to the door, but his feet kept sliding out from underneath him and was unable to advance him very far. Earl began cursing as the back of his head was being bounced along the icy surface. Finally, we crouched behind the supine Earl, rolled him over the threshold, and slammed the door behind us.

After determining the coast was clear, I returned to the Jeep to retrieve some crackers, and we finished them off. Earl reminisced about northern California, the region rife with citrus trees, while Brandon fiddled with the television to check the forecast for the following day.

"I can get a program job in Oroville at a gun shop working on pistols," Earl murmured. "Oroville is pretty close to Yuba City."

"Sounds like a good job," I said.

"It's a great place. You'll have to come up sometime."

"I hear they've got good weed out there," Brandon chimed in. "I'll be up there as soon as I can get another car."

The next morning was so cold that it took fifteen minutes of jump-starting with borrowed battery cables to get the Jeep running. I'd parked out of view from the office, so I wasn't worried about being found out anymore. I sat nearly frozen in the driver's seat and begged the key while the battery coughed and sputtered. Once the motor came to life, I fastened the rope that held the hood down and we drove to a grocery store, where I bought bread and a package of baloney. Brandon was livid.

"You bought baloney? I hate baloney. Why'd you buy baloney?" he whined.

I countered, "Fuck you, asshole. I bought it with the last of '*my*' money!"

"Kiss my ass, dipshit."

"Eat the bread then."

Earl had heard enough, offering, "Guys, we have to eat whatever we've got, so shut up and let's drive, okay?"

"You can eat the damn baloney if you're hungry," I said, insisting on the last word. Brandon dismissed it, unable to argue with Earl.

The conditions improved after we crossed the Arizona border and I eventually got us back up over 60 mph. Brandon's trailer cost us more in gas than he'd contributed for the trip, and I let him know about it. At one point I threatened to unhitch the trailer and leave it on the interstate.

In spite of the tension, we whooped in celebration after crossing into California, but the tank read empty and so did our wallets by the time we reached Corona, another two hours from the apartment. I approached a man at a gas pump and offered the mood ring that my mother had given me just a few days before. He accepted, probably out of pity after he spotted Earl's wheel chair in the back of the Jeep. The ring, before I took it off, was black. Stressed.

Denise welcomed us in with hugs and kisses. I pulled Brandon's U-Haul trailer the rest of way to Fountain Valley and parked it in front of Douglas. He was his usual self, and ignored me, while awkwardly embracing Brandon. Earl's brothers retrieved him a few days later.

CHAPTER 23

I gnoring my shortcomings, Denise let me know that she wanted us to have a child together. It took me awhile to warm up to the idea, but once I did, I eagerly did my part. Her job was secure, but mine was winding down and my dependence on my father was shifting. He'd been cordial with Denise and she'd reciprocated the formalities, but she wanted me out of his orbit even though he still slipped us a little money under the table. I'd found a temporary job in Tustin, near Orange where Denise worked, with decent wages for a laborer that would last a couple of months. Now that I wasn't working for my father, I assumed I'd keep him in my life somehow, even if only minimally. I should have known not to let my guard down, and not to go for a ride with my dad to see one of his friends, but I did.

We pulled into an empty parking lot behind a liquor store in Garden Grove and met Ronnie, the former football player I'd been introduced to during a previous trip to California. I greeted Ronnie with a nod and stood next to my dad. "I need my money, Ronnie," my father announced once we were gathered in the parking lot, "I expected to be paid by now."

"I don't have it," Ronnie admitted. "You'll get it when you get it."

Ronnie was obviously not Lonnie, who'd quickly folded after Dad had pulled a gun and demanded his vehicle while I stood by in Newton County, Arkansas. Ronnie was a solid-looking ex-running back and wasn't used to being pushed around. My father pulled a loaded gun from his pants pocket and pointed it at Ronnie's face. Dad was angry. Ellen's job was over, all his shady deals had fallen flat, and Ronnie owed him money that he didn't have. I wasn't sure what he might do, never mind that it was midday. "What about now asshole?" he threatened. "You better get it quick."

"Don't do this," I pled, "we'll all regret it." Dad's eyes darted to me, and after a brief pause, he pushed me aside.

"I'll pull the trigger," he warned Ronnie. "I got nothing to lose."

Shaking my head, no, I begged, "You can't."

"Listen to your boy, Lemus," Ronnie put in. "I'll give you what I have and I'll get the rest. I've got $500 on me and you can have it. Let's get out of here before somebody calls the police."

Ronnie slowly reached into his pocket and emptied it, and said, "I'll get you the rest, Lemus."

My father took the $500 and let Ronnie get back in his car. We did the same. I knew this would be the last time I would be riding along with my dad. The gun hadn't shocked me this time, instead, I saw the desperation surrounding him and the way my father had been taken advantage of by people he'd trusted. The fact still remained that his idea of doing something about it was pulling a gun in a parking lot. I needed to save myself and take refuge in my marriage. I needed to avoid him.

I didn't tell Denise about the incident, but she could tell I was looking to extricate myself. Out of the blue one day, she raised the possibility of a move, and I listened.

She quizzed me, "Earl likes it in Yuba City, doesn't he?"

I reported, "I talked to him on the phone and things are going good for him. The job at the gun shop and the van he was trying to get, have all come through."

"And I'll bet the cost of living's cheaper up there," Denise added.

"Let's do it," I said.

I'd told myself that on our budget, southern California wasn't all it was cracked up to be, but really the move had everything to do with my father. I talked to him about the move north, explaining the need to be closer to Earl, the terrible Orange County traffic, the high cost of living. I couldn't stand to tell him how eager I was to put some distance between us, but he had to know. In response, he informed me that Ronnie's debt had been partially satisfied with an older red Dodge Monaco that didn't run, but would eventually, and I could drive it after it was fixed. The Jeep had finally quit running, so I was appreciative of his offer.

We scrounged final paychecks before heading to the Sacramento area, which was an hour from Yuba City. We needed to be close enough to the metro for Denise to have better employment options, but far enough to avoid the mass of humanity occupying a city. About thirty miles east of Sacramento, toward the Sierra Mountains on Interstate 80, sat a modest town the size of Springdale. Roseville, California called to us and we both said, "This is it."

Aunt Caroline in Weimar, whom I'd visited in 1967, lived another half hour east on the Interstate, and Earl lived an hour north in Yuba City. From now on, they would be our family. We rented a low-income apartment on the outskirts of town, and I quickly found construction work that paid $4 an hour. Denise took a job as a secretary, but it didn't pay nearly as well as the job she'd left in Orange County. We had one car and were poor as church mice. And Denise was pregnant.

CHAPTER 24

Roseville was divided by Interstate 80. To the west, a predominately Latino population thrived, and to the east, displaced folks from around the world resided. Rarely did I meet a native Californian on the east side. A popular farmers' market on the Hispanic side brought people from a hundred mile radius to haggle with the merchants selling everything from tires to tamales.

We made friends quickly in our 16-unit complex, and the upstairs neighbors, Duane and Janice, became our closest friends. We lived directly under them, and through the poorly insulated floor space, we could hear them in graphic detail anytime they had sex. We kept a broom nearby to playfully thump the ceiling after each performance. Duane was Hispanic, played basketball on a city league team, and invited me to join after I told him I used to play. Right away, I startled myself with my hoop skills which should have deteriorated, but hadn't. We played a full schedule against other teams in the area and I loved playing ball again. Roseville started to feel like home.

Another apartment neighbor, "Turkey Joe," became my weed connection. I rarely had money, but worked out small deals with him on occasion. He went by Turkey Joe because he was Turkish, not because he looked like a turkey, though he kind of did. His Colombian Gold was the best around.

As the pregnancy advanced, I buried whatever dignity I might have had left and stood in line for food stamps while Denise went through the steps to secure Medicaid for delivery of our newborn. The due date was early January. In the meantime, I bounced from construction job to construction job, but content to just be with Denise and free of drama. This was the longest I'd been away from Lemus Daniel since my 1970 stint at the Gray House.

I finally got word from my father that he'd repaired the Dodge, and I could use it if I retrieved it. I wanted that to mean something, that maybe Dad regained a smidgen of sanity. That somewhere in the midst of his erratic behavior was a parent who was generous and protective. I considered a bus ticket but decided against it. Neither could we afford the gas money for Denise to drive down with me, so I opted for what I knew how to do: I prepared to hitchhike from Roseville to southern California, almost four hundred miles away.

I kissed my wife goodbye at seven that morning, and soon after, I had my thumb up at an on ramp on Interstate 80. It was a typical sunny California day without a cloud in the sky. Once I reached Sacramento, I considered going south on Interstate 5, through the vast wasteland of valley towns, but instead, I decided to go to the coast and take Highway 101 south, to Los Angeles. Cars stopped for hitchhikers here, not like Arkansas or Missouri. It was impulsive, but I wanted another glimpse of the coastline.

From Sacramento, I caught a ride with a retired auto parts salesman all the way to Milpitas on the outskirts of San Jose in the Bay Area, and got dropped off when we hit a monstrous freeway jam. I exited the motorized pretzel and continued south on foot until a car slowed and a slender blond woman in skimpy clothes ushered me in. I told her I was on my way to L.A.

She said, "I'm not going far, but I've got some food in the fridge and a couple of beers if you want."

Her short skirt made its way up her leg, "A shower?"

She was tempting but I was pressed for time. I considered myself happily married but my short marriage hadn't been tested like this. I told her I had better keep going, and she let me out.

The old man who followed was a change of pace after the sex kitten. His van already contained several hitchhikers. He'd picked up travelers to ensure a captive audience and ranted about a host of offbeat subjects. His wild stories about former lives, alien impregnations, and end-of-times predictions left me wide-eyed and looking for evidence of empty liquor bottles or LSD. He kept us between the ditches so we let him talk. Eventually the half dozen of us tuned him out and managed our own conversations about where we were going and why, periodically peering out the window at the scenic coastal towns. After it got dark, I was let out in Santa Barbara with a warning from one of my fellow hitchhikers to watch out for the Hillside Strangler, a killer who frequented the Hollywood area of Los Angeles. I'd followed the grisly details of the murders on television. My next ride reached North Hollywood, but no further, and I began to regret my decision to take the scenic route. I needed to get to La Mirada where my sisters had recently moved from Whittier, and where Dad had left the car, but it was so late that I gave up and began burrowing under the ice plants that covered the closest freeway onramp area. I wanted to conceal myself under the ground cover until daylight, so I pulled leaves and branches over me and laid my head down for the few hours left before sun up.

Just after getting sufficiently concealed, however, I heard a car approaching and instinctively sprang up, waving my thumb. The driver, a young woman with long greasy hair in an older compact car pointing in the direction I'd come from, lowered her window.

"Where to?" she asked.

"La Mirada."

She wasn't going that way but offered a nearby bed for the rest of the night, no strings attached. I accepted. She seemed safe enough but when I walked into her house and discovered several people scattered around the room manning telephones and carrying on grave discussions about engrams, I became wary.

"They're mostly heroin addicts," she explained, leading me to a sofa heaped with Scientology pamphlets.

"Calling the toll-free number, we help them recover."

I waited for the next move and weighed my options. The girl quickly tipped the scales for me.

"Would you mind taking a test?"

"What kind of test?" I asked.

"I can help you find your full potential."

"Take me back to the highway."

My potential was parked about an hour away, and I refused to talk about it with her any further. Scientology or the Hillside Strangler seemed like a toss-up to me. I'd lost an hour and stood at the same exchange when a big Cadillac approached, going the right way. When my thumb popped up, the luxury auto slowed. A bald man with a fat face peeked through the lowered glass.

"Where ya' going?" he asked.

"I'm going to La Mirada."

"Get in."

THE RUINING OF LEMUS DANIEL

As my luck would have it, David, a rotund businessman from Wichita, was going my way. I felt lucky because a few freeway interchanges stood between me and La Mirada and I hadn't expected to find a ride straight through, especially at four in the morning. There would be no Hillside Strangler for me, unless it was David. He started in on some racy jokes and I wondered briefly if he was hitting on me. Surely, he knew that the Hillside Strangler hadn't been caught yet.

I played along and laughed at the innuendos out of courtesy. The closer we got to my car, the more grateful I became. Turning the last corner, he asked, "Do you like to fool around with cock?"

"Excuse me?" I said. I wasn't sure if he'd said what I thought he'd said.

"Do you want to fool around?" he explained.

I couldn't think of anything to say except, "No thanks."

As I shut the door, he mused, "Well, it takes all kinds."

I tried to not analyze what he meant by that. I'd made it to the car and that's all that counted. Dad had been generous, leaving me keys and a full tank. I got in the Dodge, closed my eyes in the front seat, and waited on sunrise before going in to say "hello" to my sisters. They were both still working in Whittier and became involved with some guys from Iran, many of whom relocated to southern California after the Shah was deposed. My sister's messy apartment reflected a couple of girls that were enjoying life and the company of the well-mannered, but hard-partying, Persians. After a brief visit, I returned on Interstate 5, having seen enough of US 101. When I got home, Denise shared that Brandon met a girl in Fountain Valley named Adrianna that he was going to marry.

Adrianna spent her whole life in southern California. They'd met at a party, and he'd dazzled her with his faux bravado. She was well-read, thoughtful, and shy, which was an odd match for Brandon. He hinted that he might move to northern California.

In July, 1976, America celebrated its bicentennial and we got word that Denise's sister, Jenny, had a new husband, Robert. I'd known Robert since he dated Jackie years before, and invited me over to meet Patti, the girl who stole my virtue. He was now my brother-in-law. They came out for the holiday and we traveled to San Francisco to see a grand fireworks display. We learned from Jenny that Douglas was retiring soon and was looking to settle in Foresthill, a small town east of Roseville in the Sierras that he'd evidently had his eye on for years.

Denise's due date passed early in 1977, and we tried everything we could think of to induce labor. Our first drive up the mountain to Lake Tahoe was meant to provoke her water to break, we'd heard it could be triggered by a change in elevation, but it didn't, and instead we found ourselves immersed in the scenery. The two-lane highway wound through towering Ponderosa pine groves, and occasionally gave us a view of the gigantic granite boulders strewn along the banks of the roaring American River hundreds of feet below. Guard rails lined some of the most treacherous drop-offs, but not all of them. From the top of Echo Summit, more than 8,000 feet above sea level, we were mesmerized by the sight of waterfalls and forest aromas before we took in the brilliant blue waters of Lake Tahoe and its 70-mile shoreline. Snowcapped mountains bordered the lake. I was itching to try my luck at the casinos, but resisted the temptation.

Back in Roseville, we considered every suggestion to induce labor, but nothing worked. We couldn't have it done at the hospital because public assistance wouldn't pay for it.

When her water finally did break in late-January, we piled into the Dodge and pulled up to the doors at Roseville Hospital, and I waited in the holding room and watched the contractions break line and suit over her body. In spite of her pain, she could see how uncomfortable I was watching her wail during a convulsion. The nurse informed us contractions were far apart and that it might be awhile.

"Why don't you take a break?" Denise offered between contractions.

She'd delivered before and was telling me not to worry because the subsequent deliveries were always supposed to be easier. The thought of bailing out of the event had me feeling sheepish but she relieved me of that during her next contraction, telling me, "Go on."

After a couple of hours, a nurse came to tell me that they were making progress. I asked her if the doctor had arrived yet.

"He'll be here," she assured me, "Delivery isn't imminent."

"Should I go back and see my wife?"

"No, it's not a good idea right now," she answered. "A lot of people don't handle it very well. I'll come and get you when it's over."

"I think the doctor should be here," I said as she left the waiting room. She pretended not to hear me.

Left alone to ponder, I hoped for a healthy boy but didn't mind the idea of another girl. I fretted about my ability to measure up and be a good provider. The conception aspect of parenthood was all fun and games, but the delivery didn't seem to be going quite as well.

Many hours of labor later, they wheeled an exhausted Denise out to see me. I embraced her and she kissed me, a near death taste to her breath. She seemed delirious and not all there. The doctor had never shown up.

"It tore me good," she announced, once she'd been situated in her room and had the chance to gulp some fluids.

A whopping 11-pound baby boy lay nearby in the hospital crib. He had the Daniel face with Denise's nose and was 22 inches long. He rested comfortably while I gazed at him, and counted his fingers and toes. After he'd been measured and weighed by a nurse that I glared at the whole time for taking so long, I picked him up and held him.

After they sewed Denise up, we only had a few hours in the room, and before long, I was pulling the car up to load in mother and son. It didn't cost a dime, but I was never allowed to forget it. We named him after a musician whose name I liked, Jimmie Earl Daniel.

Things happened fast after that. Brandon and Adrianna moved to Auburn, fifteen minutes east of us, and Brandon got a job with a builder. Douglas and Donna sold their house in Fountain Valley and bought one in Foresthill. Dad finally made a trip north to meet his grandson, and there in the apartment in Roseville, with my first child cradled in his arms, he made me an offer I couldn't refuse.

CHAPTER 25

My father had connections all over the state of California. He had other siblings strewn across California—beside the aunts I'd already met—in Merced, Clovis, and Fresno. It shouldn't have surprised me when he followed me up to Roseville. He was going straight, he said, and had formed a partnership with a financier to build some houses in my neighborhood.

I was still on public assistance and desperate for work. Twenty homes were to be built in Rocklin, a mere five miles from my front door, and I said "yes" to the job my father offered, and I swallowed my pride, my dread, and my sense of failure. I couldn't look Denise in the eye when I'd told her what I'd done. She didn't scorn my decision. She'd have taken the job, too.

Right away, the new job had its own challenges apart from Dad's mood swings. It hadn't rained since we'd moved up north last fall, and after summer came, the temperature soared. The temperature often reached 115 degrees, but thankfully was a dry heat void of Arkansas humidity. Still, we hit the building site before daybreak and worked without lunch until early afternoon, when it became unbearable. Nearby Folsom Lake turned into a creek, and longstanding records cracked like baked clay as the drought and heat wave rolled through.

By mid-1977, most of my old Springdale buddies relocated to the greater Sacramento area, including Denise's dad. After

Wendy rejoined Earl in Yuba City, only an hour separated Earl, Wendy, Phyllis, Lemus, Brandon, and Brandon's new wife, Adrianna, from Denise and me.

Dad leased a duplex with Phyllis on the same block as the building site, so my job was literally right outside his front door. He kept the same schedule as before, complaining that his dogs were barking and popping beer cans in the afternoon, his gout prompting him to self-medicate. Dad took after Hemingway. "Done by noon and drunk by 3:00 p.m.," became "Done by 3:00 p.m. and drunk by 5:00 p.m." Dad started later than Hemingway, but drank faster.

In his air-conditioned duplex, felled by the heat and too much Miller Lite, he continued to ramble on about his misfortunes, while I smoked myself toward languor. He did his best to flood me in self-doubt about my newfound fatherhood. "You're in for a rude awakening, son," he declared after throwing back another beer. "You don't have a clue what it takes to make it in this world."

His callous words still stung but had become familiar. I went back to drinking with him in pool halls, sometimes getting in late. With a six-year-old and a newborn at home, Denise wasn't too happy about it, and we fought. She withheld affection sporadically, maybe strategically, but couldn't argue with the new yellow Dodge van we bought, or our new independence from food stamps. Lorene wore better clothes, and Jimmie had everything a newborn would need.

With Douglas in Foresthill to babysit, Denise, Brandon, Adrianna, and I finally made a trip to see Earl and Wendy in Yuba City. Earl was in tall cotton and eager to show how the lift in his van worked, proposing a drive to the gun shop in Oroville.

"Shot gun!" Brandon hollered.

We watched as Earl pushed the buttons to lower the lift, roll onto it, and rise. Once level with the driver's seat, he slid himself behind the wheel, folded his wheelchair, and set it aside.

"That's so cool," Brandon gushed as Earl demonstrated the hand-operated throttle and brake.

Earl's black lab pup jumped in and took the back corner, tail wagging. He knew we were going by the irrigation ditches that lined the fruit trees outside of Yuba City. Earl let him out when we reached the 12-foot wide ditches, and he kept pace with the van, floundering joyfully in the water. Earl gassed it until he couldn't run anymore, then slowed and opened the door so he could leap in and collapse, a soggy, panting, mess of happiness.

After the tour of the gun shop and a brief look at Oroville, we went back to his place. A few of his friends were gathered and it was like old times, where joints were passed and other drugs were available and used openly. I had access to some good pot through my dad and Turkey Joe, and promised Earl return visits to share it. Denise took it all in and formed her own opinions about our little reunion.

Things were familiar again, but as far as Denise was concerned, it was no more than a brief reprieve. Maybe she could sense trouble coming, or maybe she just missed Arkansas, but one day in late 1977, she announced that she wanted to buy a house in Springdale.

"We'll never be able to afford one here," she pointed out. "I want to own something that will accrue equity. I miss my sisters. I'm thinking of the kids. We can find jobs there. You're not in trouble in Springdale anymore. I want to go home."

"This is home now," I argued.

"I don't like it here," she admitted.

I felt cornered. I didn't want to be left alone with my father in California. As I laid it out for him, he stood in disbelief, and predicted, "You won't find a job worth a damn in that shit-hole."

"It doesn't matter, I have to go," I reasoned.

"There isn't any work."

I turned to walk away, adding, "I'll find something."

At the close of 1977, Denise, Lorene, Jimmie, and I returned to Springdale, Arkansas, with no guarantee of work, no telling whether the coast was clear, or a place to stay.

CHAPTER 26

B y 1978, the building business had gone into decline in Arkansas, making steady work hard to come by. As expected, the conveniences we'd enjoyed in California disappeared. We had to get rid of the van and replace it with an older, green and white Dodge pickup with three on the column and a rusty bed. Denise had a friend in real estate and sent her sniffing around for a small house we could barely afford. The house she turned up had three bedrooms and a bath and a half—an additional stool and sink off the master bedroom—but the seller knew my father. "We need $500 down and don't have to worry about the credit application," Denise explained.

Denise had a credit history, but not one good enough to purchase a house, and mine wilted under scrutiny. My father's connection seemed like a godsend. Over the course of the next few weeks, we worked and saved. On the closing date, we signed papers for the small, 900-square-foot house on Backstrom Street, and I shook Hank Howell's hand.

"Shame what they did to your dad," he mused. I sidestepped a response and thanked him, but he went on. "He was the biggest of the big time," he claimed. "Tell him I said 'hello' when you see him."

The interaction helped me realize that many people were still in his corner, but had been fearful of taking any real stand against the forces that brought him down. In Arkansas, it seemed I'd only known the negative of being his son.

The minute we turned the key and crossed the threshold with Lorene and Jimmie in tow, Denise began nesting. The house had faded blue wood siding, half high brick wainscot, and a tan shingled roof, and it came on the market after getting foreclosed, but it might as well have been a castle. The large, unfenced backyard bordered similar structures in the modest neighborhood, all within walking distance from a school. Denise knew better than I did when it came to the family's needs, but I wondered how we were going to keep up with the payments.

Howell didn't do business with Dawson's savings and loan, so thankfully, we'd steered clear of his bank for the mortgage and couldn't be denied because of my last name. Unbeknownst to Dawson, he'd been supplying my brother-in-law with construction loans through a friend of my dad's. My father kept close tabs on the transactions and on Dawson's savings and loan scandal. To fill in the two year gap in my memory of Springdale, I turned to his memoirs:

"Mr. Dawson had as much regard for this institution as he had for the ill-fated motor hotel. Hometown Savings and Loan, which was formed in the early 1960s, was the first stock savings and loan company in the state of Arkansas. A dozen or so businessmen in Springdale, including Jim and Tom Dawson, were the investors and directors of the newly-formed company. Up until the formation of the S&L, the home builders, including me, had to go to Rogers or Fayetteville to obtain financing for their projects. The purpose of the Hometown S&L was to keep the money local. Its deposits grew rapidly.

By the late 1960s, Dawson realized that it held millions of dollars in assets that he could use for his own interests if he

*could oust the other stockholders. He immediately launched a
campaign to buy out the others. He replaced the manager and
installed his old friend Robert Allenby, a man from Springdale
pioneer stock who was five years older than me. I idolized him
when I was in high school.*

*Robert was in the lumber business when he became man-
ager, and he and Dawson struck a deal, which meant that Tom
Dawson bought and owned the man. I knew Allenby's alliance
to Dawson to include loan fraud and pulling several million
dollars from the back door of the S&L for Dawson's chicken
and new swine business. Bob had a deep fear of Dawson, especially after he used the S&L for his own benefit. Tom eventually
gained more than 50% of the stock and set up business in the
following manner:*

*Any construction loan application submitted to the S&L
that did not list the Allenby-owned lumber yard was denied.
Also denied were any farm loan applications that didn't include
Dawson as the poultry associate. Dawson took second mort-
gages on the farms and Bob got usury prices on his lumber.*

*The S&L ran smoothly for three years until one man, Noble
Carter, took exception to the rule. Noble owned a local lumber
yard but seemed to have no one to sell his materials to due to
the Dawson-Allenby agreement. His first move was to interest
others to file for a charter to open another S&L in Springdale.
He was able to do so and more than 50 signatures stood behind his request. At the court hearing for the application for
a federally funded loan company, Dawson and his attorney,
Archibald Fleeman, showed up to protest the issuance of the
chapter. Their reason was that Springdale, with a population
of 18,000, could not support another S&L, and that their institution was capable of handling all the business. The charter
was denied, so Carter wrote to the Securities Commission and*

filed suit against Dawson and Allenby. They were indicted by a grand jury and the trial took place in the same courthouse where my trial took place in 1968. It was the same circus, with just a few changes to the cast.

Gary James was the attorney for the defendants, Tom Dawson and Robert Allenby, instead of Dawson's private attorney, Archibald Fleeman, who was then able to indirectly suggest to Carter to obtain the services of the same lawyers I used in my failed civil suit. Carter even went to see them, and later related to me that after five minutes of conversation with the two attorneys, he'd said, "Thanks, but no thanks." He said he felt as if he'd been sent there by Dawson and remembered what happened to me. Even though he acquired a Federal District Attorney named Barry Lunsford to prosecute the case instead, the results were the same.

Lunsford eagerly accepted the petition material and began to work closely with Carter. He convinced him that he had enough to convict as the case took shape. However, with fewer than five days before the trial, Lunsford suddenly quit his job and could not be found. Later it was learned that he decided to return to school in the middle of a semester—if that was even possible—and took his file with him.

Lunsford's replacement was less than adequate. He was seen visiting with Dawson in the hallways of the courthouse and was spotted out with him after hours. The new attorney rarely spoke with Carter and assured him he had all the facts he needed. Dawson bought 15 new Lincoln Continentals every two years and the replacement attorney was seen driving a new one just 30 days after the trial concluded.

Having avoided a conviction, Dawson and Allenby were given a reprimand by the judge: "I don't ever want to see you people back in my courtroom again."

THE RUINING OF LEMUS DANIEL

Still, Allenby worried throughout the ordeal. He described his attorney's behavior to me, that he never said a word for the five days of the trial. When Allenby gave me his version of the trial, he was unaware that Dawson already had the results in his pocket. "Lemus, I sat next to James," he lamented, "and watched him pick his nose for five days."

He later remarked that the former U.S. attorney charged $50,000 for those services. Dawson could not fire Allenby because of the million dollar loans Dawson was ordering him to make.

After the judge slapped Dawson and Allenby's hands and they returned to Springdale, you would expect that they would have cleaned up their act a little. However, quite the contrary. They became even more blatant in operating the S&L. Stockholders began to offer their shares for sale at whatever meager price Dawson would give.

By 1981, its assets reached $75 million. Hometown Savings and Loan lasted another two years before shutting down. I learned later from Allenby that, during those last two years, they raped the organization blind. Luckily for Dawson and Allenby, the nationwide Reagan-induced Savings and Loan crisis arrived and Dawson's S&L closed its doors without any more attention brought to its practices."

Even though Marty wasn't involved in any of these proceedings, Dawson discovered his loans through Allenby and cut him off. Suddenly, he was out of business and unable to provide any work for me now that I relocated. He'd been stuck with a couple of houses to pay interest on and scrambled to provide for his wife and two children.

I found limited work finishing cement with Dennis, who revived my love for country music. He'd quit drinking and still wore black every day in honor of Johnny Cash, while pouring, leveling and hand-smoothing cement. Cement finishing paid more in less time than house framing, but I never saw much of it. I averaged a little more than $100 a week. It was hard to scrape up enough cash for necessities like milk and diapers, so we ate cheap TV dinners and hand-wrung the mustard-colored shit out in the toilet, then washed the diapers to use them again. Naturally, Denise and I started fighting over money.

Until then, an "us against them" mentality kept our marriage strong, but the lack of opportunity and lingering threats in Arkansas made the pull of good money with my dad in California a formidable test of will. Denise didn't want him in our lives, and saw the house as an anchor for the family, but we were already late on the payments.

"The factory's steady work," she insisted. "I know you can get on."

So, I took a job at a paper company, and grudgingly wrapped paper sacks in bundles for less than a month. It was a mundane, soul-sucking, and a low-paying waste of time to me. I didn't want to be cooped up in a factory no matter how much the family needed it, and pined for my old job in California.

Even though a carpenter's work could be sporadic, I loved the sun, the fresh air, the smell of fresh-sawed wood, and the natural reward of seeing a home go up. I proposed a return to California, just me this time, and just long enough to make some real money and get the bills paid. Denise wanted no part of it. She said if I went to work for my father, I shouldn't plan on coming back, then backtracked, and conceded that we needed the money. I assured her it would be temporary, but I wasn't sure if she believed I would come back.

CHAPTER 27

I loaded up the tools I'd accumulated, swallowed a couple of uppers for the journey, and headed west. At 22, I was a veteran cross-country driver, and I talked to myself, talked back to the radio, and rolled the window down to freeze myself awake. Without cash, I couldn't stop and try my luck in the Vegas casinos before passing through onto the desolate highway 95 toward Reno, motoring instead through old mining towns and trailer park brothels filled with semi-trucks. I'd been driving non-stop when my mind started playing tricks on me and the never-ending highway lines were interrupted by a vision of 100 oversized rats swarming across the asphalt and the empty desert.

After a brief rest stop, I pulled into the driveway in Rocklin late the next morning and was greeted by a jovial Lemus Daniel and a surplus of employment.

"We're pouring the driveway on one of the houses day after tomorrow," he announced. "So get some sleep and we'll get to work."

At first, all I did was work. Across the tracks, Tim's Pizzeria had everything we needed for food, so we never had to wander far from the building site. At night, the train blew its horn when it rumbled across the nearby crossing and I could set my watch to it. At 10:37 p.m. every night, the whistle shook my bedroom window while I thought about my wife and kids. Denise and I talked on the phone a few times, but then stopped altogether.

Dad still drank himself to sleep every night, but managed to keep out of trouble with the law. He was easier to be around during the day and kept his three o'clock rule, never opening a beer can until then. After that, all bets were off, and he had the green light. As much as I tried to avoid it, I'd periodically find myself trapped in his vehicle while he drank and reflected.

Repeating himself, he would slur, "I love you, son," weaving on and off the shoulder. The alcohol-driven repetition was dreadful and wore me out. Men of his generation weren't known to express affection well, especially if they were drunk and marred by untreated post-traumatic stress. He drank to forget, but all he did was remember.

"I love you, too," I dutifully whispered back.

After a couple of weeks, I sent my first cash-filled envelope to Denise, and it felt good. By the time I sent another, a primal urge had emerged from the murk of my loneliness and desperation. In Sacramento, just twenty minutes down the road, I'd found a night club that booked good bands and brought temptation, exposing a chip off the old block. My esteem was in the tank. I was a sucker for the temporary ego boost, and I cheated on my wife. Denise, with a social circle in Springdale that included men that could have replaced me if she'd wanted, could never know. She took care of the children, and as far as I knew, hadn't matched my transgressions. Still, my own infidelities left me moody and suspicious.

One day while wandering through the aisles of a hardware store to break up the hours of raising walls and hanging sheetrock, I spotted Dad pocketing a handful of nails. His good standing with the law suddenly looked flimsy. I decided it was a good time to return to Arkansas.

CHAPTER 28

P ulling up to the house on Backstrom Street, I found Denise waiting for me with her hands on her hips and her hair in a ponytail.

"I missed you," I said as I emerged from the truck. I smiled and asked, "How've you been?"

"I've been okay," she answered smiling back. "Thank you for all the money. We've kept up the bills without any trouble." After an awkward few seconds, the suspense dropped.

"I missed you," she added.

Jimmie slept in the extra bedroom she'd fixed up for him, and Lorene was still at school. We went straight to bed remembering we had a reason to continue as a couple. Later, I would wake my son and hold him and feel proud I had done my part to provide for him. But niggling questions remained, ate away at me. *What would come next, a factory job?*

Again, I saw my mother, who now had a suitor, a well-to-do entrepreneur named Herbert who owned properties around town. Everybody liked him and no one had dirt on him, but she insisted it was nothing serious; she was just having a little fun. I apologized for losing the mood ring she had given me. She liked Denise and encouraged me to do all I could to be a good father and husband. Besides fixing ladies' hair and her hobby, oil painting, she was now active in her church, and asked me again to go with her while I was in town. "You'd like the preacher. You need to come with me," she insisted.

I explained, "I just can't right now."

While I'd been working in California, Denise landed a job at a popular night spot in town as a waitress. According to her, Dawson was known to show up drunk and manhandle her co-workers with impunity, but she'd been able to side-step him. Everybody feared him. Another excerpt from my father's tell-all recounts his doings with one well-heeled Fayetteville banker and leaves no question that he was above the law:

"Tom Dawson and a well-heeled banker named Michael Jones borrowed from each other through their prospective lending institutions. Michael borrowed $1,000,000 to construct a new building, and Tom used Michael's facility for such things as an escrow account for $50,000 football bets Tom made with a Dallas man concerning Texas-Arkansas football games.

Tom and Michael got along well with their business dealings, so it was only natural that Michael would turn to Tom when he began having problems with his wife, Marsha. For reasons unknown, Marsha left Michael for a south Arkansas man, whom I didn't know. Michael was jilted and didn't like it. Tom acquired the services of a local thug whom I was familiar with, Patrick Pine, to nearly take the life out of the man. Pat wasn't able to make a clean getaway and was tried and convicted, all the while remaining silent about why he had attacked a man he'd never seen or known. Tom furnished a lawyer, but the fee wasn't large enough to buy freedom for Pat.

Pat told Tom that if he didn't get him out soon, he was going to start singing. So after two months in the Van Buren jail, he opened his mouth and was promptly moved to the more slum-like Ft. Smith jail to serve the full year of his sentence."

Dawson still hovered over Springdale like L.A. smog and the smell of his chicken plants reeked like a cesspool anytime the wind blew. Soon after my brief second honeymoon with De-nise, I broached the idea of all of us going back to California, promising that I would steer clear of my father apart from work. Surprisingly, I was met little resistance.

"Lorene will be out of school any day now," Denise pointed out, "and we can lease the house while we're gone."

We agreed that construction was drying up in Arkansas, that she wouldn't have to work as much in California, and that we could come back anytime once the work there was done. We packed up and left for the west coast in the summer of 1978.

Back in California, Dad knew that Denise didn't like him, so he set out to get on her good side as soon as we got our bearings in Citrus Heights, a short drive from Rocklin. He invited us to San Francisco to an intimate venue called the Old Waldorf as guests of Rick Danko, who introduced us to Gary Busey, who would be nominated for an Academy Award for his portrayal of Buddy Holly in *The Buddy Holly Story*. He spoke in staccato-like bursts, and had white powder caked around his nose. We also met Paul Butterfield, a popular harmonica player and leader of the Butterfield Blues Band. I caught a bright smile covering De-nise's face. She was amused by Busey's antics, but also tried to play it cool to suppress any outward expression of enjoyment for her father-in-law's sake.

Despite Dad's half-hearted stab at reconciliation, our stint in Citrus Heights would prove short-lived. Fewer than a cou-ple of months in, Denise announced that she was pregnant. We didn't think it would happen, but it did. It was a gut punch to me and my reaction surprised me. I accused her of doing it intentionally. I bitched and moaned about money. I ranted and sulked about added responsibility. I wasn't getting along with my step-daughter, who had grown old enough to acquire a sassy mouth. The pressure was undeniable.

But as the months passed, I tried to be more helpful, by watching the kids, doing dishes, and housekeeping. I was glad I still had a job and we had money for a doctor. Remembering the lax care Jimmie received in Roseville, Denise found a good physician in Citrus Heights who encouraged her to feel emboldened about the impending birth.

Unexpectedly, my friend, Harris, from Springdale called and asked if I could pick him up at the Sacramento airport. I informed Denise that we might have company for a few days before he continued north to Yuba City to see Earl. After he arrived, I brought him to the job site to show him where I worked. My father proceeded to ridicule me in front of my guest.

"I don't know how I'll get any work out of you while he's here," he bitched. Standing in a deep ditch, he started shoveling out loose dirt from a freshly dug foundation and slung the dirt near my feet, then maliciously tossed the shovel at Harris' polished shoes. He climbed out of the ditch and barked at Harris, "Have you ever done an honest day's work in your life?" Harris was aware of my dad's reputation and knew better than to smart off in response. He left that up to me.

"Alright, alright, we're leaving," I said. His look said it all. My father didn't like it one bit. He smelled trouble, and hypocritically told me so.

I promised to take Harris out on the town before Earl came to shuttle him up north. Denise knew of Harris' playboy reputation, but consented because I'd convinced her it would look bad to deny a friend the experience of a Sacramento nightclub on his first visit to town. I figured that as long as we made it in before she got up the next morning, all was well.

Harris stripped me of my identity like vinegar takes the paint off wood siding. I'd gotten in the truck a married father of two, but en route to the Oasis Ballroom, found myself nodding along as he commented on the quality of females in California, adding, "And there's a lot to choose from."

At the Ballroom, the sound system boomed out contemporary music, a band vacated the stage, and the crowd thinned. Harris drifted, sipping a beer and eyeing women in the crowd. One of them eyed him back, and she had a friend. I stayed near the bar, observing the crowd and chasing bottled beers.

"She's invited us to a party at her friend's house," Harris informed me. Her friend was attractive and I didn't want to be a killjoy. I agreed to help him out without considering the consequences. We hadn't been at the party ten minutes before Harris let me know that the girl wanted him someplace more private. She'd come to the Ballroom with her friend and didn't have a car there, and Harris wanted to know if he could borrow my truck for a few hours before returning for me. Harris didn't know where he was to begin with, and it wasn't likely that he would find his way back. I said okay anyway. I wanted my friend to have a good time. Of course, he never returned.

I mingled as the party slowly dispersed and was ultimately left alone with the friend of the young lady Harris was entertaining, waiting on him to return. She was far from upset that I was there. She brushed up against me. I was a little drunk. I did not resist.

Near daybreak, with no sign of Harris or my truck, regret poured hot coals over my head. I convinced the hostess to drive me to my duplex and let me off at the corner. I would tell Denise that Harris found a girl at the bar and I'd let him use my truck and had gotten stranded, excluding the other incriminating details of the evening. I lamented that the only thing I had to be sure to do, I'd failed to do: get home before Denise woke up. I entered as stealthily as possible—for naught as it turned out, since I entered to find Denise interrogating Harris in the living room. Harris could only stand and take it. He had his gaze turned downward and held it there, her reading him his rights, and him remaining silent. She'd caught him sneaking in the guest bedroom window mere minutes prior to my arrival.

"Where were you!?" she demanded when she saw me.

I didn't know what he'd already said. I stood stone-faced, prepared to hold my cards a little longer.

"And why was he crawling in the window?" she continued, suspicion etched on her face.

I wondered how in the hell Harris had found my duplex in Citrus Heights, but not the party in Sacramento.

"He found a lady friend and wanted some privacy," I muttered. "Isn't that right, Harris?"

"That's what I told her. You were doing me a favor and we got separated."

"Why didn't you call me?" Denise hissed. "Were you at the club all night?"

The club did stay open all night, and I told her that I'd talked a stranger into bringing me home. I wasn't about to tell her about the party or the other woman. "I didn't want to wake you," I added feebly.

The children soon entered the stage and derailed the ongoing drama. Because of the late night, I dozed that afternoon, and Denise rummaged through the belongings that I'd left on the counter, finding the woman's telephone number that had found its way to my wallet. Denise got in my face.

"What do you think you're doing, Larry? When are you going to grow up?"

Careless, clueless, foolish, I had no answer. I wondered the same thing.

She ordered Harris out of her sight and told me to begin packing. No more California. My attempt at an explanation fell on deaf ears. My lack of integrity came back to bite me. Shame hung on me like an ill-fitted white suit, too tight around my ribs, with an impossible to wash out black ink stain on the pocket.

In the days before we left, Denise, who was now more than six months pregnant, stopped talking to me. Lorene clung to her mother a little tighter and Jimmie needed constant monitoring as he toddled around the duplex. I made it my mission to keep my son out of trouble. My rude awakening rang in my ears, as did Harris' explanation: "I got lost and drove all over town before I recognized the freeway and found your house. I'm sorry." He left with Earl the next afternoon. I had no escape route. My life in California, and probably my marriage, was over.

CHAPTER 29

I purchased airline tickets for Denise and the kids, loaded our trucks high, reinforced them with tarps and clapboard, and hitched hers to mine. We would rendezvous at the airport in Tulsa, and I would ferry her and the kids the rest of the way to the house on Backstrom Street, unsure whether I'd be welcomed to join her. Moved by profound guilt, I would let the chips fall where they may.

As it turned out, she took pity on me, and let me sleep on the sofa once we reached the empty house and unloaded the furniture. We were not at ease with one another, but she would be delivering soon and, aware that she needed the income I brought in, tolerated my presence in an adjacent room.

The day her water broke, I was playing basketball with friends and rushed home to take her to the hospital. I was unexpectedly invited by the doctor to witness the birth. A nurse joined us as I nervously stood by, clad in my green outfit and face mask, fearful they'd ask me to leave if I made a sound. Now that I was in there, I was eager to see it. As he emerged, I instantly regretted my resistance to the news of his conception. He was a lot smaller than Jimmie, but most newborns were. A dad again, I planned to pass a few cheap cigars around after we took him home. Denise and I embraced while I wished my former indiscretions away. Within minutes, confusion replaced our joy. The baby struggled to breathe, and his face turned blue. The nurse shook him to

229

jumpstart his lungs. No luck. I looked on in horror while Denise appeared stunned by her labor like a bird crashing into a windowpane. The nurses finally whisked our child away. When the doctor returned, he told us the infant's lungs were underdeveloped and his survival expectancy was 50/50. He'd been moved to an ICU and was in critical condition. Devastated, uncertain, and without insurance, I sat in silence while Denise looked at me and wept.

As the days passed, the doctor informed us that Clayton was improving and hope surged. Denise was finally allowed to hold him, the frail, blond, brown-eyed son she'd fought so valiantly for, and at the end of the second week it became apparent that Clayton would survive. The doctors discharged him, and I found myself standing outside the hospital on a summer's day with my wife at my side and my second son, $10,000 in debt and without a way in the world to honor it. Denise and I managed because she still needed me. I wasn't sure what would happen when she didn't.

Clayton came with a bevy of medications and instructions. His lungs were weak, and his frame delicate, his stools dried out and chronically obstructed by the antibiotics saturating his body. At times, we had to extract his impacted feces with our fingers as he wailed at the top of his underdeveloped lungs. He became colicky, and it piled on the stress and stole sleep. But as the weeks progressed, he grew stronger.

We missed another house payment and the bank sent a letter warning of an impending foreclosure. Rex Sage, the old pro at the Springdale Golf Club who'd taught me how to swing when I was a kid, now ran a liquor store and agreed to hold a check for the amount of a house payment until I could make it good. He let me know it was the first and last time he would do it. I didn't know how I would pay him back.

Denise's brother, Brandon, moved back to Arkansas and was expecting a second child. After he got settled, he came over and filled us in on Earl's life. I braced myself for his caustic personality as he made himself comfortable in the living room and started making snarky comments about the unfolded blanket and pillow on the sofa I'd been sleeping on. Since he was back in town, he wanted to have a small quarter limit poker game at the house and Denise gave her consent. I invited some old friends.

The whiskey was cheap, and Brandon got so drunk, he quickly started losing hard and turned to cheating. He did it so poorly that at first, I thought he was hamming it up for laughs. Cards he wasn't supposed to have would flutter from his hand, and he would lean down and retrieve them sluggishly and scan each of us to see if we'd seen. We'd all been drinking, and the liquor was having its way, but none as badly as Brandon.

"You're cheating," I told him. "Cut it out. Everyone can see what you're doing."

"Are you calling me a cheater?" he asked, in an incredulous how-dare-you look.

"Yes, I am," I said. "We can all see it."

He offered, "You want to take it outside?"

I looked him over and realized he was there for the taking, and something evil came over me. Years of guff from this guy streamed into my memory banks, and suddenly nothing was funny.

"Yes, I do. Let's go, asshole."

It took him a minute to figure out that I meant it, but he got the idea and started mouthing off as we exited the front door. We stood in the front yard facing each other, and I felt anything and everything that kept me from kicking his ass in the past dissolved like smoke. He hauled off, tried to kick me in the crotch, and missed badly. I saw my opening and dropped him with a kick of my own to the balls. He went down and I went after him, head-locked him, and punched him without mercy. Rage took over as I pummeled him, turning his face to mud, pounding my knuckles slick, my fingers digging for his eyes while the bystanders seized my arms and dragged me across the lawn.

"You want some more!!" I howled at the pile on the grass.

Brandon slowly rose, wobbly from too much alcohol and my fist. The small gathering grew silent, and one by one, cast a sympathetic look toward Brandon, then a disgusted one at me. Denise's gaze was the most troubled. I saw the disappointment on her face and didn't care, didn't care that Brandon was her brother, didn't care that he was drunk and incapable of defending himself. It felt good and I felt no re-morse. The scene grew eerily quiet while I slowly came to grips with how I'd lost control.

The episode tipped the balance for Denise: the cost of staying with me finally outweighed my meager financial contributions and help with the children. I slept on the couch that night and woke to her announcing that she want-ed me out.

"Please just leave," she told me as I scrambled defensively for another chance. "I don't want you around anymore."

Void of anymore excuses, I complied. I left with whatever I could grab from the closet and drove to my sister Ruth's house. Before nightfall, it became clear that they didn't want me around either. Marty's lost business had infused their lives with financial strain and left no room for way-ward brothers. I lingered until late that evening in spite of Marty's stares, aware of all I'd done to bring me here, then left several hours after nightfall and drove until I reached a desolate road. I parked on the dirt shoulder, resolved to sleep there. My jacket served as a pillow and I lay across the cab with my mind torturing me. Reeling from the lack of options and more alone than ever, I sobbed uncontrollably. Remorse swallowed me. I didn't know if God existed, but that night, in the cab of my pickup, I begged Him to help me. My debts finally caught up with me. I fantasized briefly about the least painful way to end my pitiful existence. When the sun came up, I drove to my mother's house.

CHAPTER 30

My mother always stayed out of my personal struggles, had nothing to contribute to my insurmountable debts, and didn't know how to approach me. It'd been that way ever since I ran away nearly a decade before. She offered me the only thing she knew besides the bed she let me sleep in.

"Come to church with me," she said.

"I don't have any good clothes to wear," I complained. "Is that okay?" I wasn't crazy about the idea, but figured it was part of the agreement.

"The clothes don't matter. You'll look fine," she said.

After a few days of laying around, Sunday arrived. The reverend Clinton Pettigrew presided over a flock of at least 1,000 at the Springdale Congregation Church. Short and stocky, with thick white hair and glasses, Pettigrew exuded an air of confidence. The church grew under his leadership and my mother credited him with restoring her life after the humiliation of her husband's tarring and feathering. Smiling faces and handshakes bombarded me as I followed her through the crowd. I assumed I would go through the motions and get out of there as quickly as possible.

"Please stand and sing," called the music director.

We stood and hummed along with the choir, men and women dressed in crimson robes and accompanied by well-tuned instruments. Pettigrew appeared, his short stature towering over the throng from the elevated platform.

"Welcome," he declared. "I'm so glad everyone could come today. Please open your Bibles and read along."

On and on he preached, and the words passed over me. My mother nudged my elbow when he said something she thought I should be paying close attention to. I'd already forgotten about my plea in the truck just days before, and fidgeted until the choir sang the altar call and invitation of *I Surrender All* and the congregation joined in. As we sang, I felt weight settling in my chest. They were encouraging people to come forward and profess their faith in front of their brethren.

My chest grew heavier, and emotion coursed through me, the burden of the last decade crushing me. I sank into the pew as the invitation continued. My mother pulled on me to stand. I wept and refused to budge. People looked at me. I stood, picked my way frantically down the pew, and hurried out to the parking lot with my mother close behind. We met at the car and left, while inside the church, the invitation ended.

"You should have gone forward, Larry," she told me as she drove.

"Gone forward for what?" I snarled. I didn't know what going forward meant.

"To be saved," she replied.

I looked out the window for the rest of the ride home, and she said nothing more. Pettigrew had been talking about salvation for half an hour but I still didn't understand. My tears embarrassed me.

My mother asked, "Will you go with me next week?"

I conceded, "Whatever."

I had nothing to lose. I kept up the game, pretending she hadn't seen the torrent of repressed emotion. I snuck her Bible into my room that night and read passages that stoked my curiosity even more. The words leapt off the page and spoke directly to me. I laid the book down after reading verses that forgave my past transgressions and put in a good word for the ones I'd commit in the future, figuring that otherwise, I'd never make it.

The next week I returned to church with my mother, and this time I listened, heard reaping what you sow, heard forgiveness, heard redemption, heard unconditional love, and the ultimate sacrifice on the cross. He said I could come as I was.

The Spirit fell on me. In a moment of clarity, I watched my sordid past play out like an unsavory movie and an epiphany unfolded; God was in control and all I needed was a little faith. My eyes were blown open; my feet became light and I felt the fog lift. For the first time, I believed someone had my back.

I thought of Denise and how to plead for another chance. I hoped she wanted reconciliation as badly as I did and would find justification in my epiphany. I already missed my family, had a new example to follow, and would do whatever it took to start over with my wife and children.

PART IV
BAPTISM BY FIRE

LARRY DANIEL

CHAPTER 31

I didn't understand all I knew about my newfound faith, but was sick of the road I'd been on and determined to change. I met with Denise and vowed to make things right. After my mother put in a good word for me, I took to warming a front row seat every time the doors opened, and soaked up the wages of sin. I stood before the congregation on Easter Sunday in 1980, and was baptized, knowing that a good portion of the audience openly cheered while my family had suffered in the 1960s. My friends were dumbfounded with my about-face, but I didn't care. I lost my taste for drugs and alcohol and only had eyes for Denise.

It wasn't long before I started driving one of the church buses and picking up kids from the far reaches of rural Springdale to bring them to Sunday school. After the bus route, I oversaw a fifth grade boys' Sunday school class before joining Denise for the adult service. I also joined the church's city league basketball team and played with a few former college-level players. After I became more versed in scripture, I did some fill-in teaching for the adult Sunday school class. I volunteered for anything that came my way, driven by a genuine thirst for spiritual matters. I began associating with more stable influences and learned a lot about myself that I never knew.

In the midst of a major recession, the construction industry flagged, and Dennis became stingy with his use of me. My obligations remained and my creditors were unsympathetic, so it seemed a good time to do something about getting a high school diploma. I took a trip to the adult education center in Benton County to see about obtaining a GED. After I arrived, the staff gave me a five-page pretest to gauge which classes I would benefit the most from in preparation for my equivalency. After the pretest, an administrator met with me and informed me that I didn't need any classes and could take the final whenever I wanted. The following day, the official test proved even easier, and that was that.

I took a job driving a school bus for the public schools, and augmented that income with odd jobs for Dennis, and waiting tables at a restaurant in a neighboring town on weekends. Late payment notices, foreclosure warnings, and threats from the hospital kept rolling in. On the advice of friends, we sent $10 a month to forestall further harassment. Denise opened a day care for neighborhood kids so she could stay home with Clayton and Jimmie, and after selling her truck, we learned to rely on one vehicle even though Phyllis left a vehicle with Ruth that I could borrow if I needed to.

Like our ever-mounting debts, the ghosts of my past continued to shuffle through my life. One day I answered a knock on the door to find my old friend, Jonas Strickland, on the doorstep, and smelling to high heaven. We hadn't seen each other in years, not since our amphetamine fueled ramblings in his dingy bedroom with Rory, but apparently, word of my conversion spread.

"I heard you got religion," he said, while spying what he could see of the inside of my modest home. His clothes were rotten and he may have been drunk. A befuddled fog surrounded him.

I shot back, "Got a wife, kids, any of that?"

We both knew I'd let him in, but I didn't want to show too much of my hand just yet. I didn't know where he'd come from or how long he hoped to stay.

"I've got one daughter," he answered, "but I never see her anymore. My wife left me last year. Mom and Dad both died the year before that. I've been traveling the country."

His hair looked matted and filthy, as if he'd slept outdoors, and I saw no car at the curb behind him.

"How've you been getting around?" I asked, pretty sure of the answer beforehand.

"My thumb's how. I go all over. Wherever they go, I go."

A vagabond, just like the rescue mission people I'd stayed with in Little Rock as a wet-nosed 15-year-old. "I've been everywhere," he added, a braggart's note slipping into his voice.

He'd clearly gone a long time without bathing, and now he needed money, food—whatever I had. I was faced with proving my professed benevolence, and even Denise couldn't deny the opportunity that showed up at our door. Indoors, he eased off his shoe and showed me a hollowed-out sore on his foot that was infected and oozing. I ran a hot bath, made him a sandwich that he inhaled, and washed what I could of his nasty clothes. I didn't have any money I couldn't do without, but I offered to call somebody about a job at the paper company I'd previously worked in, and he agreed to give it a try. I made arrangements and they told me to bring him in.

We found him a cot in the empty garage, I gave him clothes to wear, and drove him to work each day before setting off to work myself. He got two squares a day and came and went as he pleased, but most of the time, he kept to himself, becoming engrossed in a book he'd found about airplanes.

After Jonas got his first paycheck, I let him borrow the truck so he could look around for a cheap room to rent after another week or two of paydays. It felt good to help him get back in the game, maybe see his daughter again, and improve his life. I saw myself in Jonas, on the street, lost and struggling, and just needing someone to step up and care. I could be that somebody.

I watched from the front porch as my truck returned, Jonas wheeling into the driveway, the bed filled with plywood and two by fours.

"I'm going to build an airplane," he announced, confident that he would soon be flying his wooden plane to destinations unknown. "I won't have to hitchhike anymore."

At first, I took it as a joke but grudgingly had to accept that he was beyond my help.

"Jonas, I want to take you to see some people, okay?"

"What people?" he inquired.

From my concerned expression he understood what I meant. It gave him pause, the question, apparently a familiar one. Finally, without conceding the lumber idea was foolish, he agreed on one condition: I had to keep an eye on his wood.

I drove him to the hospital and walked with him to the psychiatric ward where he stood by meekly while I talked to the people at the desk, then went quietly into a back room to be analyzed. Surprisingly, they admitted him without any money or insurance, and I drove away feeling like he was in good hands. Still, I was determined to follow up on his care and visited him the next day.

I sat down next to him while he colored in a coloring book. His was pondering color choices and focusing on staying in the lines.

"They got a plan for you, Jonas?"

"Looks like I got some problems to work out," he replied, mumbling the last few words. While we talked, his eyes shifted, first checking for any staff within earshot, then suspiciously at me for an instant, then back at the coloring book.

"What are you coloring?" I asked.

"Heck," he blurted out, "I knew that!" It took me a minute to realize he was still stuck on the physician's line, "problems to work out." As if problems to work out could encompass what his life had become, much less the logistical issues that go into building an airplane.

He rose and demanded, "Is my lumber okay?"

"I've got your lumber, Jonas."

"They gave me some pills," he said, sitting back down, "but I only pretend to take them. They're trying to control my mind. You think you can bring my wife and daughter in here?"

I didn't know what to say. "I'll try," I promised, feeling hollow.

She hailed from my hometown and I remembered her from my sparse high school days. I went to see her at her parent's plain but well-positioned home where she now lived, and she gave me the details: Jonas' mother and father died a couple of years before after lengthy illnesses, just a few months apart, and ever since, Jonas grew increasingly paranoid, enough to warrant treatment, which he refused. He worsened, and imagined people were out to get him. He'd vanish without a word, and she decided that she couldn't subject her daughter to it any longer.

"He drifts into town every so often and then disappears for months at a time," she explained. She thanked me for trying to help, but warned me not to get too wrapped up in it. "He knows the drill at the hospital," she added.

I promised Jonas that I'd return, but when I did, he was gone. He walked out on his own volition, probably onto the road again, on some semi-truck to nowhere in particular. He left the lumber for his airplane in my yard.

Two more ghosts would visit me that year. After Wendy left Earl, he made his way back to Arkansas to see Brandon for a few days. I hadn't seen much of Brandon since our fist fight.

Earl, and his dog, Slick, drove across the country without a hiccup in his gadget-controlled vehicle. Brandon notified Denise that Earl wanted to drop by and see me. I'd always been fond of him and looked forward to it. Brandon wheeled Earl into the living room then took a seat next to him, smirking while Earl seemed puzzled.

"What's this I hear about you?"

"A lot has happened, Earl," I answered, "and my life couldn't be better." It was true, my life was considerably better. While Denise stood next to me, I ventured a discussion with my old friend, and said, "I've changed my ways." I thought maybe I could help get him clean.

Earl smiled. "Tell me more," he insisted.

Brandon bolt upright and yelled, "We're not going to sit around and listen to this shit!"

I kept his gaze. I'd already bloodied his nose. He couldn't know what I might do but he wasn't about to lose his closest friend to a Jesus freak. "Not another fucking word!" he snarled, gripping Earl's wheelchair.

Earl looked sheepish. I wanted to help my friend. He was curious and wanted some answers, but Brandon was the one calling the shots and pushing the wheelchair.

"I can drive you," I reasoned.

"I appreciate that, Larry, but I got to go anyways I guess. You know how Brandon gets."

I watched him surrender to Brandon, and the homecoming was over. I knew him when paralysis was fresh on his mind and wondering how he'd get through it. His struggle would soon be over.

Earl said goodbye, and after a couple of more days with Brandon he returned to California. Soon after, alone in his small bedroom, he drew up a little more than usual and killed more than the pain. Brandon called Denise, shaken, but ever defiant in his final analysis of his lifelong friend. Earl went out on his own terms.

Despondent, unable to make ends meet, and mysteriously drawn to find out what happened to his best friend, Brandon returned to northern California, eventually hooking up with Earl's friends. Months passed until one day Denise got a call from Douglas. Brandon, too, had overdosed, leaving a wife and two children behind. Denise was inconsolable.

I could no longer look back, only straight ahead.

LARRY DANIEL

CHAPTER 32

On a warm spring day in 1982, after mowing the yard and letting Lorene help a little because she asked to, I instructed her to put away the mower's near-empty gas can before I went inside for water. Slick with sweat, I admired the neatly trimmed lawn, feeling blessed and optimistic. The small house's utility room sat off the narrow kitchen and housed a water heater. It was here that Lorene decided to leave the gas can because the door stood open to the yard. I'd settled down to take a nap and she came inside to watch television by the time Clayton, not quite three years old, ambled into the utility room and overturned the gas can. Five-year-old Jimmie followed him and called me from the bedroom. I found Clayton sitting drenched on the cement floor and quickly snatched him up and took him to the bathtub to wash off the gasoline. Jimmie followed me in. I'd never thought twice before turning on the hot water, and I didn't think twice that day. I hadn't even gotten the temperature mix right when the explosion came from the utility room, blowing the kitchen door off its hinges. Flames lunged through the aperture. Smoke followed—black, dense, and lethal—and the smoke detector and parakeet shrilled in panicked harmony. I wasn't sure where Lorene was.

I seized Clayton from the tub, wrapped him in a towel, and plunged into the living room, where Denise, with panic and fear etched on her face, screamed hysterically for her children.

"Jimmie!"

"Lorene!"

"Get out now!"

It's curious what people do in the initial seconds of a crisis. I scrambled for a few seconds to find clothes to put on before realizing decency had become a luxury. Denise grabbed Jimmie, who'd appeared from behind me. I held onto a naked but toweled Clayton, and Lorene, up from the living room floor, led the dash for the front door. We met curbside across the street and watched the windows pop and flames feel their way like blinded fingers around the sills. I couldn't bear just standing there. There had to be something I could quickly grab now that everyone was out. I handed Clayton to Denise and headed back across the street, ignoring her reprimands.

The door was open, with heat and black smoke pouring out at shoulder level. I crouched and scanned, with no idea what I'd come for. Just then, the parakeet's squawk cleared through the smoke and I made for it. I couldn't see the top of the cage attached at the ceiling so I reached in and grabbed the bird through the gate. I crawled out under smoke and returned with a screaming parakeet in my hand, to Denise and the kids, who stood terrified and sobbing at the roadside. The neighbors trickled out to investigate, and a siren trilled in the distance.

Firemen descended from a yellow fire truck and laid down the hose. A couple of men in heavy uniforms and breathing gear entered the house through the front door with a high-pressure water hose. A red car pulled up and parked down the street. The driver got out and spoke into a walkie-talkie, apparently giving orders to the firemen. He wore a white creased shirt that displayed a gold badge over his left chest. Another man in heavy gear leaned a ladder against the house and took an axe up to the roof, chopping in it a hole to let out smoke. In a matter of minutes, the black plume turned pale and dissipated, and the man in the red car approached me. I'd witnessed an attack that equaled the fervor of the fire itself; a hole in the roof, water pouring over the front door threshold. Now it seemed I had some explaining to do.

"My three-year-old spilled some gas near the water heater," I explained. "It blew when I turned on the hot water to wash him off."

He introduced himself as the fire chief. He was tall and lanky and had droopy eyes. His black slacks and boots completed his officer level uniform. "I'm Max Johnson," he added. "I might have some more questions for you later, so don't leave town, okay?"

Standing in my shorts with a naked three-year-old wrapped in a towel, I looked on as the men collected their equipment. Denise was busy composing herself and reassuring the children while I wasn't sure where we were going to stay that night. After they left the scene, we ventured back inside to find water dripping from the blackened ceiling. Pools lay everywhere. I could see the blue through the soaked and caved in sheetrock directly under the recently carved hole. The damage extended throughout the house, from the cabinets and walls to the clothes in the closet. Thankfully though, the wooden frame seemed mostly spared.

I knew how lucky we'd been that Jimmie fetched me when he did. Otherwise, Clayton could have been severely burned or killed. I bowed my head and quietly thanked God for sparing us that misery. I restored the bird to its cage. Besides ourselves, it was all we'd salvaged.

That first night, we rummaged up enough money for a run-down motel studio in Springdale, and stayed there over a week while we waited for the insurance company to give us a number.

After a week of haggling, I finally secured a check for $16,000, which gave us some unexpected breathing room. I felt confident that my building experience would let me replace the guts of our burned-out home and honor some debts before rebuilding and have it ready to go for close to half of the settlement. We moved from the tiny motel to a modest but lovely home in town that was offered to us by a fellow church member at a reasonable price. I prioritized hospital bills and overdue house payments. I paid back Rex Sage.

A call came from my dad after a period of little contact following my shameful departure from California. He settled up with his business partner after completing the homes in Rocklin, and he and Phyllis moved to the tiny logging town of Cazadero amid the coastal redwoods north of San Francisco. He put the back-breaking work of building houses behind him. I knew he'd built the houses in Rocklin as his last hurrah, not just for himself, but also for me.

Now, he turned redwood burls into clocks and coffee tables. The redwood burl was the fallen redwood's root ball, dug up years after the trees came down, and Cazadero crawled with the stuff. Living among the massive groves of giant redwoods seemed to take the edge off his temper as he tried to decompress from the turbulent 1970s.

He accumulated all the equipment needed to transform the bare wood, including a monstrous Alaskan chain saw to ensure level slabs and an acetylene torch to score the edges and crevices. A sand blaster cleared the debris, a wood planer, and belt sander revealed the beautiful grain. A finish oil or lacquer gave the end product a glossy, high polish shine. Dad started making a redwood clock with a pendulum for me and wanted me to come out to see it. Phyllis' car was in Arkansas and he said I could use it. Really, I think he wanted an excuse to see Jimmie again and meet Clayton. He enjoyed being a grandfather.

Before beginning the restoration of the Backstrom house, the boys and I granted his wish and traveled to the redwood forest with Denise's blessing. The three of us loaded up in the Karman Ghia and drove to Colorado to visit a friend before arriving at my father's small, two bedroom cabin a day and a half later. Its dull red clapboard siding hung loose in places, and the old metal roof lay thick with forest debris. Thirty yards from the shelter, a narrow creek sung its way through a redwood grove that blocked the sun and served as air-conditioning. A mother duck swam in the clear creek, brood in tow, while the smell of fresh rain rose from the forest floor. Jimmie and Clayton pitched rocks across the water prompting my old man to crack a big smile.

My father was still damaged goods. When he talked, he still mentioned the people that ruined him, but some remorse was starting to show, and I started hearing regret from the face that sported the full gray beard of a hermit. He still drank for his gout and smoked weed for a variety of reasons, but we talked like adults for a change. He heard about my conversion from Ruth, but refrained from asking about the church. Instead, he encouraged me, announcing, "You ought to be able to rebuild that house yourself."

"I know what to do," I said." If I need some help, Dennis can pitch in." In truth, his sudden confidence surprised me, but I didn't let it show.

The boys and I took in the sights for a few days before heading south across the Golden Gate Bridge to Hazel's house near Laguna Beach for a day and a night, bringing the clock he'd made for me. On our way home, we detoured over to the Grand Canyon and took some pictures.

I got to work on the house, removing the damaged sheetrock and replacing the damp insulation. After repairing the section of roof that had gone missing during the fire department's ventilation efforts, I replaced a few damaged windows and stripped everything down to studs and joists. Denise's stepdad, Carlton, helped with the drywall, taping the sheetrock with drywall mud and texturing it after it dried. I painted everything an avocado green after he'd finished then laid down new carpet. We moved in before I finished applying the finishing touches on the new cabinets. The gorgeous redwood clock that my father made brought it all together, hanging proudly in the living room and chiming on the hour. Despite never mentioning religion, I discovered that he discreetly carved, *The Lord is my Shepherd*, on the clock's upper right corner.

CHAPTER 33

One appealing option stood before me: the Ministry. We'd strayed far under Lemus, but I resolved to bring us back into the fold like my grandfather Daniel before me. Many of the church members whom I'd befriended encouraged me. Unsure of my next step, I made an appointment to see Clinton Pettigrew to ask him how I should proceed. The receptionist showed me in. Every advanced theological study guide available stood stacked on an elaborate shelf. Pictures of him in the Holy Land with prominent figures covered the walls. I didn't know what a prospective Minister ought to sound like, so I decided to present myself as honestly as possible.

"I've prayed about it a lot, sir," I began, soft-spoken and eager to learn. "I've been faithful for more than two years and want to serve as best I can. I hoped you could direct me as to the next step. I think I want to attend a school of theology." Like my mother, I idolized Pettigrew and sat mesmerized every Sunday by his sermons. Whatever advice he gave, I would follow it.

"Your wife has been married before," he said. "Isn't that right?"

A familiar feeling crept toward me but I tried to push it down. I wanted to believe I'd put my past as an outcast behind me, and didn't want to entertain the notion that my own sins and those of my father might have followed me into the church.

"Yes sir," I said. "That's right."

"The Bible says that because you've married a divorced woman, you can't serve as an elder or pastor."

Then silence.

I'd read the passage Pettigrew referred to, but had come to him assuming that my intentions would count for something more than a single, obscure line of scripture. Maybe it would have if I weren't the son of one of the most notorious men that Springdale ever gave residence to. But, as it stood, this man of God didn't want to guide, instruct, or otherwise associate with me in any way. I nodded because I didn't know what else to do.

The pastor showing me the door turned out to be a blessing in disguise.

With the house finished and our debts erased, we resumed a frugal lifestyle. A fence finally surrounded the oversized back yard we'd lucked into back in 1978, keeping the kids in eyesight and giving us the green light for an outdoor pet someday. The kids remained close, doing coloring books together, playing games like hide and seek, and watching Saturday morning cartoons. On occasion, Lorene's dad, Fred, who'd paid a small stipend in child support over the years, would pick her up for a day out. They all wore hand-me-downs. Lorene kept a stiff upper lip, bracing for the peer pressure of her teen years that lay just ahead. The used clothes hung awkwardly off Jimmie's gangly frame, but were taken in stride. Clayton always looked adorable because of his small stature and curly blond hair. On Sunday, we still attended church. Food was followed by football on TV, then finally, an afternoon nap.

But Pettigrew's rejection dampened my fire. We kept up our attendance, I think because Denise and I both feared what we might become, and also that Pettigrew was one man, and

I still felt certain there was a ministry for me somewhere out there. In the meantime, I attended another church at the invitation of some guys I'd played church-league basketball against. One of them, a fireman-paramedic for the city, remembered my house fire from earlier in the year. Crandle Smith, a tall, muscular, dark-haired Californian with a classic handlebar mustache, joined the department soon after he'd relocated from Long Beach five years earlier. That spring, he'd gone into my house with a charged hose-line while I stood half-naked across the street with a parakeet in my hand. Gil Foster, another fireman-paramedic, joined us while we talked after church one day in the fall of 1982.

"It was fully involved," Crandle recounted, recalling my house fire. I found the hot spot in the back corner of the kitchen and blasted it with a direct pattern. If my memory serves me, the water heater exploded."

Gil chimed in, "You're lucky no one was killed."

Later, at a party hosted by a mutual friend, Crandle approached me with an idea. "You're strong, Larry, and athletic. You ever think about becoming a fireman?" Not ever would've been the correct answer, but the possibility intrigued me enough to keep listening.

"I can't say that I have. Kind of dangerous, isn't it?"

Crandle shrugged it off. "I bet you'd be good at it."

Gil filled me in. "They're hiring now," he explained. "You just take a test at the city administration building to see if you qualify. Go down to the fire department and get an application."

"And you'll have to get an EMT certificate if you get hired," Crandle added. Medical calls represented an integral part of the job, and if I put in that application, I would have a lot to learn. The more I thought about it, the more implausible it seemed. *And even if I managed to master all of that information, would I have the wherewithal to go into a burning building on purpose like they did? Could I pull mangled bodies out of cars?* I thanked them for the information and told them I would think about it, and then put it aside for a while.

Restoring the house on Backstrom Street ate up a lot of cash, and we began living hand-to-mouth again. I still waited tables on the weekend, and every now and then, Dennis called me to do small jobs. I still drove the school bus, but on one day, a Doberman Pinscher on a suicide mission ricocheted out of a yard and landed under the tires. I thought I'd cleared it until the rear tires jolted over its body, raising the kids from of their seats and evoking a collective groan. The owner, who'd witnessed the incident, didn't fault me, but after that, I felt my passengers' trust in me ebbing.

Our situation worsened when I air-nailed a sixteen penny spike through my work boot and heel while standing on a wooden platform eight feet off the floor, as I framed ceiling joists to the top of a wall for Dennis. I had to pry the nail (with my foot attached) from the wood I was standing on with a hammer to unfasten it, shimmy down to the floor, slide needle-nosed pliers under the spike head flush with the boot to pull it out. I nearly fainted. Swelling and pain aside, I couldn't afford to lose more than a half hour's wages. I hadn't seen a doctor in years and didn't have insurance.

A week later, still limping around on a foot that hardly fit my boot, I asked Dennis to drop me off at the fire station. He waited in the parking lot while I went in, dirty clothes, hole-torn boots and all, and asked for an application.

I needed a job with benefits, but even more than that, I wanted to do something worthwhile, honorable and helpful to others—something my marital status and my past wouldn't bar me from. After I got back in the truck with Dennis, I told him my plans. "It wouldn't hurt to try," he said. "I'm pulling for you."

While inside the cavernous fire house, I peeked at the long, yellow fire truck beds piled high with rows of neatly stacked hoses. I glanced at the daunting sets of dials near the elevated cabs, and at the ambulance box with its high-tech gadgetry and tricolor light bar. I couldn't even imagine what kind of test I'd have to take to earn a check here.

As test day approached, I doubted myself, and even considered not showing up at all. The specter of public embarrassment haunted me, but when the day arrived, I found myself sitting at a desk in city hall with a room full of other aspiring civil servants facing an IQ test, a test I'd never even heard of. The proctor gave instructions, and at 9:45 a.m. announced, "You may begin." I had three hours to deal with the peculiar ecosystem of squiggly lines and hypnotic diagrams that filled the pages before me. I finished in two. Walking out of city hall early had me feeling cocky, and certain I did well. But even so, I didn't expect the news I received the next day. Out of all the applicants, I finished *second*.

They put me on a list of qualified applicants. The next step involved me and three other men who excelled in tests held a few months earlier vying for the single opening now available. Crandle advised me to join the volunteer group that worked alongside of the paid department to get experience. He left no doubt that good ol' boy politics would be in play. Construction work kept me fit, but I worried about my dad's reputation, even after all these years. But after my background check came back clean, I sized up the competition. One of the other guys on the short list was good friends with one of the captains. All I could do was rub elbows and pray.

I took Crandle's advice and joined the volunteer team who, for the most part, liked the jobs they already had, or had retired, but loved the action and had friends on the paid staff. Unlike the paid staff, they got to go home at night to their families instead of working 24-hour shifts. At my first meeting, I received a pair of the traditional yellow flame-retardant pants with red suspenders that held up the weighty britches, and a yellow helmet with my last name stenciled in red across the bill. I pulled on the jacket and rubber boots, donned the fire-retardant hood under the helmet, and pushed my hands into the heavy-duty gloves to complete the ensemble. I would have to trust this gear with my life if everything went as planned.

It was starting to dawn on me how badly I wanted this job.

I continued attending fire training sessions, scraped up enough cash for an EMT class, and was exuberant when I learned the first practice burn was in a couple of weeks. The city purchased a vacant house on the outskirts of town for training purposes, and it would be set on fire so we could put it out.

On the morning of the practice burn, we gathered at the station for a lecture and watched a video about the hazards of what we were about to do. Graphic images flashed on the screen, accompanied by somber commentary on the mistakes that led to civil servants' injuries and deaths. The not-so-subtle attempt to make us reconsider our candidacy went unheeded.

The gutted structure stood by itself in an open field, its front skirted by a six-foot porch, and missing most of its windows. I clamored into my gear and sucked compressed air through the mask from the 25-pound cylinder strapped to my back. I had to be sure it worked, otherwise I wouldn't be able to breathe. One of the captains went around back to light a fire, and we waited for it to become fully involved before making our entry. Cinched up tight in my gear and uniform with my pulse racing, I fell behind my training officer, Lieutenant-Paramedic Billy Brooks, on the charged line.

"Stay behind me and hang onto the hose," he called over his shoulder. "It's your means of egress if it comes to that." The face mask muffled his every word, so he raised his voice to compensate. "Stay low!"

I remembered my own house fire and how I'd flattened myself beneath the smoke. It would be easier this time I reasoned, I didn't have a parakeet to account for. We eased open the front door and crawled into the darkness on our hands and knees. I began sweating and hyperventilating. If I couldn't control it, I knew I would prematurely suck the tank dry. We felt our way further into the house, groping, bumping into walls, and unable to see anything. To cut the heat, Brooks sprayed a fog pattern over the ceiling as we pressed forward, in search of the red glow, our enemy. But he'd waited too long. Vivid crimson flames erupted above us, spreading over the ceiling and down the walls, sealing our egress, and burning through the hose line. I knew from studying my training manual that fires like these spiked well above 1,000 degrees. It didn't matter that his mask muffled his words. I knew what to do. I'd felt the slack in the hose line.

Abandoning the door we'd come in from, I flung myself toward a large window that was visible beneath the smoke—it was thankfully free of glass—and slithered through. I didn't feel the bacon-strip sized burn on my chin until I reached the porch, but I didn't have time to nurse the sting. I swung back toward the window to check on Brooks in the same moment that he tumbled through, leading with his shoulder and sending me sprawling off the front porch. I lay winded beneath him like an upturned turtle, gasping for air. And in the sky above us, Chief Johnson's face appeared like a grinning mid-day moon.

"So," he said, fighting to contain his amusement, "you want to be a fireman, do you?"

I pulled off my mask with air I'd only barely managed to choke down, and told him, "Yes sir, I do."

I started hanging out at the firehouse after that and met a few of the full-time guys. Word spread of my chin burn and it gave me a hint of credibility, albeit for the wrong reasons. I strengthened this reputation by helping Springdale handily defeat Fayetteville in the annual basketball game, and the following Monday, Chief Johnson called me into his office and told me I had the job. "I think you'll be a real asset to our department," he said. "I'm going to put you on C Shift with Captain Hand. You'll start after a two-week orientation."

I left the station in a giddy haze. No more waiting for Dennis to call. No more rude customers at the 41 Café. No more bus routes. This job meant a regular paycheck and benefits for my family. Denise and I could have things now, pay our bills and raise our children.

But one of the men I'd beaten out for the job was a friend of Captain Hand's, and that had consequences. Hand promised the young man a job at the department, but thanks to me, he failed to deliver. On my first day of orientation, Hand approached me, and I told him I couldn't wait to get started.

Hand wore an old-style crew cut and looked just like Mississippi's infamous racist, Bull Conner. He had a reputation for snoring so loud at night that most of the crew moved their mattresses into the bay room so they could sleep. He gripped my hand in a sweaty palm and leaned in close. "My boots had better be shined, probey, and the toilet had better be clean enough to drink out of. You hear me?"

Probeys—probationary firefighters—could be let go within a year for practically any reason. Maybe everybody got hazed like this, maybe not. From where I stood, it didn't really matter. I kept up my smile and said, "Yes sir."

"You won't make it here," Hand informed me before walking away.

This job was closer to redemption than I'd ever thought I'd come. I didn't care what kind of shit I'd have to take from Hand; I wasn't going anywhere.

CHAPTER 34

Orientation consisted of riding out on fire and medical calls and assisting as instructed. Medical calls outnumbered fire calls four to one. After I passed the EMT exam, I was allowed to drive the ambulance. By then, I'd found my way around the call center, bunk room, hose bay, and kitchen, and acquired the nickname, "Preacher," based I guess, on what little the guys at the station thought they knew about me. Since I finished near the top of my EMT class, Lieutenant Brooks encouraged me to continue my education by enrolling in paramedic school. The department would pay for it, and I could attend classes on the days I didn't work. Chief Johnson was delighted by my willingness to continue schooling, and told me a small raise would come after I'd completed the 1,200-hour clinical rotation and 18 months of classes. I was grateful for the opportunity.

So far, nothing—not Captain Hand's hostility, not even the practice burn—led me to second-guess the new path I'd stepped into, but my first dead-on-arrival call as a certified EMT shook my conviction like nothing else ever had. I started spending nights at the firehouse ever since completing my orientation and Lt. Brooks kept me company by squeezing in a few extra hours of mentoring between his daytime duties. The alarm roused us one morning at 2:00 a.m., the bell clanged, and lights came on. *Squad One. . .Respond to the intersection of Old School Road and Molly Avenue for an MVA with possible DOA,* the loudspeaker roared. . .*Code three.*

Squad was a term used for an ambulance and its two-man crew, and if the squad didn't leave out of the station within three minutes of any alarm, everyone onboard would get a reprimand. "Squad one is responding," Brooks announced, scrambling to button his shirt one-handed. I grabbed my comb, but waited to use it until I'd reached the driver's seat and swung the ambulance out onto the road, siren screaming. We soon reached the scene to find a compact car wedged in a ditch by the roadside, further impacted by its collision with the concrete culvert. A police officer who beat us to the scene pointed to a body that was ejected through the car's sunroof and lay face down 60 feet away. As we got closer, I saw a woman in her mid-40s and dressed in late-night, honky-tonk attire, lying still. Brooks crouched beside her and checked for a pulse. When he rose, his face answered our questions. "Neck's broken," he announced. Then, to me, he said, "Trauma dead, stay dead, Larry. There's nothing we can do."

I could smell the alcohol in the blood that oozed from her head wound. I can still smell it as I type this now.

"That's how it is in the mud, the blood, and the beer," Brooks informed me on our way back to the station. Johnny Cash. *A Boy Named Sue.* Don't take it so hard, he seemed to be telling me. In this line of work, you couldn't afford to. Back at the station, we crawled back into our bunks to sleep. Brooks, I think, really did sleep, but I couldn't even pretend. *What,* I wondered, as I lay on my back, gazing at the ceiling of the house, *had I gotten myself into?*

The last few months had been a whirlwind, earning the job, and now, mired in the grind of paramedic school. The fear of being pulled back down into the meager existence we'd left behind kept Denise supportive, and me, motivated. It wasn't easy to get out of bed to go to church because of the tough schedule, so sometimes we didn't, but Denise remained rock solid through the pressures of my schooling. She let her hair down on Halloween night of my first year on the job and snuck into the bunk room while I was on duty. With a half dozen firemen sleeping nearby, and still in costume from a party that she attended earlier that night, she slipped into my bunk and woke me up. Startled, I immediately worried about Hand discovering her. She said she was horny.

"Quiet," I whispered, then put a finger to her mouth. She giggled briefly but then kept it to a whisper.

She grabbed my junk. "Lighten up, and let's get busy," she commanded.

Her geisha girl costume inspired me to do what needed to be done, but quietly. If Hand woke up and discovered us, it would have spelled big trouble for me, but she slipped out undetected.

My probationary year passed in a blur. Paramedic school consumed what remained of my time after brutal all-night shifts, and introduced me to the perils of sleep deprivation. In the emergency room, I learned to evaluate injuries and take control of crisis, perform endo-tracheal intubations, start IV's, defibrillate, push emergency meds, and perform chest decompressions in stranger's living rooms. I strived to be a street doctor, the first to arrive, and the one most likely to prevent deaths. My training made me a specialist in car crashes, heart attacks, gunshot wounds, major strokes, and suicide attempts. Brooks praised me, and slowly but steadily, my confidence grew.

The day I became a nationally registered paramedic, I celebrated by enrolling to become a CPR, advanced cardiac life support, and advanced trauma life support instructor, following in Brook's footsteps. I was hired in early 1983, and by late 1985, I'd run out of things to accomplish on the medical side, having racked up every certification, designation, and patch I could get my hands on. I remained inexplicably leery of pregnancy calls, though. I spent enough time in school to realize that most babies will come without much help, but if a problem arose, like a cord around the neck, a breech delivery—I feared that I might panic. I recalled the faith that Denise and I put in doctors to deliver our children, imagined someone putting that faith in me, and the thought made my palms sweat. But inevitably, the call came in one day, a request for Squad One to respond to a possible delivery at the corner of Highway 112 up in Cave Springs.

Traffic was heavy, but by dodging in and out of jams, we managed to arrive in fifteen minutes. Our patient sat on a chair outside of the market, calm, collected, and carrying a small bag with personal items in it. Her water broke 20 minutes before. She wouldn't name a husband, doctor, emergency contact, or partner. I took down her name, Lorraine, got her date of birth, and figured I'd get the rest later. While Lorraine grimaced through her contractions, the driver made no apparent effort to avoid potholes. Not long after I'd prepped her, and with five miles between us and the hospital, she crowned, causing the cramped space in the ambulance box to grow even tighter. I shouted to the driver to stop and he did.

Out the baby came, head first, covered in blood and mucous, and I caught him, suctioned his nose and heard him cry. We were still a few minutes from the ER, so I swaddled him and gently set him on his mother's chest. We drove in slowly while I observed her bonding with her newborn son. As she looked up at me and smiled, I fully absorbed the meaning my new career held. I dress bandaged her and we delivered the placenta after reaching the hospital. Back at the station, I could barely contain myself. Accepting congratulations from other experienced medics, and sharing their own unique delivery adventures made me feel as if I belonged.

In spite of all the medical training I mastered, I was never too excited about pumping a fire engine. A pump engineer provided water pressure to the men up front and required specific training, training I had very little of. I preferred being one of the men up front, on the charged line going inside. One shift, Hand found me and announced that our regular pump operator called in sick, and if a fire call came in, I would pump in his place. I protested that I didn't have the credentials. "Too bad," he shot back, "you should have been learning." Sure enough, a call came in for a house fire, leaving me to give the men water pressure and keep it. I wheeled the fire truck into place and awaited the signal to connect the main hose line to the pump to keep a consistent flow of water going straight from the hydrant. The truck held several hundred gallons for an early attack but it drained quickly and needed the backup. Proper priming was essential during the transfer. My prime was inadequate and the hose line remained limp. Captain Hand lost his mind.

"Probey!" he screamed as he kicked the limp hose that spooled off the fire truck, "Get that goddamned thing hard!"

I sidelined the fire and made myself the spectacle. Frantic, I scrambled with the knobs for a few seconds before Hand forced me aside. "Probey's nothing but an ambulance jockey," I heard him mutter loudly enough to be heard over the hiss of water dousing the fire, as he walked away.

The next day, I paid a visit to Chief Johnson's office telling him I didn't want to be under Hand anymore.

Johnson was aware of Hand's spite, but kept it on the down-low, which I appreciated. "I can put you on B shift with Captain Street," he told me. They whistle a different tune over there but maybe you can fit in." I heard the last two words loud and clear.

The department operated in three shifts, and each had its own "personality." I'd most likely ended up with Hand, a deacon at a small church on the east side of town, because of my reputation as "The Preacher." B Shift had a rowdier vibe. Captain Horace Street was a hefty hillbilly from the far side of Madison County who wore overalls when he was off duty, and knew everything there was to know about the fire service. Unlike Hand and most of his compatriots, Street didn't resent the medical side. The older pre-paramedic-era firemen mostly saw the medics as a bunch of egomaniacs who didn't respect them or the older traditions of the department. Given that the medic's workload grossly exceeded that of the non-medics, we probably didn't. Street didn't concern himself with any of that, and welcomed me to my new shift by chasing me around with a live cattle prod that he brought up from his farm. He sparked it on the bed rails and chortled, going after the other guys when I proved agile enough to avoid him.

Along with a pump operator/EMT and Lieutenant at three strategically located substations in town, there were six of us at the main station, all firemen, but divided by our specific jobs. Besides the Captain, there were two paramedics who rotated first-out assignments, along with the pump operator, and two EMT's, who also rotated first-out assignments. B Shift included Buster, a seasoned paramedic with seven years of service. The afternoon of my first shift with the B crew, a call came in for an unresponsive woman on Yancey Drive.

"Buster," Street ordered, "take Larry with you on this one."

After we arrived at an older home nestled among a few others with overgrown lawns and a little trash in the yard, a bevy of family members greeted us. "Grandma Kilpatrick's having a heart attack," a middle-aged man in dirty slacks and a stained shirt declared.

The man's taciturn wife stood with a cousin who called the son after failing to rouse the old woman. "I've read where they pass out," the man continued, sweat standing out on his brow, "when they're having a heart attack. Please hurry."

We were led inside and to a back bedroom, where Grandma Kilpatrick was lying still. We both noticed the unresponsive woman's fruity breath and pegged her as a diabetic, the coma a result of low blood sugar, or maybe high, also a problem. We didn't know yet. Buster monitored her vitals and checked her EKG, while I checked her blood sugar with a finger stick, and the family looked on, blinking somberly. "She's got a very low blood sugar," I announced finally.

"What about her heart?" the man persisted.

I answered, "We're checking, but I don't see a problem yet." I started to explain the next step but Buster shushed me and told me to start an IV, but delay pushing the sugar through until he signaled.

"You'll know," he whispered. "Just go along with it." Turning back to the family, he called for everyone's attention, ordering, "Come close and gather around. Now, close your eyes."

"What?" the old man demanded. "Why?"

"Close your eyes now and pray with me," Buster insisted without flinching.

"Oh, my," the wife gasped. Buster stood motionless, head bowed. Puzzled, they glanced at me, but I said nothing. I just began screwing the cylinder of Dextrose-50 onto its needle so I could push it into the IV port and save the woman's life. Finally, in a circle, they lowered their heads to pray, obviously the signal. I administered the sugar. After a minute of vague pleading for Granny Kilpatrick to wake up and be alright, Buster turned to the unconscious woman to summon her.

"Wake up, Grandma Kilpatrick!"

By then, the sugar circulated in her bloodstream, her eyes snapped open, and she glared up into her stunned family's faces. They might as well have seen her levitate.

"How in the world?" the wife asked. Buster peeked toward the ceiling. All for my benefit, I assumed. I didn't know what kind of regulations applied here or whether Buster might be getting us in trouble, so I hastened to get the equipment box loaded into the ambulance. Grandma Kilpatrick started asking questions.

It was a stressful job, constant exposure to people in crisis, grotesque accidents, and dead bodies, including children, took its toll on my colleagues' home lives. I took some shots for my faith, but through these trials, it helped keep my marriage working.

We'd paid our dues, and wanted to provide the kids a regular childhood and upbringing. We enjoyed the simple pleasures of watching them learn to ride their new bikes, and finding a quarter under a pillow for a tooth that wiggled free. We took them fishing and spent summer weekends at our favorite creek, swimming, skipping rocks, and grilling burgers. They attended picnics with their cousins and went to movies. We hosted their neighborhood school buddies for afternoons of touch football in our front yard, and on Independence Day, had the best fireworks show on the block. We set bottle rockets flat on the street and sent them unopposed toward parked cars, but they always fizzled out before any damage was done. The boys got haircuts with colored stripes down the sides like their friends, and for school we bought them the most popular shoes. We did trick or treat. We did Santa Claus, lights and all. We got a new car and a dog named Sandy. The kids loved seeing me in my uniform whenever Denise brought them to the station.

I'd opted to be a buddy to the boys, rather than a disciplinarian, and still handled Lorene with kid gloves, giving in whenever her mother thought she should be allowed to have something or had somewhere to go. I was short on parental advice, remembering the only thing I'd ever gotten from my father was to not have sex with anyone that I didn't intend to have a child with, something he passed on from his father. He repeated that I should work smart, not hard, and never trust anyone, throwing in how to detect police tails and listen for the hum of a wiretap for good measure. Rather than repeat the walking contradiction that was my father, I relied on the church's message of being a good person and doing the right thing as my go-to spiel to my own kids.

Eventually, I started a room addition on the house, and Denise took a secretarial job at a large manufacturing plant in town. She also became friends with the wives of my co-workers, and we started mingling socially. Since my medical training concluded, I found myself with more free time and got involved with my sons' sports activities. I coached Clayton and Jimmie's soccer team even though I didn't know anything about the sport, and when football season came around, I signed them up to play in the annual Kid's Day football program. That meant a summer full of practices and a couple of games before school started in the fall. The coach and I agreed to put Jimmie on defense, like his hero, Mason Phipps, a stand-out star on the local high school team.

I was in the midst of a normal life in Springdale, far from the turmoil of my upbringing.

CHAPTER 35

Denise and I weren't the only ones remaking ourselves. Still intent on hustling a buck in redwood, my dad loaded a railroad car with redwood burl and brought it to Branson, Missouri, to open a shop in a strip mall. My youngest sister, Iris, returned from California, single, but now with a baby girl. She eventually got married to a small-town cop and had another daughter while Ruth and Marty started a new business for an insurance agency. They also had another daughter. Doris married a curmudgeon from Texas, and he moved into the Glenda Street house with her, leaving only Hazel in California with her husband and two daughters. Slowly but surely, as families do, we'd exerted our gravitational pull on my father and brought him closer to Arkansas. In spite of our past history, I wished for things to be different and wanted the kids to know their grandfather.

After moving to Branson, Dad and Phyllis made frequent trips to Springdale, and always brought gifts for the grandkids. With them, he was a different man, his old gregarious and playful self. He assigned them nicknames, and spoke to them in tongues, christening Lorene and Clayton and delighting Jimmie with a chanting of his favorite phrase, "Igga-bigga sow's ear."

Those relationships came easy to my father. Ours presented a more challenging puzzle. He no longer spoke to me in gibberish, but after all we'd been through, some of his axioms sure as hell sounded like it. "Do what you do, do well," he told me on one of his visits. I remembered that phrase from my years in the trenches, where we'd laid the foundations of subdivisions, all of us echoing it back like a war cry, swigging dissolved meth from wine bottles to cut the summer sun. Now he said it to let me know he approved of my new civil service job. But in the next breath, he reminded me, "You know, you're working for the city that I sued."

"I don't think anybody remembers anything about that," I said. "That was a long time ago." I wanted it to be true. I wanted his approval to come undiluted by resentment or the surprise he never quite managed to hide that I, the son he always doubted, finally made something of myself.

But he just shook his head and muttered, "Dawson still owns this god-forsaken town."

Dawson did indeed hold sway over the current mayor, an old high school classmate who was morbidly afraid of him. He'd lost his grip with the local police, though.

My father's mere presence in Springdale no longer brought the hammer down, and he even started tentatively reconnecting with old friends that Dawson drove away from him. Denise quit worrying about me getting into trouble because of him. After all, we were living law-abiding lives. We had our own reputations in the community now, independent of whatever my dad did, which for the most part, amounted to carving redwood and playing with his grandkids. For a little while, I think we all worked out a way to fool ourselves into thinking that we didn't have to live in the shadow of the past anymore—that we could rewrite history, ignore it, or even bury it. We'd already paid those dues.

None of us could have predicted the death of Tom Dawson's half-brother, Terry Dawson, but once the news reached us, my father knew better than anyone what was destined to ensue. He wrote the following in his memoir:

"At the time of Jim Dawson's death, Terry was only 14 years old. Tom was old enough to be Terry's father, but did not relish taking any fatherly duties toward him after Jim's death. As a young man, Terry weighed more than 300 pounds and was over six feet tall. He didn't have the same personality as Tom either. He was a pleasant man.

Jim Dawson, of course, left a will, and Tom was the executor and guardian over Jim's estate until Terry reached the age of 25. It was said that at the time Jim drew up the will, the attorney questioned Jim as to the division of his estate between Tom and Terry because Tom was so much older than Terry, and already a big part of the family business. Jim reportedly replied that it did not really make any difference what or how much he willed to Terry because Tom would probably screw him out of it any- way. It might have taken a little longer than some might have expected, but Tom did finally end up with all of Terry's shares.

Terry lived with Tom after Jim's death. He attended the University of Missouri, which supposedly groomed him for his future role at Dawson Foods. He also got married. When Terry turned 28, he became the owner of more than $100 million of Dawson stock. To introduce him to the business, Tom sent Terry to different parts of the world under the pretense of important meetings, but Terry got involved in drinking, drugs, and gam- bling instead. These excursions turned out to be little more than busywork to keep Terry out of the way just as Tom set his up his father to handle projects that had very little to do with the com- pany. Terry might not have minded, but too much money and too few responsibilities can foster some very bad habits.

Terry Dawson's friends said that he could easily put away a half a gallon of whiskey an evening. These habits may have *led to Terry's early death at 35. On a cold autumn night in 1986 after a night on the town, he'd consumed his half gallon of whiskey and was ready to go home. A bodyguard had the duty that night of getting him there. Terry's size made getting him out of the car a real chore but, Harris eventually got Terry into his new $2 million home, where he passed out on his living room sofa. Terry was not seen alive again.*

His wife evidently was not aware of her husband's return and did not discover him with his throat full of Oreos until the next morning. She notified the authorities and Tom, and within a day, he was buried.

Terry's death was attributed to too much alcohol and strangulation from Oreo cookies. No autopsy was performed, and because his brother's death was not witnessed, Dawson compromised a multi-million dollar life insurance policy. The death was never established as accidental.

After learning how quickly Tom got Terry in the ground and that no autopsy was performed, it made me wonder about the death of Sherman Katz all those years before. Tom benefitted from Sherman's death and would from Terry's, too. In fact, two of Tom's top henchman were assigned as executors of the will, which put Terry's wife on a stipend, and Tom and his three children receiving all of his shares."

My father never stopped blaming Tom for his misfortunes, but up until Terry's death, he'd been making progress by learning not to sanctify his rival with too much attention. In fewer than 48 hours, all that progress came undone. He took his suspicions and anger to the streets of Springdale putting out a clarion call to anyone that would listen. He was opinionated and unafraid, and said what many already thought. It didn't take long for word of my father's war cry to trickle back to Dawson.

The new Hilton Hotel in Fayetteville sat just off the town square and added a beautiful, new 15-story tower to the city's growing skyline. It boasted a popular restaurant and bar that became the go-to night spot after the Gaslight burned down— under suspicious circumstances. Shirley Simpson from Dallas, Texas, whom Ruth knew from a previous job in Springdale, invited her there for a drink one evening, and after a couple of drinks, Shirley's husband, Bob, joined them. He suggested they go up to a luxury suite for a small gathering hosted by a friend of his. It was only for a few minutes according to Bob, so Ruth followed them up.

When they got upstairs, Ruth found the luxury suite empty. She asked Bob and Shirley, who'd gone to the mini-bar, where the party was. Bob casually mixed a drink, while Shirley remained silent. The room to the back bedroom opened. Tom Dawson appeared, drink in hand. Before Ruth could react, he put himself between her and the Simpsons—who seemed unsurprised to see him and made no move to stop him from gripping Ruth by the upper arm— and hauled her into the bedroom as he kicked the door shut behind them. He once grabbed my mother while my father pretended to be passed out. He taunted my sister as he tore at her clothes. She later told me that he slurred, "Relax or I'll have to hurt you." The alcohol in his system may have been all that saved her. She called for help as she fought him off, unaware that no one was listening. She knew the attack didn't really have anything to do with her. This had always been about her dad and always would be. She managed to twist out of his grip and knee him in the groin, and he went down. She heard his giddy, manic laughter as she ran past the Simpsons and fled the hotel room. The Simpsons set her up. Ruth waited a few days to tell Dad— it was what Dawson wanted, after all: to send his enemy a message—that eventually it got back to him. Calling the police on Dawson was out of the question.

A few days later, Ruth and I traveled to Dallas with my father to speak with the Simpsons. I wasn't fully briefed on the details of the incident yet, but I knew trouble was at hand. Only after I was satisfied that there wasn't a gun in his pants and that killing Dawson wasn't on our father's agenda did I agree to go. In Dallas, I put on my old henchman's hat and sat on the living room couch while my father began interrogating Mr. Simpson. He quickly blamed it on his wife, an old Dawson ally, which Bob had no control over. She was conveniently absent from this visit "running some errands."

"We had to deliver or we were finished," I heard Bob Simpson explain. The discussion then moved to a back office, while I waited in the living room.

Dad and Ruth emerged after a half hour. He was more reserved and contemplative, and somehow more understanding of the dilemma. We left without a scene and I breathed a little easier. He'd apparently let the Simpsons off the hook, but Dawson remained in his sights. "I'm going to get that son-of-a-bitch," he swore on the drive back to Arkansas.

"Don't do it," Ruth pled.

In the end, he didn't do anything. Instead, he took up his pen and sat down to put together a tell-all memoir, which began:

"After being told of a recent event that occurred between Tom Dawson and a member of my family, I have decided to fulfill the suggestion of Archibald Fleeman, a Springdale attorney, and write the full and uncut story of Tom Dawson and Jim Dawson."

Fleeman indeed suggested that my father record his dealings with Tom Dawson during the deposition from his civil suit against the city in 1968, and the suggestion lodged in my father's head. "If there is to be any money made off of this trial," Fleeman prophesied, "it will be in the form of a book."

Dad loved money, but it wasn't the primary motivation for his memoir. He needed Springdale to know the truth about him and Dawson. He needed someplace to put all the pain.

While my father began his manuscript, he contacted an old friend with writing experience, and allowed the redwood venture to fizzle. He'd made gorgeous tables, chairs, and clocks, but toward the end, he lost his taste for mercantilism and started giving his creations away. His family landed elaborate pieces at no cost, and they reminded us of him after he returned to California to work on his book. He was fearful of bringing more harm to us by staying in town. Seeing my father leave brought me relief and rage in equal measures— relief and rage because no matter how far he fled, none of us would ever really be free.

"I'm sorry for everything that happened while you were growing up," he said before he left.

An uncomfortable feeling came over me. It was confession time and he wasn't drunk. It must have taken a lot for him to say that.

"And you're smarter than me," he added.

He'd never really know the fear and angst I experienced while growing up. The time for that had passed. I suffered with him and I suffered because of him. Nothing either of us said now could change that, but I loved him and assumed that he loved me, and that was something.

My father's failure to stop Dawson, or even Knox, who finally died of a heart attack the year before, truly humbled him. Maybe it had done worse. But the unhappiness coming off of him as he prepared to leave Springdale fueled his resolve. He would write down Dawson's story. He would have the final word. It was all that was left to him.

"Don't be a stranger," I told him. "You can always show up here anytime, just like before." Before he drove off, he stuck his head out of the van window with a request, "I want to be cremated," he called to me. "I want my ashes spread over Lake Tahoe when I die."

I worried for him. I feared for all of us.

CHAPTER 36

"I'm the devil," announced Marcus Sanders, the EMT and pump operator for B Shift. I saw him around, but hadn't spoken to him much before, even since joining B Shift. Short but athletically built, Marcus originally hailed from northern California and enjoyed department-wide popularity. He was also a bit of a wise-guy and references to my church-going wore a little thin, especially since Denise and I didn't even attend services anymore. Paramedic school and long work hours made regular attendance impossible. By late 1986, Lorene was 16, Jimmie was 10, Clayton eight, and we'd quit going to church altogether. I turned away from Marcus, ready to ignore him.

"Just kidding," Marcus called after me. "You know, like the cartoon character, the Tazmanian Devil. The guys call me Taz." He did look like the animated savage that spun like a tornado, kicking up dust and trouble wherever it went with a reputation for being a little slow upstairs. I saw how the nickname stuck. We soon found that we had a lot in common and frequented the same towns at the same times in northern California. From 1976 to 1979, we could have easily run into each other on the street and never known. He worked for the Forestry Service in California before following his dad to Arkansas. Marcus was hired several months before me, and after he broke the ice, we became fast friends. I remained a mysterious loner to a majority of the department, and he began to serve as the social glue I needed. We were both fans of the NFL and discovered our mutual interest in the Los Angeles Raiders, formerly of Oakland, where I'd seen them with my dad. Marcus also liked to play tennis, and I'd been playing racquetball since my Roseville days, so we got our allotment of cardio by whacking balls across nets and off walls.

He was one of several guys gathered around the break room watching the Challenger launch when I declared out of the blue, "One of these days, one of those things is going to blow up." No one paid any attention to what I said, but after Challenger exploded and we watched the smoke spiraling into the sky with the rest of the world, he turned to look at me and asked, "What was that about, Preacher?" Good question. It spooked me, too.

Marcus eventually started to pressure me about going to parties. These were small gatherings with a few co-workers, but I remained hesitant to go anywhere with Marcus at night. We shared other things from our past too, things I didn't want to revive. I got out of one invitation by signing up to man the ambulance for the high school football game. During games, a fully-staffed ambulance parked near the north end zone of the stadium in case of serious injuries. A team doctor and trainer roamed the sidelines and summoned a medic if anyone needed emergency care. A broken bone or a serious concussion requiring spinal immobilization could warrant a wave-in from the team doctor, but it rarely happened. Still, game shifts paid time and a half—easy money. After I became a medic, I signed up for all of the games I could.

One of the players, a 270-pound defensive lineman named Mason Phipps with the nickname Mace, hitting you like pepper spray, was a highly sought-after college prospect. I still had his dad's autograph, an All-American at Arkansas and a former member of the Chicago Bears. Mace might have been the best to ever come out of Springdale.

We played Rogers that night and expected an easy win. My boys loved the games and came with their mom whenever I manned the ambulance. If I wasn't working overtime, I sat with them and our neighbors in the stands. The whole town followed the team, either in person or on the radio. Our win that night, handy and free of injuries, paved the way for the big showdown with our cross-town rival, Fayetteville, which would determine the conference championship and state playoff seeding. After checking at the station, I learned that I'd failed to get assigned the Fayetteville game because Crandle, a veteran paramedic, and firefighter-EMT Eddie Sanchez beat me to it. The boys and I decided we would go and sit with our neighbor, Charlie Cobb, who had two young boys with whom Jimmie and Clayton played touch football. Denise decided not to go that night, and stayed home with Lorene.

The stadium was packed by the time we arrived. I estimated at least 6,000 fans to be wandering around inside the fenced enclosure while countless others tuned in to listen on the radio. Just before game time, it started to rain. The field became sloppy as the game progressed, forcing the players to run more than pass. Springdale got out to an early lead behind the running attack of senior Paul Neely, and Phipps prevented Fayetteville from establishing any momentum. We retained our lead through halftime and came out ready to build on it, but Fayetteville scored first and made things interesting. With seven minutes to play, Fayetteville had the ball and was driving. They'd reached Springdale's 40-yard line after a short gain by Fayetteville's quarterback. The tackle pile, drenched in mud, slowly disentangled and returned to their prospective huddles, but Phipps remained face-down on the field. A few of his teammates ambled back over to him and encouraged him to get up, but got no response. Finally, a player signaled to the team doctor. I watched as the physician came out and knelt to try and talk to the fallen player. The trainer soon joined him. As they rolled him over on his back, I noticed one of his legs quivering. I asked Charlie to watch my kids for me and headed toward the field.

When the doctor and trainer saw Phipps' face they knew he was in trouble and started waving their arms for Crandle and Eddie to get out there. Meanwhile, I'd jumped the fence that surrounded the field and squeezed between the players on my way to the scene. All three of us arrived simultaneously, in time to hear the shaken team doctor announce, "He's not breathing. His eyes are rolled back in his head. He doesn't have a pulse, either."

A small crowd of coaches and assorted health professionals, including a dentist, had come onto the field and formed a ring around us, pressing in to help or gawk. Crandle cleared the space, ordering coaches, bystanders, and players to the sidelines where they took a knee and began to pray. Crandle, Eddie, and I surrounded the player and began the assessment. We checked for a breath and a pulse, and there was neither. When Eddie started doing chest compressions, shrieks arose from the stands, followed by silence, the fans unsure of what they were seeing. Fearing a spinal injury, we had carefully removed Phipps' helmet so Crandle could slip an endo-tracheal tube into his throat and breathe for him with supplemental oxygen. I retrieved the crash cart that held all the equipment needed and began assembling the fluid bag to connect to the IV in his arm.

After I attached EKG pads to his sweaty chest, Crandle and I both noticed coarse ventricular fibrillation. His heart was quivering, not pumping. V-fib was unsustainable with life and would have to be corrected. The longer it persisted, the less likely it could be reversed. I quickly administered the appropriate medications while Eddie continued compressions and Crandle breathed for him. I placed the conductive gel pads on his chest and charged the defibrillation paddles to the maximum setting. If we could get enough electric current through his heart muscle, it would stop the heart and allow the normal conductive system to reset itself. The medications I administered were meant to lean Mason's heart towards conversion. I warned the immediate circle of my intention to deliver a shock, and shouted, "I'm charged to 360!"

I held a dangerous level of energy in my hands. Any shock I delivered would pass through anyone touching him and continue on, dispersing through the thick, gooey field. I braced myself to feel the buzz and warned the others, calling, "Clear!" Mason's body heaved in response to the first jolt and the crowd went into complete meltdown. They all knew what they were witnessing now. I shocked him again and the entire stadium howled. I felt lucky my fear of electrocuting myself in the wet environment hadn't been realized, giving the on-lookers even more chaos to process. I glanced at the EKG to see if we'd converted him. No luck. Phipps' dad stood a few feet away and watched us work. He solemnly looked to the ground for composure, but couldn't find it, and wiped tears from his face. The kid with the big future lay supine and clinically dead on the field.

Between medication deliveries, I shocked him to no avail, the crowd remained silent except for a handful of isolated moans. As we neared 20 minutes, we threw the book at him and it was time for the emergency room. I heard the game being cancelled over the loud speaker as I pulled the ambulance out of the parking lot and headed for the hospital.

After we'd wheeled Phipps into a back room, a doctor called for blood gases to be run. Eddie continued compressions while Crandle maintained respirations. The boy's mother forced her way into the small room just the six of us now instead of six thousand.

"You can do it, Mason," she whispered in his ear. "I love you."

The blood gas results came in and the doctor administered an additional medication. "I love you, Mason," his mother kept whispering. "Please son, don't give up." The doctor turned to me and gave the order to charge up the paddles. I cleared the personnel from his body and pressed the paddles into his upper chest, delivering 360 joules of mule-kicking energy. His body convulsed up from the gurney and relaxed back down. A blip appeared on the monitor. Then, a spiked rhythm. I felt for his carotid artery and found a bounding pulse.

I participated in successful resuscitations before, but I never saw anything like this, not after 25 minutes. We all cheered and traded high fives while Mason's mother stood looking stunned and disoriented, unsure if she called her son back from the dead, or just called him home for supper.

While Crandle and Eddie stayed behind to finish paperwork, I walked out of the emergency room and into the parking lot, forgetting that my car was at the stadium. I emerged, dazed and no less disoriented than Mrs. Phipps, to find hundreds of anxious fans crowding the emergency room entrance, waiting for word. They watched Eddie still doing chest compressions as we loaded Phipps into the ambulance and wanted to know if he was dead.

"Is he still with us?" one of Crandle's friends demanded, cornering me at the entrance.

"We got him back," I answered, loud enough for others to hear.

It felt good to say it like that. *We got him back.* He was gone, but we got him back. Murmurs followed us as I walked with Crandle's friend, Tommy, to his car. Shouts of, "He's alive," vibrated through the throng.

Denise heard portions of the event on the radio before Charlie dropped by to deliver the boys and wanted to know what had happened. I was soggy and covered in mud as I entered our kitchen. I had no idea what to say.

Mason Phipps made a full recovery. The local paper kept the story on the front page for a month. The radio chirped about it non-stop for just as long. Articles appeared, written from every angle imaginable, and kept the town buzzing. A full three months after the resuscitation, I read a lengthy article in the local paper containing lines like, *Firefighter-Paramedic, Crandle Smith, and Firefighter-EMT, Eddie Sanchez, were standing by when the player went down.* I was also praised with similar headlines for joining in the battle for the player's survival.

We each received a certificate of recognition from the governor after news of the miracle swept the state, and the department reaped enormous positive exposure.

What did all this mean to me? The old days hadn't been completely forgotten. The town disrespected and kicked around my family name, and now thanks to the life I helped save, they'd done an about-face and were singing its praises. In the end, I decided the newspaper clippings would always stand as a testament to the service I did for this community. After all the town's misdeeds, my father's, and mine, I had the final word: *Clear!*

LARRY DANIEL

CHAPTER 37

After my move to B Shift, my attitude slowly started to change, and by summer 1987, things began to deteriorate between Denise and me. At work, I didn't have Hand on my back anymore, but I allowed my new friends to get me into trouble. Looking back, I gradually traded principles for acceptance, compromising my newly-formed values and giving myself over to the crudeness that prevailed at the testosterone-rich station. I played along and inhabited a different personality to ditch the loner tag. I stayed out after hours with my new buddies. I drank socially and my eyes wandered. Suspicion moved back into the house on Backstrom Avenue.

Joined together for twelve years prior under difficult circumstances, Denise and I approached another crossroads, but now with a few more bucks and a few more options. I spread my wings as local hero and chief wage earner, but Denise didn't seem that impressed, since I was four years her junior and still had plenty to learn. At Denise's insistence, I was a hands-off dad for Lorene and she smelled blood in the water. She stepped in and tested the limits, letting me know that I wasn't her real dad and that I couldn't tell her what to do. Denise readily agreed. We came through hell together, but war bonding alone wouldn't save our marriage, as I proceeded to make it worse.

Marcus and I traveled to a gathering in Little Rock that summer, where civil servants from all over the state came to discuss trends in fire and rescue. During the day, I learned. At night, I forgot other lessons and closed the bars with Marcus, slamming lemon shots and dancing with open-minded ladies. I glanced toward our table and observed Sanders shoving a miniature spoon of cocaine up his nose.

"I'm afraid I might be a bad influence," Sanders later confessed. I told him not to worry. I grew tired of feeling left out and finally had a friend who understood a hidden part of me, that was tucked away since before 1980. I told him to pass the spoon.

After Denise decided to throw a party at the house, inviting her favorites from the plant for drinks and mingling at our newly remodeled home, it was clear where we stood. She was upset that I'd invited some of my co-workers and when a couple of them showed up, she gave us all the cold shoulder. She neglected to introduce me to any of her new friends until one of them shook my hand and gave his name. "This is my husband," Denise coldly butted in, "the big shot."

An awkward pause followed, and after trading hateful looks, I retreated to the back deck where a few stragglers gathered. I spotted a lone fireman from A Shift enjoying a cold beer on the patio and we left a few minutes later for another at a nearby bar.

Denise and I somehow managed to keep it together whenever it came to the boys, who were testing out a sibling rivalry in the midst of their parents' cold war. Clayton excelled in sports, and became a leading scorer on his soccer team, and showed skill in baseball. Despite Clayton's prowess, Jimmie had the advantages of age and size, and he showed no reservations about smacking Clayton around when Clayton made too much of his own talents. Breaking up fights between the two became my new job.

When word of the Mason Phipps miracle eventually reached my dad, he called and demanded details. He'd been scarce since his departure nearly a year before, but checked in every so often with Ruth. Over the phone, he told me, "I've known that kid's dad since he played for the Razorbacks in the 1960s. All of my sisters in California are talking about it," he added, pride in his voice. "I've been bragging on you."

At his request, I read the certificate I received from the governor, putting emphasis on certain parts. "This Certificate of Recognition; as an outstanding Citizen of the State of Arkansas, having shown to the people of Arkansas, an outstanding interest in public service to this State." The governor scratched his signature across the bottom of the paper with a gold seal near his name. We both found the humor in Springdale slobbering all over me, and the state of Arkansas honoring me, the son of public enemy No. 1, Lemus Daniel. He soaked it all up.

He mentioned his book, which he'd finished, and before hanging up, added, "I'm going to have to find a job soon." I was never that keen on the book, even though I knew it kept him from doing something he could never take back.

"What kind of job?" I asked.

"I don't know yet," he said. "Phyllis is bitching. I think she's ready to leave me." I offered to lend him some money, but he shot back that never in a million years would he ever take a dime from me. I could tell that working on Dawson's exposé, especially after his attack on Ruth, left him agitated. My father returned to Arkansas to scratch that itch, but I wouldn't learn of it until later, when I read this section of the memoir:

"The most recent conversation I had with Tom was in his office. On a Monday night in August, 1987, I dropped by Larry Joe's Bar in Fayetteville. The place was packed except for a

table next to Tom, who was with a beer distributor, along with Chase Meeks, a Fayetteville playboy. Tom immediately became aware of my presence, but waited a half hour before stepping over to speak with me. He extended his hand and said my name, 'Lemus Daniel.' I asked him if he would be in town the next day because I wanted to meet with him. He said he wasn't busy, so I asked him if I could drop by his office. 'Oh,' he said, clearly disconcerted, 'well, I've got to leave town at four, and I've got a meeting.' He paused before adding, 'Come out at 8:00 a.m.' Before disappearing, he changed the time to 10:00 a.m."

Dad knew he'd find Dawson at Larry Joe's. By asking Dawson for an appointment in front of his peers, he hoped to watch him squirm, and never believed his request would be granted. Dawson didn't want to come off as a coward, so he agreed to meet. The memoir continues:

"At 10:00 on Tuesday, I arrived at Tom's office, which was built like a bank: Spacious, and with a reception desk in the middle. I announced myself to Patsy, the receptionist, who said that Tom was expecting me, and I sat down to wait. A few minutes later, a large man entered the lobby and asked Patsy, loud enough for me to hear, 'What would you do if a 6'5", 300-pound man walked in, passed your desk, and headed straight for Tom's office?'

'I know what to do,' she said.

'Well, what?' the man asked.

'I'd push the button.'

The security person disappeared and left me wondering what would happen if Patsy pushed the button. A good 30 minutes passed before Tom finally called me into his office, and I waited another five minutes until Tom walked in through a different door. Looking back, I wish he found me sitting in his chair with my feet up on his desk, just as I'd found him in my office so many times.

Tom greeted me and we sat down and talked. I asked after his family and brought up Terry, and Tom replied that it was a damn shame. Then I mentioned that I had grandchildren living in the vicinity of a Dawson processing plant, and that dirty smoke clouds hung over the entire neighborhood and filled it with a sickening stench.

'We don't know where the smell is coming from,' Tom said. 'We're studying that.'

I let him know that if he ever laid another hand on a family member of mine, I would kill him."

He didn't write anything else about this encounter. Following the visit, he returned to California to a troubled relationship.

LARRY DANIEL

R uth called me at work with some bad news. "Dad's fallen off a scaffold and has a skull fracture," she said, adding, "He's at the hospital in Davis and is in serious condition."

Davis was less than an hour west of Roseville on Interstate 80. "What the hell was he doing on a scaffold in Davis?" I asked.

"He took a job there," she answered. "He fell a few days ago, but I just got the call. He was in critical condition, but they've backed off of that a little."

"What do you mean backed off?"

"The hospital said that he's doing better."

Dad was climbing around on 20- to 30-foot high scaffolds for an hourly wage. I didn't doubt that he could still do it—though at a much slower pace than I remembered—but he raised the possibility of ending it so many times that I couldn't help wondering if he fell voluntarily.

"The company he works for is paying all the medical bills," Ruth said. "I'll let you know if I find out anything else."

The fall forced his first trip to a doctor in decades and my father benefitted from it. The fall becoming a blessing. They discovered his stress disorder and sent him to a therapist, who started him on an anti-anxiety medication and convinced him to stop treating himself with alcohol. When I checked in with him, he assured me everything was fine and that he was complying with the physicians. In February 1988, he called me with a proposal. The insurance company that covered the job site determined the employer was at fault and offered him a healthy settlement. "Come on out to California and spend a couple of weeks with me," my dad offered. "Help me decide what to do with the money."

I had some vacation time saved up and needed a break, but knew I would get opposition from Denise. On the other hand, I had to tamp down my guilt over not being there when he went to the hospital, and I felt a lot closer to my father than my wife just then. "Good," he said. "I'll pick you up. Let me know when you're set to arrive."

Denise, as expected, gave me an ultimatum but I didn't fully embrace it.

He met me at the Reno airport, sans his sidekick of the past 15 years.

"Where's Phyllis?" I asked.

"She left," he mumbled. "She packed her stuff and left before the accident." She returned after hearing he was in the hospital, but left for Fresno after he recovered. "I don't care one bit," he said. It was a bald-faced lie.

We drove north from the airport to his condo in the tiny community of Loyalton, across the border of Nevada and into California. We came across a herd of elk roaming a vast valley on our way through the towering Sierra Mountain peaks that surrounded us. He found the place while thumbing through articles in his doctor's office during his rehabilitation. The income-based residence catered to people like him, retired or otherwise budget restricted.

Before his fall, Dad and Phyllis wandered around the Sierras. They did okay at first, and got by on whatever menial job Phyllis could find while he worked on his revenge prose and sold leftover pieces of redwood. Eventually, they had no choice but to hunker down in Caroline's tiny spare trailer in Weimar, dependent on his sister's generosity. He came full circle from living through the Great Depression as a kid to sitting down in that cramped, broken-down shelter on an isolated hillside in northern California. But now, thanks to the monthly insurance check, he didn't have to worry about money. "I'm officially retired," he proclaimed in the modest condo as he put his legs up on a recliner.

He wanted to take me south and do some work on Hazel's house. I looked forward to seeing my sister and spending more time with him.

"How's your head?" I finally asked him.

"The doctors say I'm cracked but my skull's just fine!" he cackled. He recounted toying with the shrinks by acting strangely during interviews, and invoking his grandpa gibberish before finally getting bored and complying with treatment. "The Valium helps me sleep, so I don't drink anymore, but I still like to smoke," he admitted. He brought me up to speed on his late-night antics. After watching hours of late-night televangelism programs, he'd taken to giving monetary pledges to these organizations over the phone on behalf of long-time acquaintances in Springdale, including the current mayor. Just to entertain himself. "I call the number, blather on a bit, tell them I'm so-and-so, give them the address, and just like that, they get a letter demanding the money," he explained. "It's hilarious."

He handed me a bound copy of his manuscript. I was reluctant to rehash any memories at the moment, so I stashed it with my belongings. Writing it seemed to have done him some good and maybe giving Dawson a piece of his mind a few months before hadn't been such a bad idea, either. He looked better than he had in a very long time. He missed Phyllis but hid it well.

I put my clothes away and we set off for southern California. During the drive, my dad not once lapsed into the rants and complaints I always loathed. During breaks on the job, I bonded with Hazel's two daughters and visited Laguna Beach a couple of times. I always loved that part of the coast. With the front porch job completed, we packed up and went back to Loyalton.

The ski slopes of Lake Tahoe, just an hour away, beckoned me next. I wanted to give it a try ever since visiting the area years earlier. After a half day of lessons, I picked it up pretty quickly, and Dad relaxed at the lodge. That afternoon, I weathered the cold wind atop a 10,000-foot peak and looked out over the expanse of sparkling blue water that reminded me of a pricey postcard. The view was one of the most spectacular things I had ever seen. I fantasized about living there someday. It seemed a suitable resting place for my father's ashes.

After a quick trip to Sacramento for an errand he needed to run, we drove through the residential areas of a much larger Rocklin than I'd remembered, and surveyed the houses we built in the 1970s. We stopped at Tim's Pizza for lunch. "You know, you could work anywhere with all the education and experience you have now," my father said. "You could work in Tahoe at the fire department if you wanted to."

"I have a good job now," I replied instinctively. I wasn't so sure I meant it. Firehouse drama reached fever pitch by late 1987, when Lieutenant-Paramedic Billy Brooks was caught with his pants down in the company of another fireman's wife. Captain Hand, who took over as interim chief after Johnson retired, got wind of it, as did others. Brooks was ultimately dismissed and there was widespread debate over whether he should have been fired. As tempers flared and moral questions raged, I found myself considering my own options in response to the prospect of permanent Chief Hand. My job and any future promotions depended on the city's final decision, and they were taking their sweet time. The good vibes of 1986 had vanished, and left the department mired in negativity. Still, I wasn't ready to pack up and leave my kids behind.

He asked me about Denise. I'd told him what she'd said about me not bothering to come back, but immediately regretted mentioning it. I went back to my sandwich. "It's just an application," he said.

He was right, it was just an application. After lunch, we drove into South Lake Tahoe instead of returning to Loyalton, and Dad pulled his van into the main fire department office, just like Dennis did for me years earlier in Springdale. I picked up the papers. "I'll fill it out and see what happens," I promised. I didn't want to be a buzz-kill and figured it wouldn't hurt to explore my options. If my marriage remained sour, then I could very well move back to California, but this time with a good career to sustain me.

Before returning to Arkansas, we planned a trip into Reno to celebrate my potential job-in-waiting at the South Lake Tahoe Fire Department. He said it tongue-in-cheek, but I could see the wheels were already turning. Inside the El Dorado Casino in downtown Reno, the buffet drew my father's attention, and I drifted toward a blackjack table. An attractive redhead dealt cards to another gentleman, who left before long, and left me alone with Kitten, as her name badge advertised. "Kitten," I said, "I like that name."

She asked where I was from.

"Arkansas," I said, "the land of no opportunity."

I won a few hands in a row, and when I lost, she pushed the money to me instead of raking it in, gave me a wink, and kept dealing. The next time I lost, she did it again. My father returned from the buffet, so I left the table, up by $300, and wandered around the casino with him, recounting Kitten's generosity. My father insisted that we go back and look for her.

I found Kitten at a different table with a couple of tourists, sat down, and pushed $5 onto the circle. After a few hands, Dad came over and announced that he was getting tired but didn't want to be a party pooper. I had no intention of pursuing her, but Dad made a suggestion. "You should get a room here at the El Dorado," he said. "That way, you could stay out." He promised to pick me up the next day. Kitten kept glancing up and smiling throughout the exchange. I took the bait.

"I need someone to show me around the real Reno," I finally told her. "When do you get off?"

"In an hour," she replied.

We had a drink at the casino bar, and then she drove me up to a mountaintop that looked out over the glittering Reno skyline. She told me about her card-dealing life in Reno, mentioning that she'd moved from Oregon in the fifth grade, attended high school in Reno, and didn't have a steady boyfriend. I didn't share my marital status.

We descended from the mountain and sauntered into one of her favorite nightclubs, where we danced to some disco music. After a few drinks with a few of her friends at the club, we went back to her place. The next morning, I called Dad to pick me up at her apartment. He showed up with a bouquet of flowers. I told her I'd call her when I came back to take the job in Tahoe, but I had no idea if I meant it.

When I returned home, Denise met me with silence, but her ultimatum was an empty one, so I dove headlong into work at the department. My renewed relationship with my dad and my time away from Springdale left me energized, and though the possibility of moving to California lingered, thoughts of the boys held me back. If Hand got the job, I figured, I might ratchet up my interest in South Lake Tahoe, but a few days later, the city named Chief Nathan Black.

Black had been with the department for a decade, and was an officer for half that time. He more than earned his reputation for being sharp, well-educated, and committed to the department. Right away, he made some changes that the medics liked, switching the shift change to 8:00 a.m. instead of 6:00 p.m. He served as a medic himself and knew as well as any of us what it felt like to work all night then stumble zombie-like through the following day, taking calls on zero sleep, with exhaustion jeopardizing us and the public we served. Now, after a night of calls, I could go home and get some sleep. I also didn't mind when he moved me to the less volatile A Shift. Black's promotion pushed my fantasies about Lake Tahoe to the sidelines and left me feeling optimistic again.

A few weeks passed since my return from Loyalton when I got an early morning call from Dad at the station. He asked if I had sent in the application. I told him I couldn't find it and even teased the idea that Denise found it and threw it away. I fibbed to my father, and chose not to send it in after having changed my mind when Black was named Chief. Dad said he had a doctor's appointment in Sacramento that morning and instead of returning to Loyalton by Interstate 80, he could take Highway 50 through South Lake Tahoe to pick up another one and mail it to me.

"Go ahead," I told him. It was, as he said, just an application. But maybe more than that, it was a chance to humor my father, something I felt more and more compelled to do since my trip to California.

"I really enjoyed my time out there." I added.

He paused for a beat before answering, "Igga-bigga sow's ears."

After we hung up, I prepared for my shift and thought nothing more about the application or the call. The day proceeded like any other: I checked my equipment, had a cup of coffee, and got called out to a car accident in town with minor injuries. For lunch, I retired to the bunk room and was relaxing in a lounger watching television until the non-emergency phone rang. It was Marty, of all people.

"Larry," he said when I answered. "I want you sit down, okay?"

"I'm sitting," I said. "What's up, Marty?"

He paused for a moment. *Igga-bigga sow's ear,* I thought, then he said, "Lemus is dead."

I made him repeat it. "I'm sorry to be the one telling you," he said, "but your sister couldn't do it. She's devastated." I heard him swallow hard before continuing, "He was in a car accident this morning on Highway 50 on the way to Lake Tahoe. It killed him."

There were other people in the bunk room. I couldn't make eye contact, I couldn't show weakness, and I couldn't let on what was happening. I gripped the sweat-slick phone to my ear. "I'm so sorry," Marty said. In spite of my attempts to hide it, it didn't take long for the crew to work out what happened. My captain told me to take all the time I needed to settle my father's affairs. From my house, I got in touch with his brother, Samuel, and he made arrangements to travel with me to northern California.

Marty's call cut me open, and dreadful thoughts seeped in. *Was he in pain before he passed? Did he die quickly?* Fleeting feelings darted in and out: The gratitude I felt for the two weeks I had with him was chased by the guilt for my role in his death. He wouldn't have been anywhere near that highway, after all, if I hadn't lied about my application and agreed to have him pick up another one. To bear the burden of my own weight suddenly seemed impossible. To keep going was incomprehensible. I grew numb, the task arranged before me became my own anchor, the one thing I could focus on as the rest of my world crumbled and blurred. After months of my antics, Denise had little patience left for my grief. "His death," she told me bluntly, "is probably the best thing that ever happened to you."

She never understood my loyalty to him, but then again, neither had I. She may have been right in the end. I told Lorene and the boys that their Papa was gone, and they reacted as children do in grasping to accept the finality of death. I boarded the plane for Reno with a suitcase still loaded with items from my previous visit. As soon as we landed and secured a car, Samuel and I headed straight for the Sheriff's office in Placerville in search of answers.

"A young man in an old Chevy driving west on Highway 50 lost control and hit your father's Honda head-on near Kyburz," the Sheriff explained, "about 30 miles up the mountain from here." The driver had just been released from prison that morning. He was well over the limit and admitted to taking some kind of a pill. We have him in custody."

"What's his name?" I asked.

"Greg Edwards. DWI's and burglary," the sheriff answered.

Samuel asked about his brother's body, and the sheriff directed us the local mortuary a few miles down the road, where the director offered his condolences and told us cremation would cost $600. Sam pulled out six $100 bills and the director told me to drop by in a couple of days to pick up the ashes. According to the death certificate, the shoulder harness of the car nearly decapitated my father, but Sam still demanded to see the body. The director's expression changed. "I don't think that's a good idea, sir," he said. I agreed but Sam wasn't having it. He tried to force his way behind the reception desk into the back room and I had to soft tackle him. He looked at me with fire in his eyes, and lost control for a moment before he finally relented to my pleas. He'd have to recall another memory for his final face-to-face with his brother.

After I dropped Samuel off at Caroline's, I headed to the salvage yard. I could barely tear my eyes away from the tiny compact Honda that I'd traveled across the state in just weeks before, crumpled up like a beer can now, with my father's blood staining the interior. I ducked inside, the smell of death still lingering, and gathered a few belongings from the wreckage. Afterwards, I rejoined my uncle at Caroline's.

The next day, after a restless night spent at Aunt Caroline's, Uncle Willy loaned us his trailer to empty out the Loyalton condo. We drove two hours through the Sierras, not talking, and letting the dread percolate and fill us like slow-dripping coffee. At the condo, we started in the bedroom and worked our way through the living room, loading a sofa, a few tools, or anything else we deemed worthy. It didn't take long. Afterwards, I sat down at his makeshift cinder block and plywood desk, and started sorting through his personal belongings. I found a house plan, some books, and a notepad filled with his ideas, plans, and a to-do list. Or bucket list, maybe. Sitting at that desk reminded me of the photographs I'd seen of him at a much nicer one when he was at the top of his game, looking over plans for a new house or shopping center. I found his checkbook and a photograph or two. At some point, my uncle joined me. I don't know how long we sat there. "This is killing me," he said after a while.

It was killing me, too. Hauling the nearly-worthless remnants of my father's life from that miniscule condo was the saddest thing I ever did. Willy offered us a small sum to take my dad's garbage off our hands, more as a kind gesture than anything else.

Caroline insisted that we hold a memorial, even though Dad always said he didn't want one. I didn't put up much of a fight. As long as his ashes ended up in Lake Tahoe, I'd go along with the rest.

We all gathered to remember Lemus Daniel at a small community center in Colfax. After an awkward start from a clergyman, Samuel got up and said a few words, ending with a quote from the poem, *Do Not Stand at My Grave and Weep*, by Mary Elizabeth Frye.

Do not stand at my grave and weep
I am not there. I do not sleep.
I am a thousand winds that blow
I am the diamond glints on snow
I am the sunlight on ripened grain
I am the gentle autumn rain.
When you awaken in the morning's rush
I am the swift uplifting rush
   of quiet birds in circled flight.
I am the soft stars that shine at night.
Do not stand at my grave and cry
I am not there. I did not die.

After the memorial, my sisters and I drove up into the wilderness of Highway 50 towards Lake Tahoe to find the place where our father passed. We came across the site on a two-lane stretch near Kyburz, beneath the St. Pauli Girl Beer billboard. Debris lay strewn along the roadside, untouched by the rescue squad. We parked on the shoulder, got out, and stood mesmerized by a lone tree with its bark sheared off that must have kept his car from plummeting hundreds of feet into the ravine of the American River. I imagined his spirit wafting up from the crash site into the towering trees and looking down on us, telling us he'd had enough and was ready to go. Majestic scenery and all, he picked a decent place to die.

We headed back to say a final goodbye to those that'd gathered in Colfax. I gave Hazel the plastic box containing the ashes and told her I might not come back for a while, so maybe she could scatter them. I'd have planned a trip back sooner, but knew I'd stand on shaky ground once I returned to Arkansas. Hazel took the ashes and promised she'd hold onto them until I came back.

It didn't take long once I got back to Springdale for friends of mine and acquaintances of his to start asking if I thought his death was an accident or not. The same question occurred to me, hit men and contract killings, never dismissed as conspiracy theories in the house I grew up in.

Before he died, my father shared more than a few portions of his exposé to friends and others in Arkansas so everybody knew about it. There was bad blood to the bitter end, but I simply couldn't see the logistics of foul play working out even though global positioning systems came on the scene around 1983. It would have required impeccable timing and my dad's car most likely didn't have one.

I simply couldn't face another drama related to my father. I feared what I'd discover and have to deal with it,

or worse, internalize it with everything else. I didn't want
to know anything more. Energy poured out of my body and
it drained me. I couldn't afford to care. I feared going over
the edge.

LARRY DANIEL

CHAPTER 39

My mind started going strange places and unloading my burden on Denise wasn't much of an option. I was flipped upside down. Good or bad, I was in deep mourning over the loss of this huge influence in my life.

While the kids also mourned the loss of their grandfather, their grumpy temperaments began exposing the negative atmosphere at home. Denise and I agreed to separate and I moved into a duplex across town. I pulled my shifts, kept up with Jimmie and Clayton's sports activities on my off-duty time, and left Lorene to her mother. I took to being alone for the first few weeks, treading the uncharted territory of solitude in between the grueling demands of my job, but after a few more weeks, I was begging Denise to let me come home. As a pre-condition, she proposed counseling for me and I agreed. I also thought of Jonas and didn't want to wait until I was building airplanes out of two-by-fours before I got help.

I got educated pretty quick in the time I spent on the couch with the therapist. During the initial oral history, I left plenty out, but the specialist raised an eyebrow more than once as I retraced the bumpy journey of my life to her office. After some initial reservation, it was a relief to finally spill my guts and be heard. I confessed that after several years on a noble path, I detoured and returned to some behaviors that I wasn't proud of, and that I wasn't coping very well in the midst of my most recent crisis, the loss of my father. I got around to sharing more details of my spotty behavior.

"Voids that need to be filled," she interrupted.

She also said something about codependency and thought that I might be depressed. I was given anti-depressants and was scheduled for another visit.

The church kept me from certain disaster, and the fireman job wet my appetite to the possibilities, but now I needed to know myself better. The visit to the therapist launched a personal investigation into my upbringing, my past thinking, insecurities, and subsequent issues. I wondered whether I should be married at all, but decided I needed to see the kids through to graduation if I could. I read *The Adult Children of Alcoholics* by Janet Woititz to see what I was up against, as well as a slew of other self-help books, including the work of psychologist Carl Jung, who claimed that if our shadow, or dark side, was better understood, it could help us from repeating the same mistakes.

"Who are you?" the counselor asked, "and what do you want from life?" I couldn't come up with a suitable answer. It would be all uphill from here.

After I did my part, Denise and I cleared the air. I admitted things she didn't already know, and she admitted things I didn't know. She let me move back home where she tried to do her part, which included analyzing me, and we continued the tug-of-war. Good days were followed by bad days, and our resilient kids improved their egg-shell tiptoes around us. She rescued me in 1975, and I respected her maternal instincts. I may have even loved her while she carried my baby in Roseville, but her domineering style didn't work for me anymore. I suspect she hoped that without my father's influence, she'd be able to get back her compliant husband of a few years ago. It wasn't going to be that simple of a fix.

I was a caring parent and husband, but also an insecure child posing as an arrogant adult who was easily manipulated and in need of assurances from anyone that would offer them. I was also the same person that reached for the eye sockets of a defenseless Brandon in my front yard years ago, from rage that escaped the dark cave inside. I was all of these things put together, the dominant part dependent on the types of people I surrounded myself with. I didn't have the courage to acknowledge any of this until after my father died. I needed to find my own voice now that he was gone.

This book is a result of that search.

I didn't start to feel better until I started jogging, and processing my thoughts on the open road after I saw a television program promising it might be good for grief management. On a run, I encountered a couple of guys I remembered from my church going years: Landon, a local tire salesman, and an orthopedic surgeon named John.

They were doing the Los Angeles Marathon the following March and invited me to join them, promising there was still plenty of time to catch up to their training. I left feeling inspired and couldn't wait to get started. Landon promised to deliver me across the line in Los Angeles.

I'd jogged short distances before, but after a short time, I could spend an entire hour running. I called Hazel in California to tell her I was coming to run a marathon the following spring and needed a place to stay. Within a couple of months, I completed several long sessions with my fellow joggers. I enjoyed running to exhaustion while I reckoned with my dark side.

I avoided my friend, Marcus, who would later be arrested for possession of cocaine with intent to deliver. He made the headlines, lost his job, and served time in prison. I wrote to him a couple of times while he served his sentence.

I'd decided to dedicate the marathon to my dad because the big day was scheduled for March 5th, which was close enough to the first anniversary of his death. His motto of *Do what you do, do well* became my motto, and to me, doing well meant breaking four hours. Since his death, I thought of him every single day.

I got busy knocking off mileage goals, which did me a world of good. My running buddies encouraged me while we trotted down back roads and absorbed lessons about life being messy, that we were all just human, and that none of us were perfect. I ran, pulled my shifts, and went home after work.

The fire department announced an officer's exam just after the trip to Los Angeles, so I added that to the goals I set my sights on. All of the medical calls added up, and I knew that before long I'd rather be driving a red officer's car than manning the back of an ambulance. The more experienced men shared that the shelf life of a busy paramedic was around seven years before burnout hit.

Burnout was the cumulative effect of managing disasters on a regular basis before a mere mortal began to leak oil. Anxiety disorders and insomnia were typical signs, calling in sick, another. After my sixth year, the shine dulled and the "new car smell" of my job faded into a psychologically demanding task, but I'd yet to start calling in sick.

When the day finally arrived to remember my father by running over 26 miles in Los Angeles, I hoped anything that he and I had left unsaid or undone could be worked out here and quiet my lingering grief. The Los Angeles Coliseum served as the starting line, and as the time drew near, we took our positions near the middle of the pack. Brightly colored balloons bordered the boulevard and encompassed runners for as far as the eye could see. The forecast was for sunny skies and a high of 75 degrees, which was unseasonably warm for early March. The lack of an ocean breeze would also have a bearing on the conditions.

Just before the gun, I vowed to finish under four hours and prove to myself, and somehow my dead father, that I was tough enough after all. It was my motivation which had shifted from a dedication to him, to a purge, instead. I wanted to prove that I was no longer the skinny kid getting pushed around. Being tough had been important to him and now it was to me.

After 10 miles, I felt good, but my buddies were faltering in the heat, so I forged ahead and didn't look back. After 20 miles, the blazing sun forced many runners to quit, but instead, I spoke to Dad as if he was slogging along right next to me. I imagined that we were together in the searing heat of the Rocklin job site, with him doubting me, and me, determined to prove him wrong. I was almost there, but after 23 miles, I had to stop and walk. I talked some more but nobody answered. He was finally gone.

"The heat was brutal," Landon declared as he finished 25 minutes behind me. I told him my time of 3 hours 53 minutes as I grinned proudly, but didn't rub it in.

Before the race, I visited with Hazel and talked to her about completing our father's request, so later that week, she and her husband traveled north to Tahoe, hopped aboard a tourist boat, and in the middle of the dark blue liquid resting place of Lake Tahoe, emptied the ashes of Lemus Daniel.

The officer's exam loomed next and offered me an opportunity to experience fewer sleepless nights, advance my career, and cash bigger paychecks. There was only one spot available but more could qualify; the results of the exam good for a year if another position opened up. If that position didn't open up within a year, the process had to be repeated all over again. The written exam preceded an interview with six men appointed by the mayor and city council.

When the results were posted, only two people qualified, and I was the second one. The fireman in front of me had 18 years of experience. There were several of the old timers that could leave any day now. It was just a matter of time.

After Crandle, already an officer, congratulated me, he surprised me with a bit of exciting news. CBS television had been in contact with him about a new show called Rescue 911 that wanted to do a segment on the Mason Phipps resuscitation. Apparently, William Shatner would narrate the story that was to be nationally televised during prime time viewing hours. The production company was coming in a month and they wanted us to be in it, so I got a haircut and trimmed my mustache. It sounded like a big deal.

After I was greeted by the smiling interviewer, she gestured for me to take a seat at a table that had been set up in the main equipment bay room. Bright lights pointed downward at my face. When the tape started rolling, she asked me a couple of questions about what happened. I answered her in technical terms. "I gave an amp of epinephrine and defibrillated him at 360 joules," I kept repeating. She stopped me.

"Okay, but what was it like? How did you feel about seeing him lying there?" she asked. I looked away when her eyes got moist, a trick to soften me up. She wanted to know how I felt inside.

I would be speaking to America on behalf of the city of Springdale, who I knew would be glued to every word spoken. Given my history, I felt vindication with a hint of irony. In retrospect, I felt a Benevolent Spirit among us.

Initially, I felt the enormous weight of my responsibility to the young man on the field, and to his family. I felt the fear of failure in front of the large crowd. Even though I could sense Mason Phipps was in real trouble, prompting me to amble down to the muddy playing surface, I felt disbelief that the kid was dead on the field. I felt the desperation of the thousands of fans that watched us working on him. I felt the anxiety of pressing the shock paddles onto the player's chest while standing in highly conductive goo. I felt the pain of watching a father lose his son, imagining how I would ever survive such a thing. I felt the calm of being able to do my job under pressure. In the end, I was proud to have been a part of it. The lights were on and the camera was rolling.

An answer came to me and I fed her what I hoped might be a good sound bite. Afterwards, a few of our perspectives were headed to the editing room where a segment devoted solely to the resuscitation of Mason Phipps would be presented to millions of people. I couldn't help but enjoy the experience.

Nevertheless, I was still getting slammed with ambulance calls. I anticipated that it wouldn't be much longer after a rumor surfaced about an officer retiring. Things were looking up, and while I licked my chops, we got called out to the furthest reaches of our jurisdiction.

"Squad Five. . .Respond to an unresponsive man in the bathtub. . .Code three."

We sped towards the vague call. Sometimes, you just never knew what you would be dealing with.

"Squad five is responding," I said into the microphone.

At the house, I was led by a hysterical woman to a hefty man lying naked on his back in a damp bathroom floor. He appeared to have a head injury, and his face was directly under the water spigot that was now turned off. It was apparent that scalding water burned his face and his tongue was swollen twice its normal size. He labored to breathe, was combative, and weighed at least 250 pounds. The wife had not witnessed the event, so I reasoned that he had a seizure while he was in the shower, fell against the dial with his body, inadvertently upped the hot water then fell directly under the faucet that shot scalding water on his face. It was possible that the fall knocked him out. His face was purple and blistered, and his tongue, freakish-looking. I was in a rural setting and didn't have the usual back up.

My new partner, Joshua, brought the backboard into the tight space, and we prepared to arm-and-leg hoist the patient onto it so we could get him to the hospital as soon as possible. The man's wife urged us to hurry. I grabbed the man's legs as best I could and Joshua grabbed his arms, and on the count of three we lifted then swung his slippery, dead weight up and above the board. We accidently dropped him and watched him bounce off the board, onto his stomach, on the other side of the floor. I felt my left knee give out as pain shot up toward my hip. Face-down now, the man proceeded to ooze fecal matter. The odor reached my very core. Joshua retched while I wiped it up with a nearby towel and tossed it aside. The man's wife was now screaming at us. We were finally able to roll him onto the backboard, and hoisted his naked body onto the gurney. My uniform shirt was slimed in his filth. The gurney straps were too short to cover his enormous stomach which overflowed the sides of the gurney, and in his combat-ive state, he flirted with the possibility of flopping onto the ground as we pushed furiously toward the ambulance's box. A thin sheet barely covered his privates. He was turning blue, so I tried to oxygenate him with a mask but couldn't keep it on him. I needed an IV to administer a sedative and better manage his airway, but was unable to secure one because he continued to thrash around so desperately. Joshua raced to the hospital, and the rough ride knocked me from side to side. My knee throbbed as I talked to the ER on the radio. After a sharp turn from the hyperactive driver, I was nearly dumped headlong onto my combative patient. He struggled to breathe, and flailed even harder.

"I can't get an IV," I hollered at the emergency room from the module radio. His tongue was so swollen I knew I couldn't tube him. His struggle was loud and ugly. My knee was swelling.

"Squad Five, just get him here," the ER ordered.

"Hurry the fuck up, Joshua!" I shouted through the small panel window that divided the ambulance, as I held on for dear life.

We pulled into the emergency entrance and a nurse came out to help retrieve the patient. I went home after the paperwork was finished. A few days later, I called Dr. Anderson, my running partner during the Los Angeles Marathon, and he asked me to meet him at the hospital. His assistant greeted me, and I walked gingerly with him to a room where Anderson waited. I did as ordered, and pulled up my pants leg, after which the assistant began spraying something on the back part of my knee. It felt cold and my knee went numb. I barely caught sight of the needle that looked big enough for a horse as Dr. Anderson wheeled around on his swivel chair. I took a deep breath as advised and he pushed the plunger full of thick steroid directly into my knee and set me on fire, my temperature rising as he bent my knee back and forth. He said I might have sprained a ligament. After a few days, I was doing better.

The man with the swollen tongue survived.

After Clayton turned 10, he became eligible for regulation little league baseball, where real pitching replaced the machines. I served as a coach for Clayton's team, the Cubs, who won a city championship in his second year. His third and final year of little league, he made the all-star team and pitched in the district tournament.

Jimmie lost interest in baseball and was instead focused on a learner's permit and dreamed of owning a scooter like one of the neighbor kids. He and his buddies enjoyed skateboarding, fake wrestling on television, and were experts at video games, which would eventually lead him as an adult to an attractive salary in technology. Clayton, as an adult, would become an officer in the Army and certify as a paramedic. For the time being, both of the boys had a circle of friends that included a kid or two that I didn't trust. I wasn't very sure of myself raising teens, having not done very well with Lorene, who'd finished high school and moved out with a boyfriend.

After a couple of months, my knee started hurting again so I went back to Dr. Anderson and he arranged to scope my knee. After I was put to sleep, he slid a couple of thin, hollow metal tubes into the articulating joint, peeked through a telescopic instrument, and used a gizmo that allowed him to excise anything he deemed intrusive. He discovered my anterior-cruciate-ligament, shelled like crab meat. The ACL was important for the stability of my knee and was causing the discomfort. After the procedure, he tried to stay positive.

"It's not what I expected," he admitted. "Your ACL is torn. You've got strong legs, so maybe you'll do alright," he reasoned.

He cleaned the area of debris but hadn't repaired anything. I recovered from the procedure after a couple of weeks, following all of Anderson's suggestions. I worked to strengthen the quadriceps muscle that supported my injured knee to avoid a corrective surgery. I went back to work and wore a brace.

I was at home when Shatner came on the screen and set the stage in Springdale, Arkansas. There'd been a cameraman on the field, and actual footage of the player's chest heaving from my first defibrillation attempt streamed across America's households, as a close-up shot showing me pressing the buttons. Crandle appeared and said a few words, as did Eddie. Finally, my face filled the screen for several seconds while I answered a question. I stated the obvious to start things off, explaining, "It's a rare thing to find a young football player go down from cardiac arrest. We all became very emotionally attached to the situation and were putting up our best effort knowing it would be a really bad thing in front of all those people if we didn't resuscitate him."

I also remembered peeking up to see his dad watching us work on Mason, as he tried to avoid facing the fact that Mason was gone.

"He was clinically dead on the field," I said. "No pulse. No breathing. I could see what his father felt, the helplessness of what he witnessed."

On camera, Mr. Phipps said in spite of the courageous efforts of the crew, he still considered the whole thing a miracle. I sat on my living room sofa, wishing my dad could've seen the program.

I enjoyed the brief revival of publicity while it was replayed all over again, but my knee would return to bite me. I suffered a serious misstep on a sidewalk in 1991, reinjuring my knee, and was soon back for surgery. This time, the goal was to reconstruct my knee with a modification that involved the Iliotibial band, a fibrous substitute for the ligament. In the past, running kept me on an even keel and in good spirits, but I did without it long enough to notice. A long and painful rehab awaited me.

The procedure went without a hitch, but the rehab proved troublesome from the beginning. After a couple of weeks, I acquired an infected staple that had to be dug out and redone, but worked tirelessly the following six months trying to get back to where I was. I began to doubt it as the expected elapsed time for recovery passed. My employer grew impatient, and an officer's position still hadn't opened up for me. Anderson finally admitted that it could be a couple of years, if ever, before I was back to the level of standing on roofs, carrying equipment, and dragging people to safety.

I had to test my reconstructed knee on the busiest assignment in the entire department, the first out squad, so I paid a visit to Chief Black about the situation. After discussing it, I went back to Dr. Anderson and he agreed that I needed to change careers unless the department was willing to be more patient with me. My prognosis wasn't good, so after nine years, I became a retired firefighter-paramedic.

It was the end of an era, and my on-again, off-again marriage wasn't far behind. A new job opportunity sprang up that seemed perfect for me. It paid good money, was less physically demanding, and would benefit from my extensive knowledge in cardiology and patient care. The local hospital's heart catheterization lab had an opening and would provide on-the-job training.

Denise and I paid tuition to the new community college's nursing program and Denise started nursing school, saying she'd found a career she could be happy with, and where she intended to gain more independence from me.

Heart disease was the primary focus of my new duties, and I soon learned the anatomy of the pulsating muscle even more intimately. The elderly population in the area provided a harvest of chest pain and blocked arteries, so life hung in the balance on a regular basis, but the controlled environment of the hospital seemed a breeze compared with the chaotic madness that a medic faced on the street. I took to it right away. I put my head down and learned all that I could. It still mattered to me that I served people.

I worked around 60 hours a week, was on-call most weekends, and always had to pay attention. I prepped patients, scrubbed in and assisted at the table, monitored EKG and vitals, performed defibrillations, and administered medications. I also moved patients from their rooms to the lab and back again. After shifts, I wore a pager similar to the one I had at the fire department and rarely slept through the night. I eventually gained a licensure in invasive cardiology.

Technology advanced rapidly, and by my third year, coronary stenting was introduced. A stent was a narrow wire mesh tube that was wrapped tightly around an angioplasty balloon. It unfurled when the balloon expanded and stayed embedded in the inner layer of the artery after the balloon was withdrawn. This drastically lessened the need for open heart surgery, and increased our caseload dramatically. Our schedule became outrageous, and I was thrown from the frying pan into the fire. I took call after call after working 16- to 18-hour shifts, and depending on the caseload, was expected to return early the next morning for another round of injecting dye into coronary arteries and dilating them as necessary. I brought home lots of money, but was otherwise checked out and had little say in family matters.

After Denise finished nursing school, she was ready to throw in the towel, so she and the boys packed up and moved a couple of hours away. The boys, who struggled in school, were enrolled to prepare for their equivalency while Denise took a job at a hospital. I didn't put up much of a fight. My personal life was in a tailspin keeping up with the fast-paced work environment and personal dramas that came with it. After a few months of separation, I started having panic attacks.

I knew our split should be permanent, but I reached out to Denise anyway, hoping we could try yet again. Her lease was due and the boys let it be known that they hated it there. I was unsatisfied, and believed we could do better, at least for the kid's sakes. I convinced her to return with the boys, who'd by that time graduated, and agreed to call it quits for good if we couldn't make it work. She said that if we sold the house for a nice profit, and built a new one in Fayetteville, she would be interested. We sold the Backstrom house, moved into a rental house in Fayetteville, and prepared to build a new home.

In spite of our track record, I fantasized of miraculously erasing all of the mistakes with this one noble deed, but the deep-seated distrust and animosities acquired during our marriage remained the elephant in the room. After we sold the house and gathered together at the rental house, it became clearer how difficult this was going to be, but I was determined to try. I admitted being the bad guy, worked my long hours, and got busy with the contractor for the new house, hoping things might improve. Denise started a new job in town.

Following six months of cohabitation, and with the house finally complete, I didn't care if I lived in it a single day. The boys, who hadn't forgotten any of the past, begged for our marital reconciliations to end. I moved into a one-bedroom apartment, gave her the house and its sweat equity, agreed to half of the payment, and signed whatever papers she asked me to sign. I did all I could to leave her in as good a situation as possible, hoping only that my penance was now paid. I was glad the boys were in Fayetteville again. After that, I was reminded, once again, of my father.

CHAPTER 40

In 1994, my sister, Iris, called me in a panic. She received a certified letter from a district court in Washington, D.C. demanding our father's trash-talking memoirs. The FBI began investigating the Secretary of Agriculture for allegedly taking illegal contributions from Tom Dawson, and was openly soliciting information related to the case. Iris was previously married to a small-time deputy in a puny speed-trap town, and he contacted the office about the manuscript, either incorrectly imagining that we would celebrate the move, or doing it with malicious intent. We couldn't be sure. I couldn't imagine sending the manuscript to anyone, much less a bunch of curious lawyers. I'd shrugged off some of the angry ramblings that marked places in his book, but feared the backlash that might occur from his detailed record of the Dawson's sins. I had to consider the scrutiny it would bring to our family, too. An unknown number of copies already circulated in northwest Arkansas, and I had no idea who might have one or what the tell-all might have set in motion. Unpredictable enough in life, Dad left a Rube Goldberg machine of a memoir to speak for him from beyond the grave.

Shortly after the call from Iris, a Dawson representative reached out to Uncle Samuel and asked for a meeting. Sam informed Ruth, who in turn, called me. The fact that Dawson didn't want the manuscript read out loud in the halls of Congress and might even offer money to keep it under wraps made me more interested in the possibility of sending it in. But after sleeping on it, I came around and agreed to attend the meeting with my sister Ruth, and her husband, Marty. Maybe he was driven by a deep-seated sense of fairness, maybe by an oblivious sense of self-righteousness, or maybe he just stopped giving a shit what anyone thought of him. One way or another, my father's memoirs contained a self-portrait of a man consumed by anger, a man inhabited by sweet vengeance, both petty and personal. We might have had less to hide than the Dawsons, but my family's closets weren't free of skeletons, and we had reservations about dumping them out on the Capitol Building floor.

That Saturday morning, Ruth, Marty, and I arrived at Jerry's restaurant in Fayetteville and sat at a booth, across from Archibald Fleeman, now on a first-name basis with President Clinton. J.R. Hudson, a well-known local attorney, and Fleeman's protégé, accompanied him. Dawson kept both men on his dole for years. Iris declined to join us.

"I don't understand why we can't all get along?" Fleeman announced, palms up, naïve and plaintive.

I raised a hand to stop him. "Don't waste your time on me. Are you recording this conversation?"

"Of course not," he replied, smirking that I'd implied it.

"Don't."

Fleeman lowered his nose toward me, peeked over his designer glasses, and said, "I understand he dedicated the book to me." This revealed some of what he already knew about the manuscript. Because of Fleeman's comment that spurred the tell-all, my father had indeed dedicated the book to him, and had written as much at the beginning of his memoir. The thought of investigators reading about Dawson's yacht in

Cabo, and the fishing trips with noteworthy politicians on board had Archie sitting patiently with us now at Jerry's.

"So," he continued, shifting into lawyer mode, "Why'd you bring up the manuscript?"

"We didn't," Ruth said.

"You know they're just grasping for anything they can get," Hudson chimed in. In his eyes, Dawson had been unfairly accused. I ignored him and handed over the in-law's name for them to investigate. "Gary Milton. He knew about it and it made him feel important."

"We're here for the deal," Marty put in. "We want you to quash the subpoena."

Fleeman sat up a little straighter. "Good. Excellent. We'll conference call our affiliate in D.C. and sign an agreement. It'll be better this way."

Hudson pressed me to hand over a copy in good faith, but I dodged him and escaped the restaurant without making any promises. I felt dirty playing along. Retaining my copy just in case seemed the least I could do. Unnerved by doubt and feeling skeevy, I headed home for a shower.

Months passed and the investigation dragged on, but I managed to forget all about it until I grabbed a newspaper at an IHOP in central Arkansas, and found myself staring at the bold-lettered headline regarding the investigation. A reply from Dawson regarding a former friend's scandalous tell-all filled a modest-sized column. I read it as I snickered and sipped my coffee. In the column, Dawson answered questions about the manuscript, supposedly quashed and out of sight. Obviously, someone, somewhere got a hold of it, and now heaven only knows where its pages had been opened. Dawson confessed to having been young once. He admitted to doing some foolish things, and possibly getting a speeding ticket once—but he couldn't remember.

Eventually, the secretary under investigation was cleared, but Dawson had to pay a multi- million dollar fine, and two of his highest ranking officers were indicted and convicted of giving illegal gifts.

My dad couldn't have dreamed of a more fitting scenario, a subpoena from D.C. He might not have been happy with us playing along with the lawyers, but it was the right thing to do. He caused the old bastard to remember him.

Some nights, Jimmie slept on the sofa to keep me company in my tiny new living space while Clayton remained loyal to his mother. I was flush with cash but still miserable, trapped in overtime hours and stressful scenarios. I started smoking cigarettes at the break area and met an attractive woman who sold coffee in the new shop at the hospital tower. She introduced herself as Goldie. I started looking for her between cases.

After delivering a patient to the intensive care unit one day, I prepared my empty gurney to return to the lab. Rolling past other rooms, I scanned the names of patients displayed beside their doors. Privacy laws hadn't yet made such displays into violations. They probably should have. I recognized the name on one of the doors. Last name first, first name last: **Winston, Clyde.**

My heart skipped a beat. From the hall, I could see he was unresponsive, sprouting IV's and other tubes and wires. I was curious now, and stepped into the room. An oxygen mask flowed air hard enough that I could hear it whistling. I considered stifling the sound of it with a pillow while it remained attached to his face. He looked near dead and I calmed down. I returned to the nurse at the desk.

"What's the story on this guy?"

"Not good," she said, clearly not too happy about being interrupted from the chart she was studying. "He's not going to make it."

"Got any family?"

She looked up again. "He's been here for a couple of days. Somebody was here on the first day, but nothing since."

Each time I went back up, I checked to see if anyone had come to visit Clyde, but saw no one. Finally, unable to resist the temptation, I studied him from the open door. After reading my dad's account of Winston's criminal acts, I'd come up with slew of questions for him—questions I might never get to ask. Questions such as: *Did it ever occur to you what you were doing to all of us?*

It was impossible to reconcile his personal vendetta towards my father. To me, Winston was not just another disillusioned pawn just doing his job, but an evil man who relished in the pain that he delivered. But in the end, I had to acknowledge that my father bore much of the responsibility of his own demise. The next day, I saw the nurses cleaning the empty room.

Goldie left her husband of 15 years and opened a coffee kiosk in one of the hospital buildings. Like me, she was trying to start over. I learned to loiter around her small business, and developed a more refined taste for caffeine in the process. I ordered a variety of concoctions, wrote corny poetry for her, and left it under her coffee cup when she wasn't looking. She had golden hair and sparkling blue eyes—she was generous, attentive, and a free spirit who was void of judgment or expectation. She was unlike any woman I'd ever known.

Soon after we began dating, we attended a blues music festival in Eureka Springs, a tourist town with a Swiss chalet atmosphere. We both liked the blues guitarist Jimmy Thackery whom they'd booked to play at an auditorium on the east side. The auditorium held hundreds of tables and chairs lined up to accommodate the paying customers.

Not long after we'd found a place to sit, Thackery took the stage and followed the warm-up act with blistering Texas blues that had everybody nodding along, and forgetting the guitarist's Floridian origins. Taking in the electric atmosphere, I scanned the crowd and felt a different kind of shock run through me. Across the table from me, less than a dozen feet away, sat Tom Dawson. He looked sickly, shallow, and half-collapsed, as if some sinkhole that had been brooding for years finally opened up inside of him. Next to him, sat a bored-looking woman—an escort, I assumed—working hard on a piece of gum. I glanced right and left for bodyguards and saw none. Goldie was sitting comfortably, none the wiser of his presence or my long troubled history surrounding the man. Dawson squirmed while he sat vulnerable before me. He glanced at Goldie and then back toward the stage, and refused to acknowledge me. I kept staring at him before revealing a sinister grin that he simply could not have ignored. He must've wondered if I was going to leap across the table and turn him upside down like my father had at the golf club in 1967. I wondered, too. For a few moments, anything seemed possible. I survived all the chaos that my father and Dawson brought down on Springdale and had found love. The best part of life still lay ahead of me. But some wounds ran deeper than reason. I told Goldie I had to relieve myself and would be right back. She smiled briefly at me and turned back to watch the band, oblivious to the drama about to unfold. Instead of going to the bathroom, I waited just out of view until I caught Dawson ducking out through the nearest exit, like I somehow knew he would.

"Where you headed?" I called.

He came up short and stared at me. He looked fearful. He looked sick. "I don't want any trouble." His hands came up, but not in fists. Palms out, they made a plea for mercy.

I could hurt him and he knew it. He just didn't know if I would. I shot a glance toward the parking lot and he got the picture. Dropping his hands, he scooted hurriedly toward his car, never breaking eye contact until a good 50 feet separated us. One last glance before he got in his car revealed a look of relief that I wasn't following him. I was satisfied with making him leave.

Later, it came out that he had advanced liver disease. After a transplant, Dawson resumed his lavish and contemptuous lifestyle until succumbing to cancer a few years later.

While Goldie and I celebrated our fifteenth wedding anniversary at home on a beautiful spring day, local dignitaries stood at a podium and dedicated a new baseball stadium to Tom Dawson. The project took years to complete. They snapped some photos, and everybody said "thank you" to each other.

Just before he died, the city attorney who was partly responsible for my father's harassment in 1967, reached out to offer an apology for his role in the atrocity. He admitted that he was young and was coerced into doing the things he did.

At 40, my life started over when Goldie offered acceptance and an equal partnership. I was still walking uphill, but she said I could come as I was.

Now the wren has gone to roost and the sky is turning gold. And like the sky my soul is also turning, turning from the past, at last, and all I've left behind.
–Ray Lamontage, *Old Before Your Time*

ABOUT THE AUTHOR

LARRY DANIEL is a former henchman, builder, fireman, paramedic, educator, cardiovascular technologist, and small business operator. He is currently retired and living in northwest Arkansas with his wife and two dogs.

Mr. Daniel received his firefighting credentials from the Fire Academy in Camden, Arkansas and attended paramedic school at Springdale Memorial Hospital, in Springdale, Arkansas, where he also served as an advanced cardiac life support and advanced trauma life support, instructor. He gained a licensure in invasive cardiology with a specialty in cardiac intervention and electrophysiology while employed at Springdale Memorial Hospital.

Larry received a certificate of recognition from Governor Bill Clinton in 1986, for his service to the State of Arkansas, and in 1989, appeared on the CBS television show, Rescue 911. After 22 years in healthcare, the author operated an insurance agency with his wife for nearly a decade.

Larry is an avid outdoorsman who also enjoys yoga and travel. This is his first book.

CPSIA information can be obtained
at www.ICGtesting.com
Printed in the USA
BVHW030802250220
573236BV00004B/1